EVERY STOP HAS A STORY

Owen Deckinga

Chapbook Press

Schuler Books
2660 28th Street SE
Grand Rapids, MI 49512
(616) 942-7330
www.schulerbooks.com

ISBN 13: 9781943359486

Library of Congress Control Number: 2016958548

Copyright © 2016 by Owen Deckinga

All rights reserved. No part of this book may be reproduced or transmitted in any form or by any means, electronic or mechanical, including photocopying, recording, or by any information or retrieval system, without permission in writing from the copyright owner.

The opinions in this book are solely those of the author, and are the result of trial and error over 62 years in the trash hauling business. These are my memories, to the best of my recollection.

All English Scripture quotations, in this publication are from the HOLY BIBLE, NEW INTERNATIONAL VERSION ® NIV ® Copyright © 1973, 1978, 1984 by International Bible Society

Cover photo © John Deckinga, 2008

Cover design © John Deckinga 2016

Author photo © John Deckinga, 2008

To my wife Pat.

Thanks for hanging on.

CONTENTS

FOREWORD

CHAPTER 1 – INDELIBLY DUTCH

CHAPTER 2 – EVOLUTION OF EQUIPMENT

CHAPTER 3 – UNFORGETTABLE STOPS

CHAPTER 4 – THE ASSOCIATION

CHAPTER 5 – INFLUENTIAL UNCLES

CHAPTER 6 – BECOMING AN ADULT

CHAPTER 7 – MY FIRST COMPANY

CHAPTER 8 - INJURY

CHAPTER 9 – PARTING COMPANY

CHAPTER 10 – BIG CHANGES

CHAPTER 11 – SOULMATE

CHAPTER 12 – WILD WEST

CHAPTER 13 – ANCHOR ONE

CHAPTER 14 – CHICAGO COLD

CHAPTER 15 – UNFORGETTABLE PEOPLE

CHAPTER 16 – GARBIO TRUCK STOPS

CHAPTER 17 - FIRE

CHAPTER 18 – BRICK TO THE FACE

CHAPTER 19 – KINGDOM COME

CHAPTER 20 – HOURLY AGAIN

CHAPTER 21 - CRUSHED

CHAPTER 22 – WILD WILL AND THE MILL

CHAPTER 23 – UNION MAN

CHAPTER 24 – MORE CHANGES

CHAPTER 25 – ELMER HIGGINS

CHAPTER 26 – ANCHOR TWO

CHAPTER 27 – LEARNING THE ROPES AGAIN

CHAPTER 28 – HUBERT AND ERIC

CHAPTER 29 – JOB SECURITY

CHAPTER 30 - REHABS

CHAPTER 31 – THE NOISE ORDINANCE

CHAPTER 32 – CARLOTTA

CHAPTER 33 – MS LEMAY

CHAPTER 34 – BACK TO HOURLY

CHAPTER 35 – EQUIPMENT, PART TWO

CHAPTER 36 – A COUPLE OF RANTS

CHAPTER 37 – REMARKABLE PEOPLE

CHAPTER 38 - RETIREMENT

CHAPTER 39 - CONCLUSION

EVERY STOP HAS A STORY

Owen Deckinga

FOREWORD

Those of you who know me, know I'm more a story-teller than a writer. So this is me telling my story, first for my grandkids, then for you the other readers. So bear with me if I ramble a bit.

I have made a life-long career out of hauling trash. It's a job that's not very glamorous. At times it's very mundane. And at times it's looked down on as a job for a second-class citizen. But getting rid of trash is a very important part of our daily existence, and where would we be if it wasn't picked up and disposed of it properly? I've been picking it up for over sixty years, and along the way have collected a few stories. Here are a few.

CHAPTER 1 – INDELIBLY DUTCH

Have you ever wondered why some little boys are fascinated with trucks, especially garbage trucks? Who can tell? Is a part of their DNA, some ingrained quality they're born with?

My story begins like that. With a fascination for trucks. I was born on the West Side of Chicago, commonly referred to as the Old West Side. This is an area bordered by Roosevelt and Ashland Avenues, and stretching south to the railroad tracks on 16th Street, which seems like a natural boundary for what was—at that time—a solidly Dutch community. Our parents and grandparents were Christian Reformed in their faith. There was a Christian Reformed church at 13th and Ashland, which I was baptized in. Shortly after my baptism it seemed the community outgrew its boundaries. Several families moved west to Berwyn and Cicero. Other families moved south to Englewood.

My parents chose the southerly route, moving to a rented house at 6746 S. Sangamon. The house still stands. My grandfather and grandmother on my mother's side moved to an apartment building, which they owned at 6936 S. Sangamon. So we lived two blocks from my grandparents. At the corner of 69th and Sangamon was a gas station, and parked in this gas station were two trucks, muddy

1

looking trucks capable of hauling dirt or trash. Something told my young mind that these trucks were part of my family.

Now the young minds start to pick up things at different ages. I checked with my cousin Peter Laning, and he said, "Yeah, about two years old things started to kick in for me." I checked with other cousins and they said it was more like three or four when they began to have memories of certain things. This I remember, that I was bound and determined to go play on these two trucks that somehow belonged to someone in my family. As it turned out, they were my Grandpa Laning's. At home my parents had a stockade gate with a Z-brace on the inside of the gate. If you're making a childproof gate at your home, do not put a Z-brace on the inside of the gate. This makes a convenient walk up for an agile two-year-old child. I walked up to the gate, jumped over and proceeded to walk two blocks down to where these two trucks were parked.

I played around for quite a while, and then a car pulled up. I don't remember the man. I don't remember the uniform. But what I do remember is being taken to a place that had bars on it. I was given a Holloway sucker. This is one of those caramel suckers that you can suck on all day and nothing goes away except for the sticky, gooey caramel that was all over my face. I don't recall the length of time, but this frantic woman came in, my mother, and claimed her lost two-year-old son. The *Chicago Sun-Times* has a photograph in their archives, and somewhere in my family's possession, I don't know if my children have it, or one of my brothers has it, but there is a photograph of a two-year-old with his head bowed, his face full of caramel in the jail cell, which I might add was located at the police station at 61st and Racine. The station has been moved to a modern facility which is across the street but the old building still remains. I was too young to tell them I wasn't lost, just that I wasn't finished playing and when I was done playing, I would have returned home.

Was this an early indication that I was bound for carrying on a family tradition? No, I don't think so. But looking back some 70 years, maybe it was. You see, I was born into a family of four Dutch grandparents: one on either side came from Holland, the other two were born here. Nobody had a lot of money, but they did have a sense of community, specifically, Dutch community. At the time, I didn't realize it was a real blessing. I now realize why my family sticks together, why black families stick together, why Jewish families stick together. It is because they can sit and talk about their heritage. It's a sense of belonging.

You see, Englewood was a good place, a very good place, to grow up. We had three Christian Reformed churches, two Reformed churches, a Christian grade school and a Christian high school, all within a couple of square miles. We had parks, like Hamilton Park, where we could skate in the wintertime; Ogden Park, where on Monday, Wednesday and Friday we could swim; and if we were daring we went to Garfield Park or Marquette Park with our fishing poles. We could walk home in the dark in safety. We could have a pick-up game of softball on one of the public school playgrounds and meet new playmates, who were not of the Dutch community.

My folks, Annette and John, bought a house on Aberdeen Street in 1946, still quite close to my Laning grandparents on Sangamon St. These grandparents, Peter and Gertrude, had five sons and four daughters, all married with children, so my family tree was quite large. I think I had something like 45 cousins. So when we had family picnics later on in life, at the park in Western Springs, this was quite a family get-together.

My Grandfather Deckinga and his wife Marie owned an apartment building at 7032 S. Emerald, also close to my parents' house. My Grandfather Deckinga had retired from the ice and coal business, but he did tell me at one time that he had gone into the garbage business, and all he said about it was that it was not very successful. He had take a financial beating. When I pushed him for details, he refused to answer my questions, so I assumed it was not a very good venture. When the book *Dutch Chicago* came out, the author, Robert Swierenga listed in the section on the history of garbage hauling in Chicago two names which I was unfamiliar with. One was Congo, the other Nicholas, both with the last name of Deckinga. Knowing that Deckingas are all related, I began to search to find out who Congo and Nicholas Deckinga were. My cousin Marlene, who is the keeper of the Deckinga legacy, said those are your great-grandfather and his brother. So it was not until my later adult life that I realized I had a great-grandfather who spent a good part of his life hauling trash. Later on, my Uncle Deck (Clarence) bought a small route and started in the garbage business. My father did not take to the trash hauling business, although later in this book I'll explain how important it became in his life as we got older.

On the Laning side this was a different story. As I mentioned, a child's mind picks up certain things of his childhood, and they stick with him. I remember at four years old being pulled aside in the kitchen in a house on Aberdeen Street and being told that my Grandpa Laning had died of a heart attack at the Helping Hand Mission. By today's standards he was young, only 63. Lanings have always been plagued with heart conditions. I don't know if it's bad eating habits, or other bad habits. Most of my uncles smoked; I did as a high school student, but later decided to quit. So, at my grandfather's death, the business was left to his sons, my Uncle Slim (Garrett) and Uncle Clarence. I don't know the financials of it—it's not important—but those two carried on Grandpa's tradition. Two of Grandpa's other sons, Uncle Murph and Uncle Pete, each had his own operation (Uncle Pete's business was named Duke Scavenger). Another son, Uncle Al, was living in California at the time. When he came back to Chicago, he opened up a truck repair shop at 89th and VIncennes , and later became one of the first Leach franchise dealers.

Uncle Clarence Laning, being a God-fearing man, felt his commitment was to enter the mission field. He sold his interest in the Peter Laning Sons scavenger business to his brother, Uncle Slim (Garrett) and attended Reformed Bible Institute (now College) in Grand Rapids Michigan, and later became the director of the Helping Hand Mission, which was located at Madison and Green Streets in Chicago. He dedicated his whole life to helping the people living on the streets who had a battle with alcohol.

Several years after Uncle Clarence went into the ministry, Uncle Pete Laning followed in his brother's footsteps and sold his share to his youngest sister Ruth's husband Peter Lindemulder. Uncle Pete Lindemulder kept the Duke name, carried on the Duke tradition and sold it to his son Peter Junior. Peter Jr. later sold the Duke operation to Ally, the forerunner of a much larger corporation.

In the early days the garbage truck was a gold mine of stuff. Most of us were families without a lot of money. Our attention was on the church and tuition to the Christian schools for our children. And I say that because I followed a lot of my parents' traditions about church and school. But we always had enough to eat. One of the stops Uncle Pete hauled was Jewel Foods, 37th and Ashland. The building is now being torn down as part of urban renewal. Jewel has moved to the suburbs, but at that time the boxes of bread, the boxes of sweet rolls, or whatever Jewel decided to throw out because they were outdated, found their way to the Lindemulder, Laning and

Deckinga tables. Lacking today's preservatives, the food that the delivery guy put on the shelf could become the food that was thrown into the garbage in only a matter of a short time. Bread had to be sold in short order, sweet rolls only had a short shelf life and cans could not be dented. What happened when they were not up to a supermarket standards? The people at the store put them in a cardboard box and headed them to the trash. And of course the old adage "one man's trash is another man's treasure" sure kicked in when we ate like kings. In fact, my first bicycle at age 6 was bought for three dollars from Uncle Pete Lindemulder, who found it in the garbage. I was a little upset that my brother Bruce had a brand new Schwinn. He had won it on some radio show and was still too small to ride it. Why not give it to me, I thought? Of course it didn't belong to me; it belonged to Bruce. So Uncle Pete said, "Give me three dollars and you can have the bike." Which I did. Later on, when I took the fenders off, he gave me a lot of grief. He said, "I sold you this perfectly good bike and you destroyed it." But I managed to keep that bike for a long time, maybe because of his admonition about destroying things.

For some reason Uncle Pete Lindemulder and I bonded. Yes, he had a son of his own, Ronnie, but when Uncle Pete moved to 71st and Carpenter, which was half a block from our house, when I wasn't playing baseball with my friends I was at Uncle Pete and Auntie Ruth's house. Maybe because I knew he was capable of scrounging so many good treasures out of the trash, I wanted to stay near him. My father drove a laundry truck, but because it was home delivery, there weren't many treasures until he worked for De Normandie Industrial Garments.

Uncle Slim lived about the same distance from me as Uncle Pete. In fact, before Uncle Pete and Auntie Ruth bought their house on Carpenter—a brick two flat which still stands and is still in as good a shape as when they left it—they lived above Uncle Slim. I was not as close at the time to Uncle Slim as I was to Uncle Pete. Maybe it's because of a person's personality, or mannerism. But later on I came to have as much affection for Uncle Slim as I did for Uncle Pete. Slim was a principled man, God-fearing, and was not tongue-tied when it came to people who claimed to be Christians but in their daily life did not act like Christians. Slim refused to haul taverns because he did not want to subject his driver to the temptations of alcohol. He carried his mantra almost to his dying day, when his son Junior and son-in-law Jim took the business over from him. And later, as teenagers, both my friend Fred and I were willing employees of Slim, and spent many a day off of school or summer vacations working with various drivers who Slim employed. Later chapters will reveal some of the exploits which Fred and I were involved in.

Uncle Murph Laning had a one-man route, something he could handle himself with maybe an occasional helper. It was on the North Side Gold Coast, with high rises and a much different type of route. Murph's route consisted mostly of those high-rise apartment buildings, some restaurants, a few specialty shops, and his was a lot cleaner than Pete or Slim's route. But Murph lived in Berwyn, so the opportunity to latch on to a day's work with Murph was slim to none. And Murph had two boys, Peter and Bob, who in an emergency could help their father at any given time. But whenever Murph came around and got to telling stories about different places, this nephew was always willing to listen. In fact I would go to my cousin Peter's house (Murph's son) and stay overnight. Peter would do the same, come to our house and stay overnight.

One particular weekend's stay at Peter's house, Uncle Murph said, "Let's go to work at midnight. Tolee's truck broke down. We got to help him out." Peter, Uncle Murph and I left the house in Berwyn at 11 o'clock and rolled down the streets to the garage while the people were still going home from their Sunday night coffee. We then went downtown to Rush Street, pick up this restaurant, Taverns, and other assorted stops of Tolee's, mixing them in with some of Murph's accounts. Just before daylight, we rounded the corner and found a guy laying on the street. Upon closer inspection we noticed his mouth was all bloodied and all of his teeth were laying in the street. And the moans and cries could be heard for about a block. You see, this guy made the mistake of trying to rob somebody else, and got caught, not by the police but by a couple of guys that said, "We will do justice our way." And while somebody held him down, somebody else kicked his teeth out. I wonder to this day, did he ever bother to rob somebody again? I recently had lunch with my cousin Peter (Murph's son), and we talked about this because he too remembered the very incident that happened. What a horrible way to start your day, your teeth laying on the ground.

Uncle Deck's was a success story in itself. Uncle Deck had taken the reins from Grandpa Deckinga and gone into the ice business. For those of you below the age 60, that used to be—as I explained to my children—a way in which we refrigerated food. And icemen would go down the alley with his truck loaded with cakes of ice, 25, 50, 75, and 100 pound blocks. He would walk around the garage and look at a card which had the corresponding number, 25, 50, 75 or 100. Then he would walk back to the truck, chop off the piece that was needed for the house, put it on his shoulder, carry it into the house and put it in the icebox. The icebox was a wooden box with a galvanized steel liner, and the food storage would be below.

Uncle Deck made the transition from delivering ice to working at the icehouse. This is a facility that manufactures the cakes of ice the drivers used to deliver. When the ice boxes were replaced by modern refrigerators, there was no more need for the iceman. Eventually the icehouse was consolidated, and Uncle Deck saw the handwriting on the wall and decided this was the time—at age 40—to get into the garbage business. Not only did he have a late start, but he also had a very small start. The truck he bought was a nine-cubic-yard Garwood with a two- or three-yard roof rack. Today's trucks go 25 yards. But Uncle Deck was a hustler. The Dutch heritage of making something out of nothing sure kicked in when Uncle Deck got into the garbage business.

Many a Saturday Fred and I would do some of the goofiest cleanups that Uncle Deck could conjure up. He'd park the truck in an alley next to an open window, and Fred and I would shovel bushel baskets full of dirt and pass them up to Uncle Deck sitting on the window ledge. He would dump them in the truck and hand us back the empties, and we would shovel and fill some more. Even to this day when I tell somebody I'm going to "run the handle" while you load, I tell them I got the Uncle Deck's job (sitting down and bossing the help). But in his whole career, he only bought four trucks, stayed totally by himself and urged his son, son-in-law and a nephew to search for gold in them hills, as he had done.

Uncle Deck would take used wine bottles, put them in a crate and drive over to Voods Fine Wines on Jackson just off Halsted. He'd give them the bottles so they could refill them with new wine. Uncle Deck would also separate out the cardboard from his load, and make several trips throughout the day to Benny Evans, a scrap yard, which also was located just off Halsted Street. If you want to learn a lesson on recycling, you had to watch Uncle Deck. The last stop of the day was usually Weibolts. This was a warehouse for all the

Weibolts stores in the Chicago area. It was located at the corner of Ogden, Ashland and Madison. Ironically, the company I now work for on a part-time basis also picks up garbage at this very location. Weibolts has long gone out of business, and the warehouse is now a high-end apartment building. But back then we would go to Weibolts, pick up the incineration and then load the top of the roof rack of this truck with broken pallets. And there we would go with Uncle Chubby Chick (a nickname we gave Uncle Deck because that was the name of his first stop) down Ashland Avenue to the landfill. This was before the Dan Ryan, Eisenhower, Kennedy and Bishop Ford Expressways were all connected. Surface streets were the only mode of transportation.

One night when I was in my early teens, my dad said to me, "Let's go. Uncle Deck is picking us up." And we went to the near North Side. I think it was located on Ohio or Ontario about Dearborn. The name of the stop was the Milner Hotel, and we had done a large cleanup at this location about 6 months prior, and Uncle Deck had received a notice of cancellation of service. And because he was a member of the Association (more on the Association later), he had to find out who was hauling the stop. So we were doing some gumshoe operation so he had evidence before making his case to the Association membership. We waited for about an hour before a truck showed up, and three guys jumped out to haul the trash. My uncle got out and talked briefly with the driver, and got very little out of him. But he did know who was the culprit. Boy, did this excite him! And I think that he did get this stop back in time. At the time the Association exerted effective control over its members.

Uncle Al Laning told me this story before his death. Being a Leach dealer for the Chicago area, one day he got an urgent message from the Leach Corporation headquarters in Oshkosh Wisconsin, to look up a prospective client named Owen Deckinga, and sell him a new Leach Packmaster. Uncle Al looked at this letter and said, "What are these guys talking about? This guy is a 13-year-old nephew of mine." You see, yes, I had written to Leach Corporation in Oshkosh, asking for literature of various size Leach Packmasters. Because I failed to give them my age, Leach assumed I was a hot prospective client. I had no knowledge that Uncle Al was the distributor for Leach products. So, many years later we were able to laugh and joke about this very thing.

For several years Uncle Al fixed the garbage trucks that others had. He moved from his 89th St. location, down the block to 86th and Vincennes. Several years after moving, he made a deal with the owner of Ogden Hill Cement Works and bought a route from them, and started Capital Disposal. This would fit into O's life later on when he bought part of an operation from Uncle Al. And Uncle Al, like Uncle Pete Lindemulder, would play a very important part in the Big O's life. More about that later.

Uncle Pete Laning, after selling Duke Disposal to Uncle Pete Lindemulder, followed the same course of action his brother Clarence did. He moved his family, Gerda, Peter and Auntie Rose, to Michigan and attended RBI College. He was ordained and proceeded to go on the mission field. The mission field did not agree with Uncle Pete, and several years later he bought a small operation in Gun Lake, Michigan, and with his son Peter and son-in-law Dan they built it up. The distance of Gun Lake from the Chicago area, and the fact that I was already doing my own thing in the trash hauling business, made it almost impossible to visit him on a regular basis. I think later on they sold their business to Trash Management, and a few years after that he passed away.

CHAPTER 2 – EVOLUTION OF EQUIPMENT

If you read the book *Dutch Chicago* section on garbage, you get an early history of how the industry evolved from the days of horse and wagon to simple trucks, to trucks with dump bodies, then to trucks with packer bodies—which kept getting bigger and bigger—then to roll-off boxes and stationary compactors. These changes evolved over time, and many of the Dutch scavengers were brought into the next generation kicking and screaming because new equipment cost money and many did not want to part with money.

Grandpa Laning's work days consisted of carrying barrels out of the basement to the truck, up a stepladder to a first tailgate, then grabbing a rope swinging that ladder to a second plateau and throwing the barrels over into the truck. Sound like a labor-intensive, slow way of doing it? Yes, definitely. Fortunately, at this time most of the trash, except for restaurant slop, was being burned in on-site incinerators. The trash hauler had to make sure that the cans did not contain hot ashes. Fires were very common because the top of the can might be cold, but unburned newspapers, packed together, can retain fire for a long time.

But something that is so labor intensive begs for invention, and the next step in the transition from horse and buggy to modern equipment was the side loader. The side loader was nothing more than a one-cylinder hydraulic platform located on the right-hand side of the truck. When the side loader was in use, a pin would hold the platform horizontal and another pin would hold it out away from the truck. The hydraulic cylinder would raise and lower the platform to the top of the truck. So you ask yourself, how can a truck that's 7.5 feet wide go down the street with an elevator sticking out the side? It didn't. The platform folded against the side of the truck when not in use. One of my greatest regrets is that very few people took pictures of this device. Who invented this idea and where it was invented, I am not sure. But this mechanism allowed much bigger trucks because the swing of this hydraulic system would allow the platform to go much higher than a five-step stepladder. The side-loader was capable of holding two 55-gallon drums. When the operator got to the top, he would dump the two barrels over the side of the truck. As that one side got filled up, he would then jump into the truck body, slide the barrels of the side-loader platform and physically dump them to the other side, and the front and back of the truck. Trash trucks at that time would always go down the street tipped to the curbside because it was easier to dump on that side of the truck than to physically haul a barrel to the driver's side or to the front of the truck. When the operator left a stop, he was supposed to physically roll a tarp over the top of truck to keep the load in place. But many times while the truck was half full, the operator would go down the street without the tarp on top of the truck, and paper trash would be blowing all over the street.

The City of Chicago decided to put an end to this. They enacted legislation on the City Council that made it illegal for any trash hauling truck to traverse the city streets without a secure fitting steel top. Not a bad piece of legislation, looking back. Four or five steel doors were fitted on top of the truck, the side loader was abandoned and a moveable rear platform was mounted on the back of the tailgate. This system is still being used today in Coke trucks, food delivery trucks and other various applications. The only difference is that on a garbage truck the platform would go all the way to the top of the truck and was capable of hauling three barrels. When the operator reached the top of the truck, he would roll the barrels to door number one at the front of the truck, lift the door, hold it open with a steel rod attached to the truck and dump the barrels into the truck. When section one got full, the operator would jump up and down on the first door, thus compacting the garbage, and move on to door number two, where he would fill that section. And so on, till the truck was loaded. This made it easy to throw the cardboard or any other recyclables to the back of the truck. Later on, you could throw that material off at Benny Evans or one of the various scrap yards located around the city. So an operator might go with one load to the landfill, and maybe have dumped a half a load in various scrap yards throughout the city. When the truck was completely full and the load was to be dumped, two turnbuckles would be unscrewed, the tailgate would be swung open and the load would be dumped.

This invention of the elevator platform was designed by Erlinder Equipment, which was located at 122nd and Indiana, in Roseland on the far South Side. One of the pivotal innovators of the refuse industry, Erlinder to this day has not received the credit it should have in the disposable industry. Many garbage trucks had to be retrofitted for particular stops, so the steel doors could be flipped open either way to accommodates chutes or conveyor belts pushed out of buildings, which would spit out trash, residue or other things to be taken to landfill. If you had an idea, and could put it down on paper, Erlinder would build it for you. Uncle Pete had a ramp put on his platform which would allow him to roll one-yard containers onto the elevator platform. The elevator platform with the ramp on it also served another purpose: it allowed Uncle Pete to drive the front wheels of his small tractor up onto the platform, elevate the platform about a foot and dump broken concrete into the body of the truck (after the driver opened a type of Dutch doors on the tailgate). Uncle Pete would then drink his coffee, and off to the dump we would go. Many a Saturday this 12-year-old boy would spend his day working with his uncle. My sole job: to open and close the Dutch doors, run for the coffee (cream, no sugar) and talk once in a while on the way to the dump and back. Remember, those trucks didn't come with radios or air ride seats. Those things cost money

On Monday the same truck would be ready to go to a route again, the operator hauling barrels three to the platform, rolling them across the top and dumping them. Did this seem backwards? Not at the time. It sure beat shoveling dirt into a bushel basket and dumping it from a window ledge.

The rear load idea was nice because the elevator platform could be left in the half up position. And it could be mounted on both single-axle trucks, as well as tandems. The single-axle trucks were nice because the ash haulers on the lakefront would leave the platform at belt high, and those who carried the ashes out of the basement on their back would just set the can down on the gate. Then they would lower the gate, jump on and ride it to the top of the truck. This worked well for a long time since ashes didn't need compaction. They were as compact as you were going to get it. Routes that hauled predominantly ashes and incineration had little cause to separate recycling from the rest of the load. So the faster you got the truck loaded, the faster you went to the dump. Some of those routes would carry three guys in the dead of winter because that's when most of the coal was being burned and most of the ashes had to be hauled away. Very labor intensive. In fact, most guys that did that type of work, by the time they were 45 years old their careers were pretty much over with. The union had a gravy train because the retirement age at the time was 65 years old, and I could count on my one hand the number of guys that made it to 65 and retired and received the pension from the union.

CHAPTER 3 – UNFORGETTABLE STOPS

Fisher Building

This was a daily stop, located on the corner of Harrison Street and Plymouth Court. When we first arrived there, we would load cardboard barrels full of paper trash onto the rear platform, zoom up to the top of the truck, and dump the paper into the body of the truck, go down and get three more. This is rather mundane, but the memorable thing about Fisher Building was what happened twice a heating season two stories down, in the bowels of the city. That's where the Fisher building stored their ashes from burning coal for heat. Yes, it's hard to conceive that one of the mid-rise buildings in the Loop of Chicago at one time burned coal. We would open the tailgate of the rear-loaded truck and back it up at right angles to sidewalk.

Deacon Dykstra, who was the engineer of the building, would open a steel door set in the sidewalk and crank up a skyhook through the steel door. It would swivel, and he would lower the hook into the basement two floors below sidewalk level. There my father and I would take our shirts off and start to shovel. The buckets had hooks, and we would fill one while Deacon was pulling another up to the sidewalk with the skyhook. When it reached the back of the truck, Uncle Pete would swing it into the truck and dump it all in one motion on the floor of the truck. He would then jump into the truck and shovel what he had just dumped on the floor of the truck to the front of the truck. Deacon would send the hook back down with the empty bucket. We would grab the empty bucket, replace it with a full one, and Deacon would pull that one up to the sidewalk. This would be repeated over and over again.

My father and I would be sweating profusely because the basement was warm and we were busy shoveling. Deacon at the first floor just below sidewalk level was operating the controls and would be dressed like an Eskimo, since the wind would come down that hole in the sidewalk making his perch very cold. Uncle Pete would be dressed normal because he was busy shoveling. It would take us about an hour and a half to completely empty that room. This was done twice a heating season, or about every two months.

Sam L. Bingham

This was a stop located on what is now known as Financial Place. Sounds pretty ritzy. That's because the Board of Trade, or I think the Chicago Mercantile Exchange, is located down the street. At one time the streets had many a factory, mostly printing and paper supply, for the printing industry. Samuel L. Bingham was a company that made printing rollers. It was a Tuesday, Thursday and Saturday stop. We would haul the old cut-off rollers, the office paper and whatever residue the factory had.

We would back up to the dock, load everything facing Financial Place, then go around to the back of the building in the alley and park under a little steel door that was on the second floor. The driver then would walk into the building, go up to the second floor, open that steel door and push a conveyor out. Then he would turn the conveyor belt on, go to two hoppers, stick his head in each one, and take a stick and poke out the powdered rubber that was stuck inside the hopper. This powdered rubber would fall onto the conveyor belt and would go out the door and into the truck. Remember two steel doors on the truck both had to be open so that the powdered rubber could fall into the load. When both hoppers were empty, you would brush the powder from your clothes and your face. Then you would shut the conveyor off and push it back inside the building and slide the steel door shut. Go back out to the truck and close both steel doors on top of the truck and then drive away.

But at Sam L. Bingham Uncle Pete had another job and that was to plow snow in the parking lot during the winter. Now you may be thinking of a modern 4 x 4 pickup truck with air conditioning heater, plow on the front, complete with a handheld remote for up and down and sideways. But nooo! You had to remember, this was Uncle Pete. If there was an easy way to do it, he would make sure he found the harder way. I once rode with him from Englewood to South Holland to the tractor place to get a part, and I said to Uncle Pete, "Why don't you buy a cab for that tractor? They come with a heater and a radio, and you could be warm and comfortable." His answer: "No, too much money." And so ended my discussion on modern conveniences. Uncle Pete's plow was a wooden door strapped to the bucket of his tractor; his cab was a long parka with a hood and fur-lined mittens to keep his hands warm. So much for modern comforts. But when we arrived to pick up the garbage, the guy in charge of signing the ticket had plenty to say about this crazy old man who plowed the snow at five below zero. And you had to love him for his stubborn nature.

Dill Pickle

If you watched the movie *The Blues Brothers*, you might remember the scene where Dan Ackroyd and John Belushii walk into a hotel, not a modern one, more a flophouse. This hotel was located on Harrison Street between Plymouth Court and State Street. It's now an empty lot, part of the greening of State Street. But below this seedy hotel there was a restaurant called Dill Pickle. This was one of Uncle Pete's stops, directly across the street from the steel hook that came through the sidewalk at the Fisher Building. The Dill Pickle, owned by a Jewish fella, involved a couple of drums of garbage a day plus a free sandwich. Anyway, if you watched the movie, you knew that Carrie Fisher blew up the hotel in retaliation against John Belushi or Dan Ackroyd, and the real life owner had to publish in the newspaper that the Dill Pickle was still open and had not been blown up in the making of *The Blues Brothers*. This was a very popular place and some of the customers were worried that it had been destroyed in the making of this movie. It always tickles me when I watch *The Blues Brothers* because many of the things in that movie are places I've been to while hanging on the back of a garbage truck or in my growing up years.

Manny's

This is another stop that Uncle Pete hauled. Around St. Patrick's Day, whenever they want to comment about corn beef and cabbage, the press usually goes to Manny's Café, which is located on Jefferson at Roosevelt. Very popular place. And when somebody is running for office, they will go to Manny's and the press will follow them. So Manny's is quite famous. If you go back to Manny's now the garbage is in the container behind the restaurant itself. But like I said, Uncle Pete seemed to have a knack for doing things the hard way. To get the garbage, you went down this elevator which was barely big enough for one man. You got to the basement, pushed a container onto the elevator, then jumped on top of the container and went up to the parking lot. There you emptied the container and brought it back down and then reloaded the elevator with the empty boxes. Maybe three trips and the task was complete. Thank goodness for progress.

Sunbeam

This was a stop owned by the Sunbeam Corporation, which made small appliances. It was on Ogden Avenue, west of Crawford. The reason this one sticks in my mind is it had copper clippings from these electric motors and the help knew that we would scrounge through the barrels looking for handfuls of copper wire. So they would kind of gather them up and put them in a one of the barrels. Then they would point to the barrel and say, "This is the one." Every truck at that time had a toolbox located in the front of the body, and this is was where we could store the junk. When the box was full of the clippings, Uncle Peter's brother John would bring them home and sort the scrap till they got enough. This was good Christmas money. It wasn't loaves of bread or sweet rolls, but it was just as good. You could turn it into cash. And to this day I still do it, smashing television sets, sliding the core off the back of the set, gathering them up and running to the scrap yard.

Matt's Coffee Shop

Matt's Coffee Shop was a small coffee shop on North Damen. At first it was just one of those places where you parked the truck on the street and had a cup of coffee. Run by an Italian guy and his sons when they weren't in school. Very nondescript. But as time went on and the more we stopped at Matt's, I began to notice that some of these guys were just pretty fancy and had no apparent means of employment. There were no office buildings, and they were dressed very well for being a clerk in a shop. Once in a while some of these guys would have very well-dressed ladies with them at 8:00 to 10:00 in the morning, and the conversation would be quite risqué sometimes. I was about 16 years old and one day was sitting in the library in high school and had access to all the latest magazines, such as *Life*, *National Geographic*, *Time* and *Look*, and I came across an article which gave a detailed description of Matt's Coffee Shop. How it was a hangout for a street crew from Chicago Avenue and Damen. Yeah, it was labeled as a Mob hangout. I never had any conversations with the owner, Matt, or his sons about the article. But this is some of the color that a young boy/young teenager is exposed to while growing up.

Del's Gas Station

All my childhood and teen years were spent in close association with Uncle Pete, maybe because he lived closer than any other uncle. Maybe we just had a natural bond. I did not try to analyze it; I just tried to enjoy it. I knew what time he was supposed to come home, and if I saw his car I would always drop in and see how his day went and keep up with the latest news. Many times I would go to where he parked his truck, at a Conoco gas station at 75th and Halsted, owned by a guy named Del Funk. It was a one-bay gas station with three pumps. Del didn't do much car repair or tire repair, but he probably pumped more gas than most stations around that area. Five trucks, all garbage trucks, each pumping about 50 gallons a day, was pretty good for Del. Later on, when everyone started to move to the suburbs, Del had two phones besides his own, and he served as an answering service for two garbage companies, Uncle Pete with one truck and Uncle Slim with two. When Uncle Al parked there too, that made four garbage trucks, and eventually Slim and Al each added one more, so six garbage trucks lined Del's fence.

Not only did Del have the capacity to park six garbage trucks, but at any given time after school there were usually two or three retired men in the station spinning yarns, guys like Mr. Collins, a retired plumber who did side jobs. Mr. Collins had three fingers on one hand, chewed tobacco and couldn't complete a sentence without spitting at least once. Another guy named Ray lived in Oak lawn and worked at Electromotive on 103rd St. He would always stop in and everything was funny to Ray. He was always laughing. There were also a few other characters, mostly guys from around the neighborhood, just trying to stay out of their wives' way. It was always good conversation. Later on, for a short period of time, when

I was driving a linen truck, I would take my lunch break at Del's, and then go on my way.

The sad commentary on life is that for something that played such an important part in my teen years and the beginning of my adult life, I never knew what happened to Dell and his family. One day I just stopped going there because my path went in a different direction and I had no cause to go to 75th and Halsted. My Uncle Pete found a garage in South Holland to park his trucks in, and he had no cause to go back there either.

CHAPTER 4 - THE ASSOCIATION

One of the things that Uncle Pete did have at his house was a three-ring binder notebook labeled "The Association." This was a directory of the members of The Chicago & Suburban Refuse & Ash Haulers. The Association has also been referred to as the Dutch Mafia. To me the Association directory was second behind the Holy Bible as far as reading material. From time to time I would look over it, page through it, almost to the point of being able to memorize it. Later, some people doubted its existence, but I assured them it *did* exist.

Why did the Association come into being? An illustration in the directory itself explains that. One of the pages in the directory showed two teams of horses pulling in opposite directions, neither getting any further ahead because they were pulling against each other. The next illustration showed both teams side-by-side pulling in the same direction and accomplishing quite a bit. The moral of these illustrations was of course: if we work together, we accomplish quite a bit; if we fight, we go nowhere. The customer, on the other hand, had a different view. They would constantly complain that the Dutch had a monopoly on the trash hauling business. The customer had a valid point. Many would call up for a quote and could not get a direct quote over the phone. What they *would* get is "will call you back later," and most of the time the callback would never occur.

But put yourself in my Grandpa Laning's shoes. He got up very early in the morning, and with the help of his sons would go out and haul other people's trash. He would work long hours at a very hard job. Then on Sunday, a day of rest, he would file into the church with all nine children occupying one complete row in the church, and he would look over to the left, and view another family in the same business with a large number of mouths to feed. And the implication was, are you going to take bread out of my mouth, are you going to take money from my tuition fund for the Christian school, are you going to take money from my tithing to the church? And of course the answer was simply, no. So when a customer would call up asking for a quote, maybe my grandfather would make a courtesy call to the customer's hauler, and ask what the problem was, and 95% of the time it was because the hauler had raised the customer's rate and the customer did not feel he should have to pay more money. Customers were known to make twenty to thirty calls and get no response.

While you might say, what's stopping me from buying my own truck, striking out on my own, and building my own route outside the Association? You could try it. But first, you had to find a place to dump, and at the time of my childhood there were only about two or three places in the whole Chicago metropolitan area where you could get rid of your trash, two of them controlled by the same company, with the same loyalty to the Catholic Church as the Dutch brothers had to the Reformed or Christian Reformed Churches. So as an independent hauler, the Catholics wouldn't let you dump at their operation because you weren't a Catholic, and the Dutch-controlled dumps wouldn't let you dump at theirs unless you were a member of the Association. The Association said, in effect, if you're a member, we'll look out for you. And we both know that one hand washes the other. When you went to buy a truck, the Chicago area salesmen for the four major truck manufacturing companies knew pretty well which side their bread was buttered on with all their sales to Association members, and you were likely to get, "Well, we don't have anything available for you." You could always buy a truck out of state and bring it Chicago. But then you better know how to fix it and find parts around the area you bought it from. Not only did this apply to the chassis, it also went well for the body. So you see, being an independent was like pushing boulders uphill. It can be done, but sometimes it's not worth the effort.

So the idea of a trade association, made a lot of sense. It became one big happy family, each with the same goal: to make a living. And, for the most part, was done without threats of physical violence. For many years it worked well. A man with one or two trucks could support a large family, pay his bills, buy a new truck every six years and support the schools and the church. As a young kid I embraced it probably because I was born into it, and had not experienced the other side of the coin. Many routes were passed down from father to son to grandson. They retained their value throughout the years. And if one did come up for sale, you could rest assured there would be five guys banging on the door looking to buy it, usually at the price that the seller wanted. Was this fair? Depends which side of the fence you're on.

Today if you want to buy a radio license, you got to pay for it. Want to buy a TV license? You got to pay. Everything is relative. The government succeeded later on in breaking the Association up, leveling the playing field so everybody could get in the trash hauling business. Now the customer is able to negotiate with whoever he wants, whenever he wants, and maybe getting a price that is close to what he wants. Will this situation last forever? No. Compare this to the airline industry. It's a very close parallel. When the airline industry was deregulated, everybody and his brother got into it and flew every which way as long as they could park near a gate. But ever so slowly each airline died for lack of funds. The same thing is happening in the trash hauling business. Ever so slowly the independent hauler is being scarfed up by the corporations, so that in a few years this whole country will be controlled by maybe four corporations.

The Association had four divisions: East, Central, North and Suburban. Each one would meet individually every month. One of the first orders was to take care of any complaints about solicitation of other members' work, and they would hash out a suitable agreement, or agree to sit down with each party and work out an agreement. As the suburbs began to blossom and expand, the quest for new customers was quite aggressive. Many businesses that were located on the South Loop, the North Loop, or what is known as the West Loop, were feeling growing pains and decided to move to the northwest and south suburbs because expansion was very difficult in the Chicago area. Incentives were given to companies to move to larger locations because of the tax revenue. Many did, so the competition among city haulers to follow them was quite aggressive. Free service, reduced rates, and other incentives were also given by the haulers to obtain the business when they moved.

In order to combat this, many existing haulers in those suburban communities would align themselves with the local politicians or donate large sums to existing re-election campaigns so that they could restrict the licensing of trash haulers that were eager to follow businesses that were relocating. Sometimes they were successful because the size of the account was not worth the legal and financial hurdles that a new trash hauler would encounter by going to these particular suburbs This happened to me later on. A suburban license was available for the price of $2000. It would've taken me one year to pay the $2000, so that meant I would have to work for nothing for one year just to obtain said license from that community. The best thing to do was turn the work over to somebody that had an existing license.

The Association served another purpose: it policed its membership into doing a good job. If you got behind in your dump bill, you got a call not only from the dump, but also from the Association to make sure you paid your bill. If you failed to pick up your stops, the Association stepped in. In one case, I know the husband had too many taverns on his route, and his stops were not getting picked up and the wife appealed to the Association. They helped her get it taken care of and urged the man to get help so that he could keep a tight rein on his business. The customer also benefited from the Association's interventions, although he didn't realize it.

The Association developed cracks in its armor about the mid-60s. New suppliers found landfills, or opened up their own landfills. They bought trucks out-of-state and brought them into Chicago along with a good supply of parts and the technology whereby they could fix them. Also the federal government helped destroy the Association by imposing legislation that said if you had the money to pay your dump bill you could not be shut out. And then to add salt in the wounds, they levied a heavy fine on the Association for price fixing, which was passed down to the members. This, along with the advent of Trash Management, Factor Brownstone Industries and Garbage Services of America—all nationwide corporations—was the beginning of the end for the Association.

The trash hauling business can be compared to an airlines back in the 40s and 50s. It was a controlled business. The Association controlled the trash hauling business in the Chicago area until the government decided to step in. I like to compare the government's attempts to control the trash hauling industry to its attempts to control the airline industry. The government first tried to regulate airline routes and gates, but finally realized this was counter-productive, so they relaxed all the restrictions and subsidies on the airlines. At first, each airline decided to compete head-to-head, offering better service, more comfort and most of all, cheaper prices.

What they wound up with was planes flying half full. When the price of fuel went up, it really started to put the pinch on these airlines. They wouldn't scale back the number of flights because they were afraid of competition from the other airlines. They couldn't raise prices, although they tried, and the minute the planes turned up half empty, they would lower the prices to match their competition. Then, ever so slowly, they went out of business. My first flight was at age of thirty. I flew from Chicago to Dallas. On an aircraft capable of carrying hundred and eighty passengers, they were lucky if they had thirty-five on the aircraft. Now it doesn't take a math or an economics major to figure this out this flight was at a loss. My second flight was to Acapulco, Mexico. That plane was lucky to have twenty people on it. Once again easy to see that this flight was not making any money. Gradually one by one they failed. Some even failed many times, and finally went out of business. The ones that survived are the ones that said, "Okay, this flight at half-full we're not making it till we fill it up. If that means waiting two more hours, we will do so." Now, I know people complain while the service is terrible, the flights are not always on time, and you might as well ride on a bus. But what they do leave out is how much it costs to make that flight from Point A to Point B. Most of the time it's a little over double what it would take you in fuel to drive, not including the time it took, or the motels it took you to stay in while you were driving. So you see, the consumer wants it both ways: good service *and* a cheap price. The cost of aircraft never goes down; it always goes up. The cost of labor very seldom goes down. It may remain the same, but most of the time it will go back up

    Once the monopoly on trash hauling was lifted in the Chicago area, it became a free-for-all. Anybody who could buy a truck was able to haul trash and dump it, as long as he had the money to do it. From the mid-60s up until the present day it has been the Wild West as far as trash hauling. No longer does the Association make sure that you do a good job and treat your customers well. Now the major trash hauling corporations tell the smaller haulers, if you don't take care of business, we will. This, along with governmental controls, basically makes sure that everybody does a good job. Labor costs have continued to go up, the price of fuel has continued to go up and the price of trucks would be beyond the comprehension of my uncles and my grandfather. No longer are landfills ten miles from the route. Now trash is being trucked 75+ miles away to landfills at a price which is about 300% above when I first started in the mid-60s. And the customer still asks, how low can you go in your pricing, not how good can you get. He expects good service. It is no longer a business for mom-and-pop operations. It requires very deep pockets, with much patience for a return on your investment. Some drivers would make a career out of picking up garbage, twenty or more years, and may have worked for four different companies in the course of their twenty-year career. I have to give the modern technology, and the fact that trash hauling is controlled by so few companies, a tip of the hat. No longer do haulers go fifteen or twenty minutes between stops. Now one company might have fifteen to twenty stops in the same two or three block area, thus eliminating the waste of time and fuel, as well as the wear and tear on the truck, to go to next stop. With the big corporations trash hauling has become much more productive.

CHAPTER 5 – INLUENTIAL UNCLES

Uncle Pete

The fabric of my growing up, both my pre-teen and teenage years, revolves around Uncle Pete Lindemulder, Uncle Slim Laning and Uncle Deck Deckinga. My Uncle Al Laning had boys who were capable of helping him out, so my association with him was kind of minimal until I got to be an adult. There was one stop Uncle Pete hauled, which was a hospital located on Harrison Street. We'll call it the Pres. When I first went there as a pre-teen, it was a small old hospital, but as time went on, it began to grow both in physical size and in the knowledge and technology of modern medicine.

Trash haulers were always concerned about the welfare of their customers: the more a customer grew, the more trash they generated; the more trash they generated, the bigger the monthly check to the trash hauler. This was the case in the Pres. A stop that started out as once a day, maybe picking up fifteen or twenty heavy galvanized cans, and maybe ten 55-gallon drums of incineration, suddenly exploded to a three-times-a day pickup. The morning and noon pickups were fitted into Uncle Pete's regular route. The evening pickup was a different story; it involved the Deckinga family for many years.

That is where my father came in. During the day he drove a truck for a linen supply company located at 75th and State Street. That company rented, among other things, coveralls and work uniforms, so they had a ready supply of coveralls for my father. So, after he pulled in and unloaded his linen supply truck, he would pull on a pair of coveralls, and off he would go, to work for Uncle Pete. He would drive over to Dell's gas station on 75th and Halsted, pick up Uncle Pete's truck and come by our house at 71st and Aberdeen. Three of us boys, his sons, were in a rotation, so that two of us would have to help my father. We would wait for him, he would grab a sandwich and off we went down Ashland Ave., north to Harrison St. (Note: the Dan Ryan Expressway was not yet built.) He would back into a courtyard at the Pres Hospital. We would take an elevator down to the basement of the hospital and push twenty-one 1-yard containers through the basement back to the elevator and one by one up to the truck waiting outside. Bear in mind, this was not a packer type truck, but the open truck with the rear elevator platform, and steel plates across the top. Two of us would push a box onto the platform, run it to the top of the truck, push it across the top, and then dump it into the open door. We would take the empty back down and grab another full one. Meanwhile, the guy in the basement would bring up another full one and return an empty to the container storage area.

After about a year, the hospital said, "Wait a minute, this is working real good. Let's just discontinue the use of our incinerator. It is cheaper for us to pay the garbageman to haul the loose paper and other residue that we generate. We can have our employees do something else." Several companies in my career made the same decision, realizing that a full-time man or men to incinerate trash cost more than letting the garbage man take it out on a truck, and get rid of it on his terms. So now, four carts loaded with canvas bags, all containing trash, were a added to our nightly ritual. This loading procedure took about an hour.

When we were done, the three of us would go up to the cafeteria and order our supper. My father would give the lady cashier some money, and most of the time the change he got back was pretty close to the amount of money he had given her. After eating supper in the cafeteria, we would fire up the truck and return home. My father would drop both kids off at home, and we would take a bath while he parked the truck.

Throughout my life my father and I were always disagreeing. If I said it was day, he'd say it was night. I'd say black, he'd say white. But now I realize just how much of a sacrifice his working a second job was. He was doing this to pay for our educations at private Christian schools. Attending Christian schools, as well as attending the Christian Reformed Church, were two very important things not only in our family, but also in my uncles' families. The only reprieve my father got was he didn't have to haul trash on Saturday night. My Uncle Buck (my Mom's sister Auntie Gert's husband) would do this task then. Uncle Buck and my brother Bruce got along fantastically, and Uncle Buck would not take anybody else but Bruce on Saturday night. You see how easy it was to make money in our family. Not a lot. Just enough so that we always had a couple of nickels to rub together. I learned this work ethic early, and it has stayed with me well past retirement.

Uncle Pete kept hauling this hospital stop throughout his entire career. He sold Duke Scavenger Service to his son Peter Junior. Peter later became one of the building blocks of the Ally Empire. To this day Ally still services this account. Unfortunately, Peter Junior died of cancer at a very early age (50). Uncle Pete died of heart trouble, and one of his brothers died of cancer, both in their fifties. By contrast, Uncle Pete's brother Paul lived to almost 90.

Many college tuitions were paid for with the labor of students who would work throughout the summer, as helpers or even as drivers, doing vacation routes for various scavenger contractors. The money was there if you were willing to get up in the morning, without excuses, work hard, collect your paycheck, and say thank you for the opportunity to have this job.

As time went on, my father stopped working on Saturday for De Normandie, washing their trucks. Uncle Pete decided that as long as my father had the garbage truck out on Friday nights and was down on Harrison Street collecting trash at the Pres Hospital, why not do a little bit more than one stop? And over the years what I found out was: if you were willing to raise your hand and ask for more work, you could rest assured, you were going to get it. So Uncle Pete gave him a list and said, "Here, knock your socks off." So, with the help of two sons, we did the hospital as well as a partial route. The nice thing about that was we got to dump the truck at the incinerator, which was something that we very seldom did except for Friday night.

That incinerator is no longer in existence. The story behind that is: several west suburban haulers decided to build an incinerator just off Cicero Avenue, at about 31st St. between the Hawthorne and Maywood racetracks, if my memory serves me right. It is now a Trash Management garage and or transfer station. Uncle Murph (Superior Scavenger Service) had initially put money into the incinerator venture. He bought stock in it, and part of the agreement was that he was required to dump so many tons a month into the incinerator at the going rate. As time went on, the cost of the incinerator got higher and higher, so it was not economically feasible to use it, except for extremely light loads. Our hospital and the list of stops Uncle Pete had given us qualified for a light load, so that made Uncle Murph happy because he did not have to pay that dump bill (Uncle Pete did), and he could still fill his quota.

When I was twelve years old, I learned a very valuable lesson. One Friday night Dad and I got an outside flat on the truck while working at the Pres Hospital. We called Uncle Pete and were told a tire was in the corner of the hospital courtyard, and a jack and wrench were in the toolbox of the truck. He told us to jack up the truck, crank off the nuts, take the wheel clamps off, and install the new tire. Sounded easy enough, that's exactly what I did (while my Dad watched). The nuts and clamps came off, outside wheel came off, new wheel put on, tightened down tight, put the tools away, and set the flat tire in its proper storage area in the corner by the building. Then we drove straight to the incinerator, pulled on a scale, and the scale house guy said, "Hey, you guys, you're missing a tire." I got out and looked. Sure enough, the tire I had just put on was missing.

We had gone down the Eisenhower, (yes, that one was built by that time and was called the Congress Expressway), and the inside tire, by some miracle, had stayed on. When we returned by way of surface streets to the Pres, we rounded the corner and the security guard was standing there, right where the tire had came off at the first turn. I was later shown that a Dayton wheel has a slight ridge on one side of the rim. This ridge, with the clamps bolted down, is what holds the tire in place. But I had put the wheel on backwards. Yes, a lesson learned the hard way. Only twice afterwards did I have to locate a missing tire: one came loose from the truck while it was standing still, and the other fell out of the hopper in transit.

One of our Friday night excursions turned out to be a little different than just being handed a list of stops go out and pick up. On this particular night Dad and I were in one of Uncle Pete's trucks, and he was in the other. We went down on Lower Wacker Drive. Now for people outside of Chicago, Lower Wacker Drive is a street that runs under the downtown area. It's basically a loading dock area for some of the hotels and high-rise buildings below the structures themself. Many a movie has been filmed using Lower Wacker Drive, *Batman* being the most recent. This particular night we were backed up to a loading dock below Merchandise Mart. We could see the river.

This was not one of Uncle Pete's regular stops. He had been called to help someone out, a Jack Ter Mitt, the owner of the regular trash hauling company. Jack had requested my uncle help him haul some extra trash away. This was done quite often, one hauler lending a helping hand to another hauler, of course, for a fee. Hauling this extra trash made Jack Ter Mitt look good in the eyes of his customer. And if you ever needed a favor in return, it was always something you could ask for. After we got done at the Merchandise Mart, we all drove up to Franklin Street, double parked in front of a restaurant/bar, went inside and Jack sat down with my uncle, my brother and me. Jack motioned the waitress over, a seasoned veteran—the waitress that is—and said to the three of us, "What you guys having?"

Uncle Pete never was one to eat a complete meal while working. Coffee and donuts, yes; a quick hot dog, maybe; but never a meal. Us boys, on the other hand, would eat anything, any time, anywhere. It being one in the morning, the donuts had not arrived yet, so timidly we each said, "Yeah, I'll have a cup of coffee." The waitress scratched this on her pad and left. A few minutes later she returned with the biggest, fattest steak I'd ever seen in my life, and set it before Jack, or should I say, Mr. Ter Mitt. The steak was still sizzling as she brought it to him. She set it down with the condiments, then took two shot glasses out of her apron and poured a shot in each glass. Mr. Ter Mitt quickly downed both shots and proceeded to attack the steak.

Now, why bring this up some almost 60 years later? Well, it left such an indelible impression on me, that if you're going to do this job, you better not do it on an empty stomach. We drank our coffee slowly, waiting for Mr. Ter Mitt to finish his steak, which he did, then got up, paid the check and we left.

Now there is more to this story. Some fifty-five years down the road, I volunteered to go to Texas with the young people from our church on a volunteer project. I agreed to drive, and one of my passengers, another chaperone named Jeff, was a guy I grew up with in high school. He still goes to our church, and he and I always talk of childhood things when we get together. On a 22-hour trip you're bound to talk about everything, and I happened to bring up this story, and it turns out the man I was riding with, Jeff, is a nephew of Jack Ter Mitt. While I was unfolding this story, Jeff revealed to me that his uncle was, yes, indeed, a hard drinker, and that at some point in his life, he completely swore off the use of alcohol. After he sold his business, he became very active, both in the church and in helping young people. I met Jack Ter Mitt only that one time as a kid, but what an impression he left on me, not only for his moxie as a businessman, but for one other thing he did, which some sixty years later, I am still telling about.

And it goes like this: most guys around the trash hauling business know what a roll-off is. It's where a truck raises up its body, and the box rolls off. The box is left at a job site and filled at the customer's convenience. Later when it is filled, the box will be removed and replaced with another one which is empty, or removed entirely. This explanation seems rather mundane in today's modern equipment era, but in the late 40s and early 50s roll-offs had not come into wide use. And to the best of my recollection the only one with drawings on the table, and I'm not sure if it had been in production yet, was the Dempster Dinosaur, made in Tennessee. That company was working on an idea to be able to leave containers at a job site, to be filled at the customer's convenience and picked up later. Prior to this most factories had incinerators, with trash rooms next to the incinerator. Items that were not to be burned were hauled by hand onto the trash hauler's truck.

This is where Merchandise Mart and Jack Ter Mitt came into play. Merchandise Mart wanted a truck at their building at all times. This was an expensive proposition, to leave a truck at a stop without utilizing it on a route. Jack must've gone to Erlinder (Remember them? At 122nd and Indiana?). What he did was take the box-body off the truck, install two rails to fit on the top of the truck frame rails, leaving the two hydraulic cylinders which normally raise the body up in the air. Then he mounted a heavy-duty winch, with a cable, in back of the cylinders so that the empty or full box could be pulled onto the truck. The box had rollers on it, which helped the box roll onto the truck. The truck also had a tailgate on the back, which would go up and down and could be used on a route.

Every afternoon, a driver named Bradford, would pick up the truck at 82nd and Halsted, with an empty body on it, go to the Merchandise Mart, pick up the full box, come all the way back 119th and Vincennes, dump the load, pick up several stops, and return to the Merchandise Mart, pick up a full box and leave an empty. Then he would go back to 119th and Vincennes with a full load. He had a key for the landfill, would dump a load and that would complete his day. When this was explained to me after our excursion to the Merchandise Mart, my respect for Jack doubled. Not only did he eat right when he worked, but his entrepreneurial spirit had gone into overdrive, and he had come up with this fantastic idea to satisfy his customer and make a living, all in one shot.
When I explained this to my rider friend Jeff on our trip to Texas, he had no clue that this was his uncle's idea.

Now I know there is going to be some discrepancy here. Somebody is going to tell me, "Nooo, nooo! Heil had this on the drawing board and somebody else had it on the drawing board." But as a twelve-year-old I had not seen anything comparable to it. So I will stick to my story that his was the idea behind the roll-off. I will give credit to Dempster for the idea of leaving boxes at a customer site, but I won't give Heil credit for coming up with the roll-off concept. I never asked when Jack had put this idea into use, so I have no way of double checking the exact timeline. This was the basis for my earlier praise of Erlinder because they would fabricate any screwy idea somebody had. It might seem screwy to the guy doing the fabrication, but when put into practical application and fine-tuned, it made a lot of sense.

In his book *Dutch Chicago*, Robert Swierenga gives credit to Herman Mulder for inventing the first Leach box, and I'm sure Robert knows exactly what he's talking about, that Herman had an idea that instead of hauling one barrel on your back and rolling one, you could take this steel container and put three barrels into it, push it to a truck, dump it and return it empty. Thus for each trip you were gaining one barrel. Herman gave the idea to Elmer Leach of the Leach Corporation, Oshkosh Wisconsin, and Leach patented the idea and marketed it to the buying public. And all Herman Mulder was looking for was a better way to build a mousetrap.

One of the times I was at Stanton Equipment, the Chicago area Leach distributor, a salesman was pitching to me the idea of plastic carts capable of holding two 55-gallon drums, dumped on a gizmo on the back of the truck. I fell off my seat laughing. My logic was: when you put hot coals in a plastic receptacle, it will melt. My operation at the time was where people were constantly dumping hot charcoal, or throwing lighted matches into steel containers, thereby scorching the paint. The fire did not destroy the container. All you had to do was re-paint it, and it was good as new. But once burnt, a plastic container will not ever have any use. But there were ways around that too. Now people are responsible for their own carts, and are required to pay a replacement fee. And if you ever try to use somebody else's cart without their permission, you will be read the riot act. But the bottom line is, every time a cart is dumped, it's the equivalent of two 55-gallon drums. So maybe if I'd stopped laughing at that salesman at Stanton that day and listened to what he was saying, sorted it out, I would have seen how practical this idea was. Later on, I will get into a rant about the progression of equipment over the years, how as wages got higher, the equipment got faster, so that now much more volume is being hauled faster with less manpower.

The system that was used to get rid of the trash at the Pres was changed dramatically in the mid 60s. At that time the hospital acquired a stationary compactor and placed it on the loading dock. This did away with the labor intensive system of moving containers up an elevator to street level and then returning them to their place in the basement of the hospital. Carts of trash were dumped into the compaction unit, a button was pushed and a ram would then get rid of it into the roll-off box. When the box was full, it would be dumped and replaced, so there was no need to go to the hospital three times a day. The system that Jack Ter Mitt had pioneered back in the 40s and 50s was now being fine-tuned so that the compaction feature gave the basic roll-off an even better feature right at the customer's location.

Uncle Slim (Garrett) Laning

This uncle was very influential in my future as a trash hauler. Peter Laning Sons was the name of his company, the name of my grandfather who died when I was four. The company probably started in earnest after my Uncle Slim had moved to Roseland. I came home from school one day in 1958, and my father said, "Pack a bag for an overnight trip." So I grabbed a Jewel Food Store shopping bag, a toothbrush, some socks and underwear, and questioned my father, "Where are we going?" His response: "Shut up and get in the car. Don't ask so many questions." And with that we went to Dell's (not the Wisconsin Dells, but the gas station on 75th and Halsted). And there was a brand-new truck with no body, temporary mudflaps and taillights, and we jumped in and my father started to drive. The drive took us to Oshkosh, Wisconsin, the home of the Leach Corporation.

Anybody even close to the garbage industry knows the Leach Corporation represents the ingenuity of the Leach family, who invented, perfected and marketed a class product for many years in the disposal industry. I know some say Heil did a better job, and they are also correct in some ways. For many years the Heil body served many a hauler whose main load content was ashes.
Anyway, when we arrived at the Oshkosh Corporation about 10 o'clock at night, we pulled up to a service door and rang the bell. A man came out and directed us to a car and gave us an address of a motel. He informed us that the truck would be ready at approximately 11 a.m. the following morning, wished us a good night's sleep and closed the door. We jumped into this rather well-worn Ford sedan, started it up, drove to the address given us and went to bed. Next morning we ate breakfast and at 10 returned to the Oshkosh Corporation, and the truck we dropped off now had a brand-new body on it.

This was a social event for many a hauler from the Chicago area. They would take their wives, or children, or wives and children, to Oshkosh get a new body mounted on their truck, and then return the next day with the complete unit. Sort of like a business trip, which is exactly what it was. You could get the Stanton Company to make the trip for you, but they would charge you, and who wanted to pay for that when you can get out of town for a day? I don't know why Slim gave my father the privilege of taking the truck up there, but I was sure glad he did.

Slim's route was much like Uncle Pete's: same neighborhood, same type of material. The only difference was that Slim had followed one of his customers to the far north suburb of Niles. A. B. Dick had many years earlier moved from the north side of Chicago out to Niles, and Slim had no problem with licensing, so he followed A. B. Dick when they made the transition. This would prove to be a juggernaut for Uncle Slim. Slim's driver, Kenny, lived up there, and Slim would go maybe twice a week to make sure Kenny was still alive and give him his paycheck, say hi, make sure the route was in order, and the truck was okay. Kenny and Slim had a relationship that lasted twenty-five years. Most of the time Kenny got the new truck because the maintenance was a lot less on a new vehicle. The city route was manned by a guy named Jake. He too was with Slim for twenty-five years. I think Jake took his retirement from the union when he left Slim. In fact, Jake was one of the few people I knew that made it to 65 and was able to take a full pension from the Teamsters while still in good health. To this day I am acquainted with Jake's son and his grandsons, who followed in their father's tradition and haul trash. Even one of Jake's granddaughters married a guy who is very active still in the trash hauling business.

So Slim did not have to do a route every day. The main thing was to make sure the customers were happy, make sure Kenny on the North Side was happy and make sure Jake was happy on the South Side. Slim had a very smooth operation. Slim's son and son-in-law carried on after Slim's retirement, and also kept up the tradition of hiring family members. Later on, Peter Laning Sons was sold to Ally, and five of Slim's family members went along with the acquisition. Son Junior died of a heart attack in the early 80s, while still in his 40s. Son-in-law Jim retired in 2014 after spending the rest of his career with Ally. Jim's two sons struck out on their own. One later sold to Ally. Jim's son James JR is still working at Ally. The other is still active in the trash hauling business on his own.

After Jake's retirement, Slim hired a young 26-year-old driver named Leonard. Leonard was cool. That's the best description I can say looking at it from a 14-year-old's eyes. Leonard dressed well, had a way with the ladies, had the gift of gab and drove a 1959 Ford Fairlane 500 with a retractable convertible top. You know, the one where the hard top went into the trunk. What I didn't know was Leonard had quite a spotted track record, and Slim, being one who was full of Christian love and compassion, hired Leonard, assuming that his wild oats sewing days were over.

At first, it appeared that way. Leonard was able to hustle up new stops because he was gifted with a salesman's ability. This pleased Slim immensely. Someone getting the route done and doing a little salesmanship on the side, he had acquired the whole package in one. But that was short-lived. Soon Leonard began to show his true colors. He would get Fred and me to go with him, and he would back up to the dock, tell us to load the garbage, and wake him up when we were ready to go. Then he would drive to the next stop, and repeat the process all over, telling us to wake him when we were ready to go. For two 14-year-old guys this was the greatest thing. We were in charge of running these routes. Eventually he didn't even bother to wake up, and with simple instructions we were able at fourteen years old to drive to the next stop. This was not known to Slim, and of course me and Fred weren't about to tell him, one reason being that if we did, Slim would make changes, and Leonard would also make changes. In fact, one time I did get caught in the middle when I gave a truthful response to something Slim had asked me, and Leonard gave me a verbal tongue-lashing and was not so quick to invite me along after that. I was a relative of Slim's, Fred was not, so there were a few times I was left at home.

One night around eight o'clock, while walking by Dell's gas station, I noticed Leonard getting into the truck with another guy. Leonard did not see me, and I never asked him for an explanation. But I knew that that truck had no business leaving at eight o'clock at night, and I had been around these trucks long enough to know that something was not exactly kosher. Leonard's drug use finally came to the surface, and Slim had no choice but to let him go. Leonard latched onto a few jobs, but they were not in the trash hauling industry, and I finally heard that he had been arrested for trying to pass bad checks. He did some prison time, moved around quite a bit, did some more prison time and eventually died in the late 2000s. My childhood cool guy had feet of clay.

One of the stops Slim had was Driscoll Inc., a company that blended and manufactured printing inks. It involved backing up to a loading dock on Canal Street every Wednesday morning. The truck would not fit flush against the dock; it was at an angle. So the trash would have to be muscled off the dock into the truck. Before we started, we had to put on a coverall that was strictly for use at Driscoll. When we finished, the coverall would come off and be folded and put back under the seat of the truck. The secret was to tape both the cuffs and the wrists and the neck so that the dust from the black dye that was used to make ink would not filter into your clothes. If you were so unlucky to leave gaps, you would be brushing up against black ink on your clothes all day long, or everything you touched or got near would turn into black ink. Driscoll moved to Lincolnwood, next to Niles, where they merged with Richardson Pigments, and Slim kept the account even after the move.

After Leonard was shown the door, Uncle Slim hired Uncle Buck, Auntie Gert's husband. Uncle Buck attacked this job with much vigor, and for the most part, did a pretty good job. After going to work for Slim, Uncle Buck and Auntie Gert sold their house in Englewood and moved to Lynnwood, where they bought a house with some acreage. Uncle Buck was a farm boy, being raised in a rural area in Florida, so he decided to buy three piglets and raise them for fattening to market.

By then I was out of high school and starting to work, so I had a few bucks that I could fool around with, or so I thought. So I bought one of the piglets; I'm not sure if uncle Pete bought the other one. But suddenly we were farmers. Now, I have no clue what a farmer is supposed to do. I didn't at that time and I still don't. What I do know is that pigs have to be fed. Uncle Buck devised this plan: he would take three buckets to work each day. Each bucket had a tight fitting lid, and at Ricardo's restaurant on Rush Street next to Remington Rand, while he was waiting for the place to open in the morning, the night porter from Ricardo's would fill the buckets with leftover scraps of food.

Now, this truck did not have a toolbox, so there was no place to put three buckets of ripe food for the rest of the day, except right next to the driver, two on the passenger seat one on the floor. Needless to say, this did not set well with Slim. Garbage trucks were dirty enough without adding to the mix. But Slim was a patient guy, so he held his tongue and said very little about three buckets of used food being in the cab of his truck. At the end of our work day, Uncle Buck would take the buckets from the truck, put them in back of his station wagon and take them home, where he would feed the food to the hogs.

I think I was charged a fee for his efforts on behalf of my pig, which was fair. He did all the work. He also did it on Saturday, driving his own station wagon all the way downtown to Rush Street at six in the morning with his three buckets and filling them with used restaurant food. Then he would drive all the way back home to Lynnwood so that the hogs could have food for the weekend.

Eventually I gave up on this venture and sold my interest back to him. I think I made a few bucks on it, but it taught me a good lesson on get-rich quick schemes. Most schemes require quite a bit of work, and to Uncle Buck's credit, he *did* work to raise his hogs. His old house still stands; the garage still stands. I don't know how much of that land back there is still part of that same house, or if it was sold to build new houses in back of that house. Eventually Uncle Slim and Uncle Buck had a falling out and they parted company. For many years there were hard feelings between the two families.

Slim was a real hustler, much like all other garbage men, the motto: "you snooze, you lose" very much in the forefront of their thinking. Slim had some real nice stops. As anyone in this business will tell you: it's a luxury to back up to a dock, load half a load, or even a full load in one shot, go to a dump and do that again. And Slim would haul these nice stops, rather than pay one of his drivers to do it for him, and he would usually take Fred or me with him. We were the go-to guys. We would go to places like Cotton Felt at 22nd and Halsted. Now it's in the same building as the Service International Union. We would back up to the dock, put on our dust masks, and a guy would bring us these big bales of used dirty cotton, which we cut open, and dumped in the truck. Then we would cycle the blade on the truck, and just about the time that bale got into the truck, the guy would be back with another one. And we would repeat the process till all the bales were in the truck. If the truck was full, it was a straight shot to the dump.

He had a similar arrangement with the store at the corner of Jackson and State. We would back into a very narrow alley on the north side of John Marshall Law School, which now occupies the whole block between Jackson and Harrison, with its entrance facing Plymouth Court. Before the truck backed up to the dock, the helper would have to get out, walk to the back of the truck and jump up on the dock, because a fire escape blocked the passenger door once the truck was up against the dock. The driver was able to squeeze out or climb out the window. The store help would then load the elevator with excelsior, a wooden fiber that looked like straw, used as packing material before the Styrofoam peanuts became such a common nuisance. Excelsior was the go-to for packing glassware. It's a much a superior product because it does not separate or blow around the way Styrofoam peanuts do. But I suppose it's a lot more expensive to manufacture than the Styrofoam peanuts, so now those peanuts have taken over.

These days I have a rule of thumb: if you are too stupid to tape a box of Styrofoam peanuts and they blow away because I have grabbed that box, then you're going to pick them up, not me. This goes back to the day when I was pushing a container away from a wall on South Chicago. I opened the cover, and the wind caught about a quarter of the loose peanuts in the container and blew them all over the place. The guy working for the customer said to me, "You either pick them up or we will quit as your customer." I bit my tongue because I had just started with City and wasn't in the mood to start looking for another job at the time. But after I finished picking up all loose peanuts, I looked at that man and said, "You just witnessed the last time I will ever do that I don't care what the circumstances are."

But I got away from my story a little. Back at the store on the corner of Jackson & State, the store help would bring down boxes and boxes of, yes, taped excelsior, and I would load them as fast as I could. Just about the time they ran out of boxes, I would run out of room. Slim had a similar stop on Wabash, boxes of trash stored on the second floor, brought down on an elevator by store personnel, then thrown in the back of the truck. You loaded as fast as you can, hoping you didn't run out of room before they brought the last of the boxes.

To this day, I count my blessings, that I had uncles with such dedication to their faith in God that it transcended into their business life. All of them were hard-working men dedicated to the worship of God, their families, their church and their schools that supported their churches. What a heritage to take into adult life!

My teenage years were like most other kids. I was not a particularly bright student, did not like school, did not excel in sports. But one thing I did like was to work. During my high school years I had some of the most mundane jobs that you can imagine, for example, pushing sticks in taffy apples. Most teenagers would have walked away from them, and preferred to stay home and do nothing. Myself, on the other hand, did not mind getting a paycheck every week. It gave me a sense of independence, free from the begging from my parents that I would have had to do if I didn't have a job.

All three of my summers in high school were spent attending summer school. I went to Lindbloom Technical High School, located at 61st and Wolcott, and one of my assignments was to write an essay on the meaning of success. I wrote a very detailed account of how we associate success with money and physical adulation and fame and fortune that goes with it. But the gist of my essay was this: do something you enjoy, make it a game, feel good about your accomplishments, and this is success. Many times I think about this essay. Now that I've reached the downward slope of my life, I realize that I have been successful beyond my wildest dreams. Financially, no. But I always had two nickels to rub together. If I wanted to buy something on time, I could see my way clear to purchase it. I have made it to retirement and beyond, and God has provided for my spiritual as well as my mental well-being.

The last year I attended summer school, my father got me a job at De Normandie, the linen supply company at 79th and Dante. After taking three buses from 61st and Wolcott, I would arrive about 12:15, grab a sandwich at a carry-out place on the corner, and punch in by 12:30. I would operate a huge drying machine and four smaller ones. I would work till 6 o'clock, punch out and then take a shower and head for home. I made a mark for myself at De Normandie. Peter Sellers (not the comedian) was the plant foreman and he liked the way I did things. I also met the De Normandie clan: the father, who I knew only as Mr. D, and his sons John, Roland and Grant. This played an important part in my life later on. I moved up to driving a truck, like my father, after I got married.

After the summer I returned to my senior year of high school and began to date. Nothing serious, till I met a niece of Uncle Deck. She was from a western suburb and went to the Christian high school there, the rival of Chicago Christian High, my high school. My association with her led me to meet a number of people, some whose fathers hauled trash just like my uncles. Some had done quite well; others were just doing their job. But to this day, I will meet the sons of these very people I got to know, and we can talk shop just like the old days.

In fact, one story I tell is the time me and my friends drove out there from Englewood, and we arrived just as church was letting out. And the girl said, "Come on, we got to go to church." My response was, "What are you talking about? You just got out of church." She said, "No, we're having a prayer service." Of course, I inquired what it was for. Her reply was, "The Mob has muscled their way into the garbage hauling business, and we're going to have a prayer service to ask God for guidance."

And this is exactly what had happened. The Mob had connections on Rush Street, since most of the bars and restaurants there were owned or controlled by certain factions of the Mob, and they had decided to muscle in on what previously had been a Dutch-controlled business, namely trash hauling. Being someone who was close to the trash business, I went to the after-church prayer service. To this day, I believe in the power of prayer, and I know God does indeed answer prayer. The Mob later made a deal with some of the larger Dutch-controlled companies, and offered to remove themselves from the trash hauling business, for a price, of course. The Association was still active and they made an agreement with the Mob to buy back the businesses the Mob had taken over. The scuttlebutt was that the Association was willing to sell the stops back to individual haulers who had lost this work to the Mob. This did not set well with some who lost the work; they felt it should be given back to them free of charge. But the Association had to pay for the work—the stops bought back from the Mob, and who was going to pay the Association back?

    I never had conversations with the Mob sellers, so I don't know what their motivation was. Were they going to make it a lifelong occupation, or were they just going to "pump and dump." Or did they find out that hauling trash meant you had to get up every day, work your butt off in all kinds of weather and at odd hours, and put up with rats, smells and all the things that go along with the day-to-day grind of hauling someone else's crap?

CHAPTER 6 – BECOMING AN ADULT

Marriage

I graduated from Chicago Christian High School in June of 1961. After spending three summers in summer school, I was able to walk across the platform at Calumet High School in Chicago (our gym and auditorium were too small to hold a full-size graduation). My first job was not on a garbage truck. None of my uncles were looking for the kind of help that a high school graduate would demand salary-wise. So I went to work for Basil B. Hur, a landscape contractor my friend Herman was working for. So it was an easy transition from my high school graduation one day to the next Monday being gainfully employed.

The money was not very great, but I did not have a lot of expenses, not even a car yet, or enough money to buy one. I figured that if I saved enough, I would be able to move to a better paying job. Uncle Pete had given me some advice: he said, "Do you think that someone is going to hunt you down and pay you big bucks just because you are you?" The more I thought about it, I knew he was right. I would have to earn a place on the garbage truck.

With the landscape contractor, I worked at the Sears administration building on Hohman and Arthington, on Chicago's West Side, planting and taking care of flowers, and also mowing the grass. The mower was self-propelled, and that job was a piece of cake. I would cut the grass, and then to look busy I would keep walking behind the thing and cut all the dirt that Sears owned. This would take about 2 days. The rest of the time I would make myself look busy. Two months after I took this job I decided that I should work somewhere else, and

Uncle Deck knew of a job at Davis Packing in the Union Stock Yards. And because the landscaping job had winter layoffs I took it. Funny thing: two months later, Herman was hired at Davis because Davis asked if I knew of anyone looking for a job, and Herman had just got laid off for the winter. Not long after Herman came to Davis, another classmate came to work there. And in less than a year we about gave Mr. Davis a heart attack. I tore up two cars that were leased from the local Ford dealer, so they would not send me on deliveries. And the three of us called the Union and forced a vote to make Mr. Davis pay us double the pay we were hired in at.

And adding insult to injury, Herman found a job on a construction crew making three times the hourly rate he was hired in at Davis packing for. And I was able to get hired on a construction crew at Ceco Steel at laborer's rate, which was three times what I was hired in at Davis Packing for. Herman and I quit within a couple of days of each other and went our separate ways in the workaday world. Herman went to work in concrete construction; I went to work setting steel forms for buildings.

By that time my parents had moved to Lansing, Illinois, which was about 20 miles further south than Englewood. In less than a year the whole Dutch, Christian Reformed/ Reformed neighborhood I grew up in had moved to different parts of the south suburbs, some to Lansing, others to South Holland and some even went west to

Tinley Park. My old neighborhood was no more. The problem that arises with moving so far is you need a car. I had bought a junk car despite my father's pleading not to, because I didn't think I could afford a brand-new or almost new car, but mainly because it had multiple carburetors. As it turned out, it had more carburetors than I had brains.

At my job at Ceco I would get a late afternoon order to report to a job maybe fifty or sixty miles one way, and it was nothing to travel just under 100 miles in one day. My car was not built for that type of travel, and in a matter of six months I was looking for something a lot better than I what I had originally purchased. I had a small note from Amity Bank for about $600. When I got it down to within the last two payments, I traded that car in for probably one of the better cars I've ever purchased. It was a two-door hardtop 1961 Chevrolet, candy apple red with a gray interior and a six-cylinder engine with a standard transmission and 18,000 miles on the odometer. I was able to get 21 miles to a gallon of gas, and when Ceco said, "Go to Melrose Park," which was forty-seven miles one way, I put the key in and went. When the day was over, I would put the key in, start it up and go home.

They say that some women are attracted to cars, some are attracted to six-pack abs, some are attracted to good looks. But whatever it was, this 16-year-old girl was attracted to me. And so ensued probably the biggest mistake of my life. I could probably go into graphic detail about those ten years of marriage, but suffice it to say, it was a marriage that country and western singers sing about. It was about a self-centered girl who never grew up, never took care of her children, and the only time a husband was necessary when pay day came, and she knew she could have the housing, clothes, and car obtained by my making a living. She always demanded that she look good, and when she was dressed up, she did look real good. The problem is, this comes with a price. And since I was the primary breadwinner, I had to pay the price.

Shortly after the Justice of the Peace in Berrien County, Michigan, pronounced us man and wife, we proceeded to try and make heads or tails out of being married, and the mechanics that go into it. I was employed by Ceco Steel at the time, but there were a lot of layoffs during the winter months. So if you didn't work, you didn't eat. Being a member of the Laborers Union, I went to work at Republic Steel, which was closer to home. At first it was forty hours a week, nothing spectacular. But then the floodgates erupted, and basically they wouldn't let us go home. This was all done according to union guidelines, and for a couple of months I thought the heavens had parted and money was raining down. Of course, my wife and I spent it as fast as I was able to earn it. This only lasted a few months. Then the layoffs came. So I went back to the union hall thinking, *I got that last job very quickly. I should be able to get another one quickly too.* Surprise, surprise! The approximately 150 guys who had got laid off ahead of me were all sitting on folding chairs waiting for the next assignment. They had been there approximately two months. So, with my high school math, I could see that this occupation was not part of my future.

Searching for a job, cold, without networking, is quite scary. You are putting yourself out to total strangers, and trying to convince them to hire you based on first impressions. They ask you for education, transportation, family structure and work history. I'm convinced most of them do not check work history. They just go with their gut reaction on how you present yourself. One interview went fairly well. I had background in steel because I had been working for Ceco steel, but the hitch was, I had made too much hourly while working for Ceco. No amount of convincing was able to sway the man's decision to hire me, the reason being that I would always be looking for the kind of money I was making at Ceco.

Another interview was for delivering donuts. Well, I could do this. I like donuts. The interviewer was a character sent from central casting to play Al Capone. He barely put his cigar down and continued to bark at me, "What makes you think you can deliver donuts?" Needless to say, I did not get that job.

The blushing bride had a part-time job at one of the department stores that dotted the landscape. I think it was called E J Corvette. She dressed up nice, went to work, did not make much money, but was able to contribute something towards payng the rent. One night she came home, and true to form, verbally slapped my face with the fact she was making money and I was not. I had tried to go on unemployment, but there again, I questioned, "How hard can it be to find a job?" In the past the jobs had all seemed to find me. When I was in high school if I did not have a job, I didn't spend any money and the roof still remained over my head. And in time, employment would come my way. Now it was a different story. I had to provide a roof over my bride's head. I had to make enough to keep her from verbally slapping me in the face again with the wage disparity. And I had to put food on the table. I remember the driver of a bread truck selling bread, honey and butter door-to-door. We purchased from him and made—you guessed it—honey and butter sandwiches. He would take payment every week, and he got paid every week.

I then looked at things practically, and thought, *Wait a minute. I have five uncles in the garbage business. I have worked for all five at various times. I can call some of them up and see if they have any work.* I hoped that maybe I would be able to piece together two or three days a week from them, and find an extra two on the outside. I had told myself after I got in the construction field that I really did not want to haul garbage again. The work, I felt, was too hard. And if I stayed in construction, I could make as much or maybe more than I would hauling garbage. But my thinking was changing very quickly.

Uncle Al Laning said, "Yes, I got one day for you." Uncle Slim said, "I have another." Two out of five is not bad. So hauling trash even two days a week, money-wise, earned me as much as the blushing bride made all week. So I took the two offers. The first day working for Uncle Al, I was with a man whose name I only knew as Case. He did not say much and chewed on a cigar all day. I sat next to him for a couple miles, no words exchanged between us. Finally we stopped, and he motioned that I should follow him down this flight of stairs at a place called People's Theater, which was located at 47th between Ashland and Marshfield. A heavy snow had fallen earlier that morning, not the light fluffy kind but the heavy wet stuff. We walked down this flight of stairs, half of them broken, and got to the basement, two stories below street level. Case pointed to a 30-gallon ash can and indicated that I should shovel it full of ashes. When it was full, he put it on his back and walked up the steps to an open door at street level. No Deacon Dykstra operating the cable to pull this can to the street. Your back was the cable, and that's how the ash cans got to the street. I filled my can, walked up the steps, just about broke my back because this stinking thing was so heavy, and made it to the truck. Case was quite a bit ahead of me, having done this many times before.

About the third trip, the door blew shut, and I was in total darkness. When I hit the first landing, I did not know where to go. So I started to walk in the opposite direction of where the second stairway was, and I found myself walking all along the stage where the screen was hung. Bear in mind, I had something on my back in the neighborhood of 150 pounds and I was about ready to drop it. But I could hear the repercussions from the theater owner and my uncle about dropping this can of ashes on his stage. I was just about ready to do so when I heard the roar of the truck because the tailgate was going up. So I headed in that direction and found the door to the outside street, where the truck was located. You talk about something that would take the wind out of your sail, I was totally convinced this was the stupidest way to make a living, but I had to prove to the blushing bride that I was capable of taking care of her, not only to the blushing bride, but to the rest of the critics watching closely the union between her and me. When I told Uncle Al about my adventures at People's Theater, he laughed uncontrollably. In fact, twenty years later when he would mention People's Theater, both of us would grin from ear to ear. The rest of that first day I was shot. I did the job, but after the first stop the wind had gone completely out of my sail. My second day was with Uncle Slim. That was a lot easier, so I could kind of nurse my wounds and rest up till I had to tackle the People's Theater again.

Working only two days left me some time to search around, which I did. I convinced Uncle Slim to take me for my chauffeur's license. By getting this I would be able to drive a truck. I pretty much knew the ins and outs of doing it. It was just a case of studying and taking the test. In those days a fifty-dollar box of cigars on the seat of the truck would ensure that you could pass, even though you might have made a minor mistake. Slim took me to the 99th and King Drive site, and I passed the first time. (I'm not sure if I had to raise the lid on the cigar box or not.) Now I had a lot more leverage; I could list myself as a driver.

But most companies still employed driver and helper combinations. The three days I had off, I made the rounds of various garbage companies. One was Southwest Towns Disposal, located at 95th just east of Cicero. This garage is now a Chrysler dealership. I talked to the man behind the counter, told him who I was, and what experience I had, and what companies I had worked for. He informed me that he did not have anything full-time available, but asked if I would be willing to work during the fall cleanup, which was approximately a month's worth of work. Now I was faced with a dilemma: do I tell Slim and Uncle Al that I could not work for them two days a week because I had another opportunity? I approached both uncles, and they said virtually the same thing: "Of course, if you got an opportunity, you better take it." I did not tell either of them it was probably only for a month or two. So I took the job, and it had to be the hand of the Lord that guided me to make that decision.

The first day I showed up at Southwest Towns, I was handed five white T-shirts with the company logo on the back. Bear in mind, nobody on a garbage truck wore white T-shirts. But this company did, and so, with my white T-shirt on, I began to throw 30-gallon cans in the back of a garbage truck. Nothing bigger than 30, nothing heavier than a galvanized can with house garbage. Over time, I could grab two in each hand and walk to the back of the truck with them. Each house had a limit of cans: no more than four, unless they paid additional for six or eight. We loaded up the first load by 10:30 a.m., and went 3 miles to the landfill at 103rd and Central. We stopped for coffee or breakfast on the way back and made the second load, were dumped and in the garage by 12:30 p.m., maybe one o'clock.

I asked the driver, "Are we done?" "You can go home," he answered, "See you tomorrow." I looked at my white T-shirt. Now when it comes to working, I'm used to dark work shirts and pants. And they still will show the dirt, something about getting into your work. But after one day of work for Southwest Towns, my T-shirt was still white, no ink stains, no spilled soup or lettuce. I could still see it originally was a white T-shirt.

Next day I was there bright and early, ready to tackle it again. This day was even better: one-yard containers on both sides of the street in Hometown. I would dump one, put it back, while the driver was dumping another one on the other side. Length of the day: six and a half or seven hours. Boy, do I like this job. Union scale. Boy, I gotta get on this gravy train. In fact, some of the drivers who had been there a while had second jobs, which would start at the time they were supposed to still be on the first job. The boss knew this, but he didn't care. The work was done. Now for me, I had to figure out how to make a career out of doing this.

One particular day we were in the town of Worth. This was a little heavier. We had to take everything: furniture, mattresses, stoves. When we were done, it was about 2 o'clock in the afternoon. Still not a bad day, only eight hours. The driver headed to a restaurant/bar where about eight other trucks were parked, all with their engines off. We went inside and ordered ham sandwiches with a glass of beer. Boy, I had died and gone to working heaven. This is how you haul garbage. Yes, I wanted a big part of this train, but I could see that this was going to be a hard thing to do, that is, get a permanent job with this company. Who in his right mind would quit a job that paid union scale, you wore a white T-shirt to work, did not get it dirty, and could have a second job that would overlap your first job? The answer to that was: no one.

So after about two months of doing my best, this dream job came to an end. But the Lord was looking out for me again. I had a chauffeur's license in my pocket, so my father had arranged for a job at De Normandie. Although we never spoke about it, I'm sure he did not want to see his oldest son and the blushing bride living in his basement. He could not stand her, and now I can see why.

More experience

I had worked for De Normandie during my last year of summer school, and I had left on good terms with a good work record. So I was able to make the transition from the gravy garbage train to the linen truck. I was informed by John De Normandie, one of the owners, that I was to service the large accounts, restaurants that lined 95th St. And it was my job to take care of all the linen needs that such places like the Martinique, Jack Kelty, the Barn, and Branding Iron had. This was a very good job, almost as good as the garbage truck at Southwest Towns.

I would pull out at about six, six-thirty, in the morning, and would be finished with the actual work about noon. The route went right down West 95th St., and I was able to pass Southwest Towns garage almost daily, one of my accounts being directly across the street from their garage. So every once in a while I would stop by Southwest Towns Disposal, and put my head in the door, and tell them I was still interested in a full-time position, with benefits. They informed me that I was first on their list. About eight months later I got a call from Southwest Towns. Would I be willing to go to work for one of their sister companies located in Markham? I thought to myself, *you mean there are two of these gravy trains around?* Out loud I said, "Most definitely yes!"

So I gave John De Normandie my two weeks' notice. John pulled me aside one day shortly before I left and informed me that if I decided to return—meaning if I had made a mistake in my choice of future employment—I was welcome to come back one more time. He was satisfied with my performance and with my dealings with the customers of the larger restaurants. The biggest one was Martinique, about which I failed to mention, Tony De Santis, the owner, was very good to me. Once a month when a new play would come to town, with such name stars as Diana Dors , John Payne and Doris Day, he would present me with two tickets, and sometimes throw in a dinner for me and the blushing bride. This was a nice perk. You were able to get a taste of how rich people lived at no cost out of your own pocket. So you see giving up De Normandie was quite hard. My father, who also worked for De Normandie, complained about the job. But when I worked there, I kinda liked it.

John and I talked about the fact that I wanted to buy a garbage business. John kinda laughed at me at the time. He said, "That's next to impossible. You know how tight that business is. You been around long enough. You would probably have to pledge your first and second born to be able to purchase a route." At the time John was right. Like I said, when somebody decided to sell, or even thought about selling, five people were knocking on his door. The Mob had no future aspirations about getting into trash hauling again. And from all appearances, the Association pretty much had it sewed up.

With my two weeks' notice given to De Normandie, I touched base with Alter Disposal. At the time I was living about three miles from their garage, and they asked me if I could come to work that same afternoon. Why not? I was game. After finishing my workday at De Normandie, I did like my father when he went to the Pres Hospital when we were in high school. I grabbed a pair of work pants off the shelf at De Normandie, hung up my De Normandie uniform in the car and just before entering the Alter garage, I put on a nice clean white T-shirt. They directed me, "Go to an area at 147th and Crawford, in Midlothian. A storm went through there and blew down a bunch of trees and branches. Start throwing them in the garbage truck and run the blade. That'll chew them up. When you get done with one house, move on to the next one. When you get done with one street, there's plenty more on the next street." After one hour of continually running the Packer blade on the truck chewing up trees, an Alter truck came around the corner, and the mechanic who was driving said, "Time to trade trucks." I said, "This one's not full yet." He replied, "If we let you keep it and fill it, you will burn up the packings in the cylinders from the fact that the truck has run continuously since you started. This way we give the truck a rest, and the cylinder packings will remain intact. The truck we are giving you has part of a load on it. Do this till about 7 o'clock, and then go to 138th & Cottage Grove, and there will be a little house on the north side of street. Drive in the west driveway and the landfill is in the back." I did what I was told, found the driveway and the landfill, came back out and a man stuck his arm out the window, and I signed the ticket. I took my copy and was on my way back to Alter at 167th and Kedzie. I put fuel in the truck, parked it and went home to my blushing bride.

My official start at Alter was on Tuesday morning. The work week was Tuesday through Saturday, picking up homes on the first four days, a commercial route on Saturday. Something I could handle. No long commute like the days at Ceco Steel, no donating my car to a long commute. Union scale, union benefits, and yes, of course, white T-shirts. I jumped on the back of the truck and began to throw garbage. Finished one load, jumped in and went to the dump. Only this time the dump trip was not ten minutes to and ten minutes back; this was one hour up and one hour back.

I loaded the truck again, assuming we would park it loaded and somebody else might dump it. No, we jumped in and had to drive another hour to the dump and another hour return. I entered a third subdivision and proceeded to throw garbage at three in the afternoon. Since this was my first day on the job, I did not question the driver if this was standard procedure, or if were we helping somebody else out. Instead of pulling in at 12:30 or 1:00, like the days at Southwest Towns, this was more like 4:30 to 5:00. Even with simple high school math, I could figure out this was a 10+ hour day. These subdivisions did not have the big tall leafy trees like Oak Lawn and Worth, but only little saplings that offered no shade. My tongue was hanging out of my mouth and scraping the street because I had failed to bring a jug of water like the driver had done. I was also starving because I had failed to bring a lunch, assuming we would stop at some convenient restaurant and order off the menu. No such luck because there were no restaurants nearby. And the faucets on the outside of the houses were all well water, which tasted like they had passed through the junkyard and picked up all the iron they could on the way to your mouth. The white T-shirt which I had put on that morning was soaked with sweat, and the dust from the unpaved roads had collected on my wet T-shirt.

John De Normandie's comments of the month before kept going through my head: "If you feel you've made a mistake, you're welcome to come back again," Had I once again outsmarted myself? Had I reasoned that I knew best for my future? *Well*, I thought, *I'll give it a little more time and see what happens.* The second day was a bit of an improvement. Different subdivision, and this time I took a jug of water with me and a small sandwich in a bag so that I would not pass out from thirst and starvation because non-stop action sure does burn up the calories. Thursday, my third day, was a big improvement, only about eight hours of work.

Friday, on the other hand, was the craziest thing I've ever seen. We were in a subdivision in Markham, cans in front of each house, and the driver skipping houses. Every other one, or one in three, we would pick up and leave the rest. I asked the driver, "What gives?" Was told two separate companies haul all the garbage on the same day. "Why don't they put the garbage on two different days so a guy knows where he's going?" I asked. Driver's response: "Village does not want it that way." "How do you know which ones to pick up and which ones to leave?" "You just do." "Boy, I hope I never have to do this route myself." "Wait till you do," was his reply.

Saturday was, for the most part, a good day. The first Saturday I was directed not to follow the route book, but take one of the cab-over trucks, an International with this contraption on top of it. Drive to Park Forest, find this address and dump a 10-yard container that has a Star label on it. They gave me about a one-minute tutorial on how this truck with its contraption worked. I drove all the way to Park Forest, backed up to the 10-yard container full of trash, hooked the hook up to the back of this container and started to pull the container up. Halfway up it stopped and would not go up or down. I checked the controls in the front that activated the power take-off, then went to the back and hit the side of the truck with my fist. After about fifteen minutes I was no further ahead than when I started. I thought, *I can't sit here all day.* So I walked to a phone booth (remember those things?) and called the shop. I told the guy there I had this big box hanging on the back which was full, and I could not drive away with it. What was I supposed to do? Was told, "Go figure it out."

I went back to the truck and decided the best thing to do was first empty the 10-yard box and then try again. I jumped up into the box and kicked the cardboard and trash into the hopper while running the hopper. Not the safest thing to do as I found out later but it got the box empty. Upon completing this task, I jumped down, and maybe the movement of the body or something must've activated the controls and the box went down as I pushed the Down button. Not taking any chances, I unhooked the box, pushed the Up button with the cable in my hand and the cable went up all the way. Well, I must've done something right. So, I was on my way, still had about twenty more stops to do. The driver of the other truck—only two of us went out on Saturday—was picking up some of the slack.

    One of the stops I went to was in Midlothian. For lack of a better term, it was the Watermelon Man. This stop had instructions to pick up a 4-yard box loaded with watermelons off the ground, drive across the street to an empty lot and dump it. When the 4-yard container was empty, I went back with the empty container and left it where I had originally gotten it. Because I had wasted so much time with the other nightmare and was totally unsure that it would not happen again, I picked the box up, and dumped it exactly where I was. The winch, or whatever the gizmo is called, this time worked fine. But when I picked the box up, I could see why they wanted it dumped across the street. The juice from the watermelons spilled all over, and the pits and the flies all came out of the box at one time. The water/juice went all over the ground, and as it hit the ground, a guy came running out shaking his fist and yelling that this box was supposed to be dumped across the street. Of course, being new to the job, I pleaded dumbass, and vowed it would never happen again. He explained that the reason for dumping it across the street was that nobody had to work around the flies there. But now that I had made a mess out of the work area, the workers would bitch all day.

After dumping several more small, uneventful stops, I came to the last stop of the route, known as the Dorchester Club, located at 154th and Dorchester, a big hotel-like structure about four stories tall. To this day, I cannot figure who built it or why. There's no expressway interchange at this location to make it easy for traffic to get off and on and use this facility as a hotel. My understanding is that the Teamster pension fund pumped a lot of money into this building, which makes me question it even further. It has no frontage road and has to be accessed from either 159th St. or 147th St., since 154th St. is a residential street with no truck traffic allowed on it. This stop had one 6 and one 4-yard container, and of course when I got there, there were cars parked in front of the containers. I was able to swing the 4-yarder around and dump it. But when I tried to push the 6-yarder with my back, I said to myself, "If I try any harder, I won't be able to come to work Tuesday." So I transferred the trash from the container to the truck by hand. Upon completion of my Saturday route, I once again drove back to the little house on Cottage Grove, dumped the load in the landfill, signed the ticket and returned the truck to Alter, thus completing my week, slightly more than 40 hours, which I was getting paid for. But I was still unsure about the job. Let's see if it improves as I improve. Or I can always go back to John De Normandie with my hat in my hand.

After two weeks at Alter I could see that this was not an easy job like the one at Southwest Towns. Here the customers had no limit to the amount of garbage they could throw away. But I was starting to get a handle on it. I had pretty much decided to stick it out. Then they threw me another curve. The driver, who did not talk much to me, informed me that I was going to do the route while he was on a two-week vacation. Surprise, surprise!

In the 60s the area west of Tinley Park was all farmland. There were some subdivisions, but much of that route was individual farmhouses. Some stops you had to back up the driveway and dump the cans by the barn. Others the cans would be by the street. But to me, a city boy, I didn't know one country road from another. The north and south streets might as well have been east and west streets. So, after I got lost the first Tuesday and Wednesday, they decided to give me a helper who knew a little bit more of the geographical layout than I did. He was a college kid whose mother worked in the office. Thank goodness, he was a big help. Somehow he and I slogged through the next two weeks with no customers quitting and going to the competition.

The second month was a lot better. The regular driver came back, said a few words to me and yelled at me quite a bit. But I determined I would be the best employee anyone had ever hired.

After the second month I was called into the office, my knees wobbling a little bit, uncertain about what they were going to tell me. The boss, whose name was Lambert Becker, owned a controlling portion of Alter and would play a very intricate part of the future of disposal industry on a nationwide scale. Later accounts of this man would be met with different opinions. Some were negative, but if you looked at him in the grand scheme of things, he definitely was a visionary, who played a very important part in several aspects of trash hauling nationwide. No, let me correct that. World wide.

The purpose of him calling me into the office was to inform me that a portion of Alter had been sold to a new company, and I was the last one to be hired, so, according to the agreement with the union, I would have to go with the new company. There were three of us that went with the new company, appropriately called New Way Disposal. This company, three owners later, is still in existence. I was introduced to a relatively young man named Ronald Heiser. He was to be my boss for the next five years. He, along with his two uncles, owned the original New Way. Besides three of us from Alter, there were two from an Alter subsidiary in Joliet, so five employees were initially employed at New Way. Ron had a background in trash hauling, having sold an interest in an operation in Chicago. So with a sigh of relief that I hadn't been shown the door, I proceeded to attack this job with much gusto.

The situation with the blushing bride was not improving, so to substitute, or sidestep her, work became my focus, my hobby, the thing that drove me. Not only did more hours mean more money, but by making more money I could pacify the blushing bride. A new car and new clothes were purchased, as appeasement for her demands. The hours I put in were not ridiculous, under 50 hours a week, but the hourly rate was halfway decent. We were living pretty good.

What changed five years later was that New Way purchased a portion of a city route. I would leave home about midnight, go to Orland Park and pick up the truck, make a swing through Bedford Park for two stops, then on to Blue Island for one, go to the 95th and Cottage Grove and pick up two more. This would be approximately a half of load on a 25-yard Packer. If I did the West End first, I would dump at 122nd and Torrance. If I did East first, I would dump at 103rd and Central, the same landfill that I used to dump at Southwest Towns. Ironically, I think this landfill is part of the parking lot for what used to be First Christian Reformed Church in

Englewood—the one I attended as a child—which had moved from 71st St. to 103rd. After the Dutch Christian Reformed and Reformed people left Englewood, the churches moved west, and some south. It was not a large landfill, but it needed to be filled, and yes, garbage served the very useful purpose in filling that particular wad of ground. A little later I will really get into the concept of landfills.

After dumping, I would return to Orland Park and begin to haul another load of residential stops. I did this without a helper because sometimes you were not always on schedule, and it would have been useless for a helper to wait for me each time I went to the dump. The second load would take me approximately five maybe six hours by the time I got back from the dump, so I was putting in twelve-hour days, running from midnight Monday morning to 6 o'clock Saturday morning. No homes hauled on Saturday or Sunday. This route was pretty good. It kept my blushing bride home at night to watch the kids, and I was able to be home during the day, although I had to sleep in the afternoon.

This arrangement worked very well for several years. Get up at midnight, make a partial load in the city, return to western suburbs, make another load, go home. What it also did was give me a taste of how to haul a lot of garbage without a lot of physical, backbreaking exertion. I had told Ron that I would be leaving, not right away, but in the near future. I had been making plans to find another job, preferably hauling trash in the city of Chicago. There's nothing wrong with hauling house garbage, but after a while every house looks the same, every garbage can looks the same. There's no interaction with people, and I could not see myself doing that for the rest of my life. Nothing wrong with the industry itself; it was just that house routes were boring. Strange. It just seems congested traffic, irate drivers, people swearing at me to get out of their way, is all part of the allure that big cities hold for me.

CHAPTER 7 - MY FIRST COMPANY

But Ron told me, "Don't get jumpy. I have some plans here, and you're included in part of my plan." New Way was growing by leaps and bounds. Every week new houses, new stores and new factories were being built. And this required someone to haul their trash. So Ron was quite busy out west, and an interesting thing happened with a few of the stops in the city. In a later chapter I will go into detail, how one account went from four 4-yard containers a day to almost three-quarters of a load a day. No longer could I knock this out in short order. The swings through the city would take a good part of six hours to complete. This put me in a bind when I would get out west. A 12-hour day suddenly was being stretched to longer hours. And I could only guess how long this was going to continue. Was it just a flash in the pan, or would I be doing this for years to come?

I was twenty-six years old when the idea was proposed to me by Ron Heiser and his uncles. We would start a new sister company; New Way would cover the suburbs, and the new company (called Mercury) would cover the city routes. The two uncles would have a third, Ron would have a third, and I would have a third. I would run the operation, be responsible for the pickup, the maintenance of the trucks, and the rest that goes along with it except for the billing and collection. This would be handled by the New Way office, which made a lot of sense to me. One big hitch: I didn't really have the money to swing the deal. It wasn't much, this $5000, but my relationship with my father was not such that I could go and ask him for this kind of money. I did not want to ask my parents because I had already established a very independent streak, and I did not want to drag my parents into my ventures. They had already gotten dragged into my family fiasco, as my blushing bride turned out to be a worse parent than she was a wife.

So I began to hunt for money. The SBA lends money to friends and families of politicians. But when I asked for money, bankers fell off their chairs laughing. Lend money to a 26-year-old kid who was going to buy into a garbage business, untested, with no proven track record? You can see why they couldn't stop laughing. I finally found a guy that would guarantee that kind of money. The only problem: the juice on it was 40%, and I had to put up my house as collateral. The loan was made at Chicago Citibank, 63rd and Halsted. To this day that bank is still there under the banner of US Bank. So I signed my life away, just on the faith that I could do it. The Association, known to bankers, politicians and to anybody close to the trash hauling business, was crumbling. Did I have a vision? Maybe I did, because we had picked up some accounts cold, and also had joined the Association, weak as it was. We were in the East Side branch, and at one meeting someone complained that we had taken one of their stops. But it was quickly brushed aside. So I could see that the Association as it stood when I was a kid, as a guide for how this business was to be run, was no longer a determining factor. They knew if they continued to flex their muscle, the heavy-handed government would soon be on them. So they chose not to try to control the dump situation, the truck situation or anyone who supplied things to the disposal industry.

My new company was named Mercury Waste Disposal. I still have a bowling shirt in the closet with that name on the back, sort of a sentimental vestige of that first company. We bought a sizeable account from another trash hauling company, and put it with what we already had. That account was a very large printing company, which printed Sears catalogues, *Time* magazine. Look magazine, and I think, even *National Geographic*. My equipment consisted of one Packer, which had a new body and an old chassis, and one dump truck, which was used exclusively for hauling wood from this one account. This stop required a pickup at 4 a.m. with the Packer, the dump truck coming at 5 a.m., a noon pickup of four hoppers of restaurant garbage, and then a 4 p.m. pickup with just the Packer. The printing company had two locations, and each time both trucks would get a load. When I arrived with the Packer, a fork truck driver would get from a location inside the plant what is known as a Roura Hopper. This hopper is counter-balanced, and when you trip a handle, they dump. It was a very quick motion to trip the handle, tip it forward, dump the stuff out and flip it back. Then he would go get another one. There were about forty of those hoppers at the morning pickup, as well as at the evening pickup. While he was getting another one, I would cycle the trash into the truck, wait a few minutes and he would come back with another one. In the morning after the Packer was loaded, the other driver would load the dump truck with pallets and big wide paper skids.

    The dump truck never seemed to have enough room because dump trucks have sides. So later on, after the dump truck blew an engine, we bought a flatbed from the other partner, fitted it with chains, and after watching how these pallet trucks came from Mississippi and Missouri loaded with pallets, I decided this was a better idea than using a dump truck. The cost of the flatbed was probably the same as what it would cost to replace the engine. So for the duration of the contract we use the flatbed, which worked very well. When I got to the landfill, I unhooked the chains, took a pipe, jammed it under the stack of pallets and rocked them off alongside the truck. Then the guy on the bulldozer would come along and very carefully push the stacks of pallets out of the way. And I would drive off. That landfill was newly opened (more about this landfill later), so the number of loads coming in was kind of sparse. The operator, whose name was Martin, introduced himself, and it turned out he was a friend of my boyhood friend Fred. So we talked from time to time. He was about my age and he would always ask me, "How is business?" Little did I know he would play a very important part in my later years.

Because the Association was breaking up, several landfills had opened up as free enterprises, one being Mob controlled, and the only thing they cared about was, "How soon are you going to pay us?" These dumps had round-the-clock operations. Whether two in the morning or two in the afternoon, you could dump there. Saturdays, Sundays, holidays, they didn't care, as long as you brought green. The landfill at 138th and Cottage was replaced by one farther east, a giant hole created by a brickyard that had mined all the clay out of the land to make bricks. This landfill had regular hours: six in the morning till four in the afternoon, and till noon on Saturday. No Sundays, no holidays. And another landfill—Sanitary Industrial Development—opened up. Their landfill stretched from 130th and the Calumet Expressway, south to the Calumet River at 138th St. (I will talk about this dump in later chapters.) SID had unlimited hours: Saturdays, Sundays, holidays, as long as you put the ticket in the box and paid the bill.

The problem with a small operation like mine, with limited funding, is you're doing everything on a shoestring. But I had been thrown into the big leagues. Since bankers were not particularly receptive to guys hauling trash without proper collateral, such as property, real estate and more property, getting money was very hard, especially expansion cost money. No longer could I put a few barrels out at a cost of about 15 bucks and begin hauling somebody's garbage. I was now are buying containers at $115 apiece, and I would have to put maybe eight or ten in the particular building. So for maybe the first ten months, anything I garnered from hauling garbage would go to paying for the containers. In the meantime, I had pay my dump bill, maintain my truck, pay my help, and pay for all the other odds and ends that went along with running a business. No longer was this a good business for mom-and-pop. Most small trash haulers would not have enough collateral to finance a truck, let alone the necessary containers to build up a route. The term "investment banking" was not in most people's vocabulary yet. If you had a proven track record, meaning your father had gone before you, truck manufacturers had ways of getting you financing for new trucks. Leach Corporation, the major supplier of garbage truck bodies, had not really got into the financing arm at that point.

So this presented a problem: to do this right you should have new equipment, meaning new chassis, new body. But the fact that the Association no longer controlled this business put everybody in uncharted waters. The old-timers suddenly had routes for sale, and it was taking them a little more than a few months to sell them because, of course, they wanted to get paid, and the only ones interested at the time seemed to be the young whipper-snappers like myself, short on cash or credit, or the large established companies that had established lines of credit, and were able to buy equipment and put large expenditures into an account before turning the first dollar. Yes, the trash hauling business that I knew as a kid was definitely changing.

No longer could you raise prices, and have the customer make fifty calls and get no response. Now you would raise prices and the customer would show you fifty business cards of haulers that had agreed to do it for a given price which was probably lower than your price before you raised it. So any price increase was strictly out of the question. As the new young guns came on the scene, guys like myself: eager, hungry, swimming in the shark-infested waters, many had no clue what they were getting into.

The customer was also getting very savvy, leaving out certain aspects of what was involved in taking away their trash. They would show you maybe ten empty containers after the current hauler had just left and say, "This is what we got." They would then leave out the fact that he had probably cleaned out five more yards of cardboard which was on top of the containers. You would set it up, only to show up for the first pickup and surprise, surprise, five yards of cardboard besides the ten full containers. And when you would complain, the customer would pull out forty-nine more business cards and say, "You want to pick the next guy to haul this?"

Competition was very much alive in the trash hauling business in the late 60s, and guys would walk around saying, "I'm going to haul on volume." What a joke! It still took you so much time per load to haul the trash; and your cost to dump each load, and the cost per truck, and the expenses of tires and fuel were pretty much the same. The only difference was you could probably get a break on labor. The union had somehow lost its effect on keeping this industry in control. So, it was nothing to hear that somebody was making half of what the next guy was making. During the Association days, the Teamsters Union had gotten complacent.

The closest I ever came to throwing in the towel during those early days was one night I went to an Association meeting. My truck had left for its 4:00 pick up at the printing company. I had a relatively new driver, but he had done the pickup for several weeks now and didn't seem to have any problems. After the Association meeting was over, I took some time to chit-chat with other owners before heading home. When I got home, my blushing bride told me, "You better get your work clothes on. Something's happened. Your partner called. He could not get a hold of you." (Remember the days of payphones, before everyone had cellular phones in their pockets?)

So I called my partner Ron. It was about midnight. He said, "You better come out and get one of my trucks. Your truck is at Mack." Mack Trucks was located at 33rd and the Dan Ryan. It is now one of the parking lots for US Cellular Field, home of the White Sox. Seems the driver broke a rear spring, and the body came to rest on the tires. This was something that had happened before, and we knew how to fix it. But the driver had continued to drive on the tires with the body loaded, and twisted the wheels underneath the truck. The tow truck had taken it to Mack, where it was sitting inside the Mack shop, fully loaded, with the wheels twisted underneath. At the time I was driving the pallet truck, so I loaded it up and went to Mack, and was informed that nothing could be done with the load on the truck.

Uncle Slim's son-in-law, Jim, was in charge of Peter Laning sons, and they had a roll-off division. So I corralled Jim and told him the best way to solve the problem was put an empty box in back of the truck. Then I would lift the tailgate, and push the load into the roll-off. The box Jim brought was thirty yards; the truck I had was twenty. In theory this should work. I said "in theory" it should work. As I did this, all I succeeded in doing was push the box away from the load, so that when I was done pushing the load out, I had an empty disabled Packer, an empty roll-off box, and a load of trash in between.

Now I failed to mention that the load was one that had ink slop and other messy things used in the day-to-day printing operation. This load was laying right in the middle of the floor of the service area of Mack Trucks. Jim looked at me and said absolutely nothing, but I could read his mind. To borrow a phrase from Laurel and Hardy, and I quote, "This is another fine mess you've gotten us into."
Fifty years down the road, I can laugh about it. But at the time it sure was not funny. The service manager at Mack said, "You know you are going to have to pick it up." Now when you think about this for

a moment, twenty yards of compacted, sloppy, ink-soaked garbage on the floor of a commercial establishment, lotta good a shovel would do. But do I think about jumping off an overpass at the Dan Ryan and end it all? Or do I sit down at the curb and cry? Maybe. But the fact remains, that trash had to be put in that box.

The printing company, from time to time, would utilize another company for roll-off work, Metropolitan Disposal Corporation. Whenever they would break out a wall, or do some construction on their plant, and they would call Metropolitan. To this day, a very big tip of the hat to Metropolitan Disposal Corporation and its owner, J. Bullock, who I don't think I've ever met. He had a real hotshot front-end loader driver named Marty, last name unknown. Their location was about a mile from Mack Trucks. I ran over there. Just to explain, Marty used to load his front-end loader into a roll-off box, take it to a job site and load the box. Then he would empty the roll-off, load the front-end loader, back into the now-empty box and return to the garage.

    I got out my kneepads and begged Marty, "Please help me out." I explained the situation that I had a load of trash in the middle of the floor at Mack Trucks. Marty's response was, "I would like to help you, but I got no boxes." I said, "Marty, there's a 30-yard box there waiting to be loaded." Well, in one half hour Marty had that 30-yard box of Jim Lytle loaded and there was no more trash on the ground. Marty, you are a saint! I was able to track Jim down, and told him he could get his roll-off box out at any time. It was completely loaded and ready to go. Mack had a tow truck and were able to tow the disabled Packer into their backyard.

    And then I had the big task of cleaning the floor. The first thing I did was go to their sanding box in the back and carry two buckets of sand at a time and spread it all over the floor. I took their broom and worked the sand into the ink on the floor. Then I grabbed one of their containers and loaded the oily sand into the container. After that, I proceeded to use soap and water to clean the floor. In the space of nine hours I had the floor completely clean, just like it was before I had tried this stupid stunt. Gave me a very good lesson in looking before you leap.

The truck chassis was never fixed by Mack. After much debate about what to do, my partner and I decided that we could not afford to buy another truck, and I located a company that was able to bend the frame back into place. We repositioned the wheels, remounted the body and continued to use this truck as long as Mercury Waste Disposal, under the guidance of Ron and Owen, was to remain in business. To this day, I don't know what the bill for that Mack fiasco came to. Ron was kind of closed-mouth about how much I was spending.

This incident was an eye-opener about the caliber of driver I should use to operate this truck. Not everyone who said he could drive a truck was able to. The guy who gripped the steering wheel was very important to a smooth operation. So later, when I looked for help for the afternoon shift at the printing company, I tried to get experienced drivers, guys that would get home at two in the afternoon, take a short nap and then spend three hours driving in the evening. The pay was halfway decent, and the job didn't involve a lot of physical activity.

CHAPTER 8 - INJURY

Chicago is blessed with a lot of great landmarks. Oh, I know Buckingham Fountain comes to mind, but what I'm talking about are the kind that are along the expressways, the kind people pass on a daily basis. One used to be the Magikist sign, with time and temperature and a big imprint of a set of lips on it. There was one on the Eisenhower at Cicero Avenue and another at 75th and the Dan Ryan. The North Side had similar ones. The Magikist signs are gone; Magikist no longer exists.

But there is a blue sign that used to hang over the Dan Ryan Expressway at Cottage Grove and 99th Street. It is no longer visible from the expressway, but If you get on Cottage Grove, you can still see a blue circle with white lettering that simply says "Jay's," the brand name for Jay's Potato Chips. I might thank them for being instrumental in getting me in the garbage business. But when a bankruptcy auction was held for them in the early 2000s, I pulled off at 99th Street and did a war dance. This company should have sent me a bill for college education because they did more to educate me about economics than I'll ever care to admit. Let me explain.

The early night operation I did when I worked at New Way involved going to Jay's in the wee hours of morning, where I would back up to three 4-yard containers, dump each one and be on my way. From time to time I would see this dump truck—not your standard dump truck—that had two pipes coming out of the back of the truck body. If you ever go by Jay's along the expressway, you will notice a railroad track running parallel to the building. This special dump truck would back along this railroad track, and a man and his wife would load barrels, lined up on the loading dock, into the dump truck. The barrels would be loaded with the potatoes which were rejected during production of the potato chips and the skins from the potatoes. I would just get the paper, the rejected bags, and be on my way. However, I could not help but ask Tommy, the fork truck driver, what the dump truck was doing. Tommy's response was, "They feed them to their hogs." Of course!

I remembered my experience with Uncle Buck and his three cans of slop sitting on the passenger side of a garbage truck. I was somewhat familiar with the feeding of hogs with restaurant garbage. This is the ultimate form of recycling. What normally would go into the trash could be used for animal feed. Makes perfect sense to me. Sure beats throwing it into a landfill. (More rants on recycling later.) The two pipes that were sticking out of the truck, Tommy explained, were steam jets. When the guy got to his farm, he would hook up to the pipes and force hot water at extreme pressure into the truck body, and would cook the potatoes and destroy any bacteria, thus preventing harm to his hogs. Man, was this a good idea.

Then one day Tommy came up to me and said, "Would you bring us another container?" "Of course," I answered. "That's what I'm here for, to satisfy my customers." But when I dumped the four containers, he would fill them again with barrels of potatoes, and I would dump them again. So, instead of three or four containers an evening, I would be dumping eight. When the eight were dumped, Tommy said, "Would you move over to the dock? I got a couple more barrels for you." "Yes, of course." Then he would give me about ten more barrels of potato material.

A footnote to this is some stops are charged on a monthly basis, but many are charged by what comes out. Fortunately for New Way, at Jay's it was what came out. Instead of twelve yards a night, I was doing twenty-four to thirty yards a night (three 55-gallon drums equal one yard). Well, anyone knows potatoes do not pack. A yard of potatoes is exactly that: one complete yard. So the truck was pretty much loaded every night when I left there. I inquired with Tommy what happened to Rayford, the hog farmer? His reply was, "He sold his land to a shopping center and quit raising hogs. So he don't need no more potatoes to feed them." I informed my partner that this was the case, that we were now hauling about twenty-four to thirty yards a night, which was equivalent to almost a full load.

Of course, this is a big problem for the customer. He is used to getting a procedure done for nothing. Rayford needed the potatoes to feed his hogs, so he was happy to get the hog feed. Jay's did not have to pay for this procedure, and both parties were happy. But take Rayford out of the mix, and what happens? Those potatoes have to go somewhere, and so, twenty yards of potatoes were dumped in our big old lap. But hauling garbage is not a charity drive; it's a business. And a business must charge for what it does. No longer was the bill for hauling Jay's garbage a few hundred dollars a month, but was… Well, you do the math.

This did not set well with Jay's. Always in the back of their mind, they were now paying big bucks for something that they used to get for nothing. So the guy breaking his ass and getting these unwanted potatoes out of their way was now their adversary. This is a common problem in our business. A lot of customers just assume that this extra garbage should be hauled for nothing by some magical formula. But no longer did I have the luxury of folding twelve yards of fluffy paper bags into a load. I had to go straight from Jay's to the landfill. And not only are potatoes heavy, they are very rough on the equipment.

One Friday at 6:30 in the morning I ate breakfast at a diner on Cottage Grove, then went to Jay's. It was about six below zero that morning. There were four containers full of paper bags with water-logged barrels of potatoes dumped on top. Those containers had back outriggers for stability, which would tend to get hooked on the loading dock when picked up. So you had to position the truck about a foot away from the trunnion of the container, pulling the container to the truck so that you could pick it up.

The problem was the splashing water would freeze in front of the container and cause the container to go from side to side and not find the back of the truck. To solve this, you would take the chains on the blade which were used to pick up the smaller containers and put them on the trunnion, activate the blade, and this would pull the container straight to the truck. I had done this procedure thousands of times without much thought. When the container was to the point where you could pick it up from the back, you would release the pressure from the chains, hook them up out of the way and pick the container up from the back. Most of the time the container would raise the truck into the air so that the front wheels were off the ground. That's how heavy they would be.

This particular morning that never happened. My left hand was wrapped around the hook, and I activated the handle to give the chain some slack and release the hook. But I moved the lever the wrong way and instead of the hook releasing, it went forward and my finger was between the hook and the trunnion. In a split-second a sharp pain went through my body, and I thought, *Well, I won't have that finger for long.* I shook the glove off in one motion and stared at a completely smashed, folded-over finger. I knew I could kiss that middle finger goodbye. There was an old man on the dock, stacking the empty barrels. I jumped up on the dock and said, "Where is your first aid?" His reply was, "What you do?" Mine was, "I just took my finger off," and I showed him, and he pointed. "Down that way." I ran along the dock, holding the palm of my hand so that the blood would not drip all over their loading dock. Partway down the dock, I asked another guy, "Where's first aid?" "Oh, shit," he said and pointed to the end of the dock. I started to run again, and all I heard was the sound of him tumbling into the empty barrels he was stacking. He had passed out. "I gotta take you to the hospital," was the response of the plant foreman. "Jump in the back seat of my car." I did so, laying across the seat and holding my hand over his floor mat so I wouldn't drip blood on the back seat of his nice Oldsmobile. He took me to Roseland Community Hospital.

Remember what your mother used to tell you: "Always wear clean underwear because you never know what's going to happen." Well, my blushing bride, who could not find her way to the washing machine, had left me no other choice than to put on my last pair of underwear. Both the T-shirt and the briefs were the most despicable pair I owned. I think a car wash would have rejected them. The first questions they asked me at the hospital were, "How'd you do it? and "When did you eat last? I answered, "Well, about a half hour before this happened." The reply from nurse was, "We're going to have to give a shot, put you in bed, and let your body digest the food naturally. We do not want to have to clean up your finger and the other end of your body at the same time." So that's what happened. I laid in bed till about 11 o'clock. I informed my blushing bride that I was in the hospital, and would she call my partner and tell him where the truck was and that I would be incapacitated for a little while. At 11 o'clock they wheeled me into the operating room, put me under and proceeded to take the rest of my finger off.

At first you get the crude jokes about your missing middle finger. As I got older, my grandchildren would want to touch the stump. Or they would explain to their friends, "My grandfather has no middle finger." Most garbage men have similar stories. Uncle Pete was missing a thumb. His brother Ben was missing an index finger. So you see it's not uncommon for most of us to go through the same type of accidents.

As time went on, the hostility between Jay's and Mercury continued. We kept hauling their garbage and billing for our services;

they continued to make overtures that they were looking around for someone to haul it cheaper. Now in the trash hauling business, the word "lowball" comes up quite often. This is the term that people use when someone will go in and offer a ridiculously low price to a potential customer just to get their foot in the door. They will set up the account, then figure how badly they got burnt by this low price. And then comes the hard part of figuring how to get the price back up to what they should be getting for what they are doing.

When I see the modern-day TV ads about cable companies, satellite dishes and cellular phones, advertising how cheap they can go, I am constantly reminded of the term "lowball." As you know, you sign up for a cable/satellite dish, and the first year seems to be a hunky-dory and you sort of forget about it. Then all of a sudden, the bill will catch your eye, and you say, "Why in the world are we paying this ridiculous amount for the ability to watch TV?" And a husband will ask his wife, or whoever pays the bill, and the response will be, "Well, they raised it once, and then six months they raised it again, and then six months later they raised it again." And now you're paying a lot of money for something you thought you were getting cheap. The same thing happens in the garbage business, a hauler has to raise his price and the customer gets upset and starts looking around for another provider.

With Jay's, it was especially painful for me because the trash hauling company that was barking at my heels was the company that hauled Jay's before I did. This is done quite a bit, the big guy baring his teeth at the little guy and saying, "Don't you dare take it. I will make you pay." And they can make you pay. In the case of Jay's, that other hauling company promised to spend about $10,000 in a stationary compaction unit and roll-off container, and haul Jay's for about the same price as I was charging them. No amount of finesse or salesmanship can solve these situations. It's something you learn by experience. Even doctors, who go to college and medical school, garner most of their education when they are put into situations where they have to apply their book knowledge to their everyday situations. And this is my gripe with colleges. For example, a business college could not have prepared me for this type of situation, where the customer has a lowball figure, is threatening to quit, has milked the old supplier for all he can, and is ready to allow a fresh supplier to work his magic.

Yes, sometimes a new supplier has a better idea and deserves a chance. In the case of Jay's, was the stationary compaction a good idea? No. The first one split like a bomb went off because potatoes don't compact. But the smoke and mirrors of selling the compaction unit as a way of saving Jay's money was all that was needed for the new hauler to get the stop back. They eventually turned the pressure down on the machine, thereby making the load less dense because all it was doing was shoving potatoes into the roll-off box.

So we pulled our equipment out after being told our services were no longer needed, licked our wounds, and said, "Well, it's better to not have that stop than to take a loss every time we go there." What the new hauler wound up charging when Jay's sold to Borden's later on, I don't know. But that hauler stayed with Borden's for many years afterward. Jay's was sold to Borden's, but later Borden's reneged on the deal with Jay's, and Jay's wound up with the whole kit and caboodle back, and then went bankrupt for a total of three times before the company was bought at auction by Snyder of Pennsylvania. Now when I go by and I think about it, I raise my left hand, and given them the abbreviated finger.

Good riddance!

But thanks for the education.

CHAPTER 9 - PARTING COMPANY

Any driver who has ever done a route will tell you that the bigger stops are the ones that they enjoy hauling the most. This is true for the owner of the company as well: one truck, one driver, one bill. Usually the same driver goes to a large account and pretty much knows just what to do to make the customer happy. The problem is that if your bread-and-butter depends on a few accounts, then if you lose one or two, you're in a world of hurt. Like putting all your eggs in one basket and then dropping the basket. Maybe you didn't drop it on purpose, or it wasn't your fault. But you still have no eggs. This is what happened several months after we lost Jay's.

We were put on notice again with the printing company, a very large account for us. The civil rights movement was in full swing, and black people were demanding a bigger share of the trash hauling pie, and what better way to get a bigger share than go after the big pie. This is what they did, and my partner said, "Well, we could possibly keep the account if we drastically lowered our price." But then you're faced with the same dilemma again: you work for nothing to keep it. Do you walk away, dust yourself off and see what the future holds? After several months of agonizing I decided, *No, I don't want to donate all my time and energy to one or two accounts who are bound and determined to beat me up one way or another.* This is what I mean by what they don't teach you in a classroom. Do you lower your price to keep a customer and hope, somewhere along the line, you can juggle your way into profitability? Or is there another way you can do this, and still make a living?

After we lost the printing company, my partner, Ron, said to me, "There are a couple of small routes for sale. Do you want to buy one and continue the partnership? Or do you want to buy me out? Or do you want to sell out? (Ron and his uncles had sold New Way and were free to go in other directions.) After much soul-searching, I decided that even though Ron had been a mentor to me and had showed me as much about this business as any of my uncles had, it was best for us to part company, and each go our separate way. So we decided he would keep Mercury Waste Disposal and I would look for something else.

After we separated, Ron combined the route we'd had with a new acquisition, and approximately a year later sold the whole operation to another individual. Ron later bought a resort in Montana. The sad commentary on this is that after we shook hands and parted, I never did see him or talk to him again after he moved his wife and two kids to Montana. Not out of any hostility or animosity. Just neglect. All I know is, without his guidance in my first venture, I certainly would have failed. I worked for six months for his brother, and during this time I was making phone calls, looking to line up my next venture.

CHAPTER 10 - BIG CHANGES

The early 70s were a time of real transition in the trash hauling business. In my early exploits most factories had full-time guys that would do nothing but burn trash in incinerators located near the back of factories. Most grocery stores had a similar setup. The factories outside city limits might also have burning pits, where they would take big crates, cardboard, or whatever, and on an overcast day, throw a match to them. Apartment buildings were no different. They burned coal, and every morning the janitor would go up to the porches and grab all the garbage that people would leave by the back door. Then they would go to the basement and stoke the furnace, add some coal and proceed to burn the garbage.

On any given day you would see in the City of Chicago big plumes of black smoke emitting from tall chimneys on these apartment buildings. A twenty-four or thirty-six-unit building could generate quite a bit of garbage, and this was drastically reduced to a few barrels of incineration dumped a couple times a week. That's why drivers on the north and south shores of Lake Michigan wore leather pads on their backs to protect themselves as they hauled barrels of incineration and small cans of ashes out of basements of apartment buildings. This system was in place when my grandfather started in this business, and I followed in his footsteps. Some routes were big generators of incineration and ashes burned by coal. Coal trucks used to dump loads of coal on the street, and a worker would wheel it to the basement and dump it there. Coal was a cheap form of fuel, but it has always been a dirty type of fuel. Couple that with the garbage being burnt, and it provided a cheap way to heat a large building. Keep this in mind for further discussion: every argument has two sides.

My three uncles—Pete, Slim and Deck—were affected when the EPA made a decree that all buildings in the future would have to burn low-sulfur coal, at such a steep price that building owners were being nudged to either burn fuel oil or natural gas. The refusal to "grandfather" these buildings forced many an owner to convert to natural gas. Converting to natural gas or fuel oil eliminated the chamber in which to burn garbage, which was the whole idea behind this edict from the EPA. No longer did they want to see large billows of black smoke every morning when all the janitors burned their garbage at the same time. They did give some latitude on the use of coal because they realized that the gas company could not provide natural gas to all these buildings at one time. So many owners applied for permits for future conversion. Uncle Al was actually a beneficiary of this rule by the EPA. His operation suddenly doubled, maybe tripled because garbage could no longer be burned along with coal, and had to be hauled separately from ashes. He was faced with what should he do? Buy more trucks? Or sell some off. He chose the latter. He put a For Sale sign on one route. Routes at that time were bought and sold mainly on the basis of location, location, location. Suburban routes were the first to be sold, at a higher price. Loop and North Side routes were second. A distant third were those South of the loop, commonly referred to as the inner-city. This much now-unburned garbage being placed into the waste stream all at once created quite an opportunity for both the existing contractors and the new breed of black business owners. Many of them were able to buy a truck, a few containers or drums, and were able to start a new business.

Uncle Al did not want to go head-to-head with the other scavengers, so he put one of his routes up for sale. I approached him and said very plainly, "I will buy one route, at your price, but I do not want any stop to exceed $200 per month in its billing. I do not want People's Theater (which, of course, was our inside joke), and I don't care how hard it is to haul. I will figure it out." I should have left that last part out; I got every basement carry-out that he had. Part of the route was around 71st and State, a few stops east of State, but most of them were west to about Ashland Avenue. The route was very compact, so I had no complaints there. Uncle Deck also approached me and broke off a piece of what he had in the same neighborhood. So I put the two together and made one operation. Bought a small truck from the two brothers that bought New Way out west, and was in business.

The thought process behind this was very simple. No longer did I want to be at the mercy of a customer who said, "This is what I want hauled and this is what I want to pay, and if you do not agree with my terms, you can walk out the door the same way you came in." I wanted to reverse this procedure, by making the work much harder than flipping a handle on a Roura Hopper and running the blade at dock level. I figured the 4- and 6-yard containers would come later. I might add, this was a very good way to approach my second venture. Yes, it was hard physically, but it did open up many doors which I was not used to.

I then went to my blushing bride's brother, who was a real straight shooter. To this day I still talk to him and thank him for being a very understanding individual. I asked him to do the billing for me to ensure that I would get the bills out on time, regardless of how hard I was working, and that the money would come in at a given time. I also said to him, "I want a breakdown on what each stop pays per pickup and give it to me in a book, so I can ask myself, 'Is this stop worth what I'm getting?'" This worked very well. If I would lug a couple of ash barrels out of the basement, was this worth $20? If I lug six barrels, and two of them are ashes, is this worth what I'm getting? If not, this customer needed to have his price raised in six months, and I did raise several. One guy in particular went to Uncle Al and said, "I'm going to quit." Uncle Al asked me, "Do you want this stop? My response was, "Is he going to pay me what I want?" "Well no, but you can have it at the old price." So I told Uncle Al, "He can find someone else."

I began to notice something: my theory was right. When something is hard to haul, large companies have no interest. It's when these stops generate big revenue that they catch someone's eye. In this case a competitor took two stops, and within a week I had two more to replace them. The human body can only do so much in a day, and if you are hauling less, you have time to haul more. This sounds like a contradiction, but it's not. Certain days were a little bit lighter than the other days, but by being in the inner-city, you always had garbage. The existing trash haulers would do what they had to do, but most of them would not haul extra trash. So if you came along and hauled the extras, hey, that was money in your pocket. But boy, some of those stops are real hard to haul. I don't know how many pipes I banged with the ash can on my back that sent shockwaves down to my toes.

What I also began to notice was that the new upstarts in this neighborhood had not been schooled like I had. They had maybe been drivers in the past, so they knew how to drive and pick up garbage. But a very important part of this business is the maintenance of the truck and, of course, what containers you got. There are horror stories of how help who had no clue about what made these trucks tick totally destroyed them because they did not have the knowledge of what it cost to fix them. Greasing was an important part, as was using clean fuel with winter additives. This helped insure that you would make it through the day.

What you didn't want to do is be halfway through the day and have to stop because something didn't work, and you had to go to either Heil or Erlinder and get a repair done, and then return to the route to finish. Because my operating principle was: do the stops on the days they're scheduled; don't move them around. That way you could pretty much keep everything in order. Many other guys would slide stops off to the next day, or the next, and you could imagine what their schedules started to look like. You got to remember, there were still about 300 companies of various sizes in the whole city. It was you against the other 300. So you had to rise to the top and be the best in your given area.

What I did notice was that if you were good, then people would come to you. If your price was higher than the last guy, their coming to you gave you an edge because you could always say, "You're not coming to me because I'm cheaper. You're coming to me because I'm better." Does this seem self-centered? Maybe. But that's what big corporations do now, offer better service. So the growth was slow, but every once in a while I would buy a couple new containers and update an existing stop. Remember the Herman Mulder Principle: you can haul three barrels with one container. And if you had a container in the back of the building, this was quite a trip saver.

About a year into this quality operation—that's Quality with a capital Q—I replaced the truck I had gotten from New Way with another truck that I bought from TV Scavenger. Tom Ritterhorse was in the same business I was, one truck working by himself. He had gone to a bigger 25-yard truck, and I bought his smaller 16-yard truck, a small cab-over Mack with a diesel engine. This was a pretty good truck at the time, and it cut my fuel bill in half.

I hired my cousin Rusty, Uncle Al's second son, who stood as tall as I did and could work as fast as I could, and Cedric, a black kid who lived on the route and from time to time helped Uncle Al. Cedric was from a family of, I think, about four children. He had an older sister and two younger brothers, and lived on the second floor of a building at 72nd and Stewart. So on Saturday morning I would pick up Rusty at his house in Roseland, then go down Halsted Street, pick up a few stops, and we would go to 71st and Stewart, where Cedric would have set out all the containers and cardboard at that stop, so I could just back up and we would throw them in the truck. Then we would jump in the truck and proceed to haul about 75 more stops that day. There would be one dump trip to SID partway through the day, then we would return to the route.

Before we were finished, we would stop at Muses Waffle House at 75th and Vincennes, where Cedric, Rusty and I would hang on the feed bag. Borrowing from my days at the Merchandise Mart with Jack Ter Mitt, we would eat good. Then I would drop Cedric off, pay him, and take Rusty home, and bring the truck in with a partial load on, ready to start on Monday morning. This was a very productive day: a total of ninety stops picked up, a load and a half. I forget how much each stop would pay, but it wasn't bad. Labor was cheap, dump was cheap, and I didn't have to worry about twenty-five or thirty yards of rotten potatoes breaking the truck.

To Cedric it was a way to earn money. He had an asthma condition, which required him to use an inhaler, and I remember from time to time him asking for his pay when he first got in the truck. And I knew what would happen: his asthma was acting up and he needed the first drugstore to buy an inhaler to aid his breathing. Cedric got to meet my brother Glenn, and to this day Glenn still talks about Cedric. The sad part is the last time I saw Cedric was when I opened the back door of a liquor store on 83rd and Cottage Grove to throw the garbage out, and Cedric was walking down the alley with another guy. This was several years later. The conversation was brief. And we parted. Many years have now transpired, but every once in a while I think about him and wonder what happened to him.

Early one morning I was at 71st and Harvard and was dumping some cans when Uncle Al pulled up in back of me, put on the brakes, jumped out, walked up to me and asked me, "Do you want to sell your route back to me?" Needless to say, I was taken aback. I sat down on the curb and looked at him and said, "Would you repeat that?" Which he did. Okay, then the floodgates of questions came to me: why, when, who, where? Uncle Al explained. "Sell it back to me so I can run two trucks with my sons Rusty and David." Rusty was working part-time; David, his older son, was no longer in high school. I told my uncle, "Well, give me a couple of days and let me think about this." He said, "Okay, give me your answer in a couple days," and left.

What to do? Sell it back to him, or not? There was little money to be made. I still owed him quite a bit for the initial purchase. But I had built it up, so there was a profit margin in the equation. What would I do in the future? Well, I could probably take David's job. He was working for Uncle Slim at the time on the North Side. That might not be a bad idea. Just take a break, remove myself from this business as an owner/operator. My marriage to the blushing bride had ended in a shambles. We were beginning the early stages of a divorce, starting to hash out the financials. The business part was mostly debt. The house had some value. Maybe this would be a good time to step back and reassess what my future would hold.

Later, when I was single again, I might think about dating, but it was hard to date with these kind of hours, and with this kind of lifestyle, you could not present yourself to someone as a future husband. I could understand it; someone coming in from the cold could not. These were things that ran through my mind for the next two days, and based on them, I gave Uncle Al an affirmative, that I would sell lock, stock and barrel to him in a month and a half. It was arranged that I would take David's job, and David would take the keys to my truck. A promissory note and a release of the note with

Uncle Al was drawn up between ourselves, and the deal was done and Quality Disposal was now owned by Uncle Al.

CHAPTER 11 – SOULMATE

The breakup of my marriage was something that probably should have happened five years prior. I realized how serious a mistake our getting married had been. But two children, aged seven and six, were the best result of this relationship. The blushing bride had not got any better. In fact, she had gotten worse. At age sixteen, she wasn't allowed to go into bars, so for about three or four years that problem was postponed. But once the bars opened to her, she adopted this as her element, with only brief interludes of remorse, in which she tried to become a mother/housewife. However, she would always return to the dark lights of the bar. My parents were granted custody of the two boys, and may God bless my mother's heart for accepting once again, the responsibilities of her irresponsible oldest son. My father, on the other hand, issued this edict: "Don't bring none of those floozies around here." Me? I had just been let out of marital prison. No more did I have to babysit a fully grown adult woman. I could concentrate a little bit more on two young sons.

My job with Slim was to go to Slim's house in Calumet City, ride with cousin Junior to Niles, pick up the packer at A.B. Dick while Junior picked up the roll-off, and do a route consisting mostly of record companies. (Remember those round vinyl things with music on them?) One of the stops was Richardson Inc., a later version of Uncle Slim's messy stop in Martin Driscoll where we had to put on a coverall and tape my wrists and my ankles and my neck. At

Richardson I didn't have to do all that because I was careful to open the cover of the one-yard containers and dump them. And as I was dumping them, I would just walk away. Sure was a lot easier letting the truck do the work. The landfill was on Willow Road in Glenview, and we would return to A.B. Dick about one in the afternoon, and grab a bite to eat at Jack's Restaurant, which is scheduled to close in July 2016. Then we would beat the traffic all the way back Cal City before it got to be the evening rush hour. Truly a sweet gig. I would haul straight loads of records, and I don't want to ever see another Al Green record or Jackson Browne. But in my basement I have a few treasures absconded from the loads, one of them being a Neil Diamond *Hot August Night,* which was presented to me on my first day on the job. This gift was intended to make my pencil a little lighter when I made out the ticket.

On Saturday I had to haul two stops. One was the Learner Shop on State Street, where they had all the boxes piled up on the curb by 8:30, and I had to be there on time to pick them up. Sounds easy, but now I can admit there were a couple times I sure didn't feel like getting up, and if I was ten minutes late, they were on the phone. Then I went to a stop on Hubbard and Ashland, and picked up long strips of wood from a woodworking company. I forget the name of that company.

With some of my earnings I bought a small boat, with a good outboard motor. We kept it for ten years till 1986, when I sold to Rev. Al Vander Griend, the former pastor of Peace Church in South Holland. A few months ago I talked to him in person for the first time since we made the exchange on US 94 in Bridgeman, Michigan. He said his kids learned to ski on that boat, and then he sold it. I bought another boat, which I still have.

Working at a route that was not physically demanding allowed me to go home and take a nap after work, then go out in the evening. This was not something I was used to because in the past I was usually burnt out physically by the time I got home. I joined a group called Parents Without Partners (PWP), a group for single people with children. Remember me telling you about the Dorchester Club, which was at one time owned by the Teamster Pension Fund? Well, this had a purpose in the Big O's life. The club had a banquet hall on the first floor and one time PWP had a party there. After the party this tall attractive woman walked into the bar accompanied by a much older and larger man. I was there, unattached, talking with my friend Roger and another guy. This woman came up to me and started to converse, much to my amazement. The following Tuesday we were meeting in a PWP focus group on the problems of being single and having children. She was there. That's all I can say. After the meeting was over, she walked up to me and said, "I have tickets for a Johnny Mathis concert at Arie Crown Theater. Would you care to go with me?" Whoaa! I had to pinch myself. "Yes, of course. Where do you want me to pick you up, and at what time?" "Pick me up at seven at my house." I had a gray suit that was still in the plastic from the dry cleaners, and that night I put the suit on with a bow tie and escorted this fine young lady to Arie Crown Theater to attend a Johnny Mathis concert…where I fell sound asleep, woke up at intermission, fell asleep again and woke up at the final applause. So much for first impressions! I apologized profusely, begged forgiveness and asked her if she would let me make restitution for this breach of etiquette and take her to a concert in the future? She agreed and allowed me to pick the concert. Today, forty-two years later, this woman, Patricia Mary, is still by my side. Johnny Cash is still my favorite singer. Yes, this was the concert I took her to and this time I kept my eyes open. For our 40th anniversary I did make restitution also by attending a Johnny Mathis Christmas concert near our anniversary. Thanks, baby. I love you.

Patricia, my new soul mate, accompanied me a couple times on Saturday to pick up the Learner Shop and the woodworking place.

About a month after I met Pat, she introduced me to her two-year-old boy, named Edward, who was cute as a bug and well behaved. So I braved the anger of my father and walked in the kitchen of my parents' home in Lansing with Patricia and Edward by my side. I said, "Mom, Dad, I want you to meet my new friend Pat and her little boy Ed." We sat down and had coffee and cake. My mother, being gracious as she always was, made my new love feel quite at home. The next day my father came up to me and asked, "Can you adopt that little boy?" My response was, "No, Dad. His father's a doctor and lives in the Olympia Fields." I think he asked me the same question once again, and my response was the same. Pat and I were married December 28, 1974, about eight months after we had first laid eyes on each other. Like a lot of things, you get a reaction inside of you that tells you, "Forge ahead. You're on the right track." And forty-some years later I can look back and say God was definitely guiding me down that path. And I thank Him every day of my life.

CHAPTER 12 – WILD WEST

After the death of the Association, the hauling of garbage became like the Wild West. No violence, of course. Disgruntled customers could make a few phone calls up and have a new hauler by the end of the day. And there wasn't a whole lot you, the old hauler, could about it. Routes which in the past had high-value were now selling for next to nothing. Guys would build them up, take a look at the slim profit margin, and say, "There's nothing in this for us." Drivers who were of any worth would pretty much run the show, most of them sitting in the cat bird seat. In fact, what was ironic, when the use of coal came to a screeching halt, the coal haulers, who had a similar organization like the Association, suffered a different fate: too many suppliers, too few customers.

So the government, in its wisdom, decided to extend SBA loans to these coal companies to soften the cushion, since many of them were facing extinction. Several of those coal companies decided, "Well, we hauled coal for some of the bigger real estates. Why not make a lateral move into the garbage business? So with the help of our government they took the money and bought trucks and hired salespeople and proceeded to rip what was left of the Association membership apart.

It was not unusual for a scavenger contractor to get six or eight postcards in the mail every month informing him that his services were no longer needed at this or that location. The cards were printed by the coal companies and mailed by the coal companies to the existing scavenger contractors, and when the contractors went to their customers to see what was happening, most of them were told the same thing: "These guys are a lot cheaper than you." In a short time one coal company put on about twenty-five trucks, all top line, and the routes to go with them. Even some of the smaller coal companies were able to put on two or three trucks each.

So the trash hauling business was in utter chaos, no value and routes, stops changing haulers like you would change your socks. The big push came just before I sold Quality Disposal to Uncle Al. What little conversation I had with some the coal people was just basically their drivers, but what I did observe is that for trucks that were less than a year old there was some major things wrong with them. Whoever was behind the maintenance was asleep at the switch. And when one of their foremen told me, "We're going to bury you," I said to him, "I probably will be around in this business longer than you will."

Now that I was no longer an owner, I was approached by a couple of the people, asking if I wanted to acquire a route, their reasoning being that if I assumed any liabilities, then it was off their shoulders. At first I was tentative and agreed to look into it. But I knew deep down that in time these coal companies were going to start to fall by the wayside. The profit margin was not there to sustain them buying a second round of trucks, since their trucks were not going to last the ten or twelve years required to get the full life of a new truck and chassis back out of what you had spent for it. By my hesitation I could get a gauge on what was going to happen. In six months I was approached again. The particular party that approached me had gotten hit some more by the coal companies. And so in September 1974 I agreed that I would take over the company and see what I could do. Did I have fear? A little bit. But I knew I could put work on faster than they could take it from me. I was single at the time, dating Pat, so I figured the best thing to do was to get this up and running before we had to make a household together.

CHAPTER 13 – ANCHOR ONE

One time, when a customer told me face-to-face that he was going to cancel, and I was able to talk with him, turn things around, and keep the stop. Another time I was informed from the start that I would be losing a pretty good size stop, which was paying $350.00 a month. But I kept this one too, and developed an almost forty-year relationship with the owner of the building (more about that later). This route was pretty complete with containers, so I did not have to purchase a lot from the start. In late August 1974, while riding up to Niles by myself wondering what in the world was I going to call this new company, I came along side of a car carrier named Anchor Transport, with a rope and anchor logo. And so Anchor disposal was born. But I first had to check and make sure no one else had this name. I went to SID, the landfill, and asked Jim Becker, a staff person at the company, if anyone was using that name, and he told me, "Well, we got nobody coming in here by that name." So I took it.

Only later did I find out that there was an Anchor Scavenger. When I did, I had already registered the trademark and name with the State of Illinois. Pat, who is perfect for details of this nature and works in a law office, had suggested that. And she was able to do that in a very short time. When I found out that there was a company called Anchor Scavenger, I told the grapevine to let that company know they should contact me, and I would work out an agreeable solution, maybe change the spelling or something like that. I was never contacted. So years later, when I met Russ Meyer, the original owner of the Anchor Scavenger name, by accident while buying parts...well, what can you do? You apologize. But this was five years down the road, and we never had a conflict because we worked different neighborhoods.

The birth of Anchor was September 1974. I had learned some lessons from watching several new upstarts, brash young guns who were eager to make a name in the trash hauling business. Two brothers started a company called Action. They had bought a garage with another single operator in South Holland. The name of his company was Nation. The truck I had purchased was originally housed in the same garage, so I agreed to remain parked there. This was a good idea, especially in the Chicago winters with below zero temperatures. It gives an operator an important edge when it comes to starting his truck in the morning and getting out the door. Your day is pretty much shot if you spend two hours in subzero temperatures, trying to start a truck that someone failed to plug in. Or once you got it started, the brakes wouldn't release because the air lines were frozen because of moisture in the tanks.

A block east a similar garage housed several upstart companies, all one- and two-truck operators eager to make a name for themselves, as well as a living for their families. Most of our days would start at five in the morning and by 2:30 in the afternoon most of us were back in the garage. We would break out the basketball, go to the refrigerator, grab a beer and play some ball.

Not all of the time in the garage was spent playing basketball. We also had time for some practical jokes. One afternoon I was working and I found a fur collar in the trash—the kind that women used to wear around the neck. It was made of four or five foxes snapped together. At the time we were having problems with rats at the garage. They would stay in the loads if a guy parked his truck with trash still on it. Rats have a habit of gnawing on things, and at times we would find chicken bones and other leftovers in the intake manifolds on these trucks. Besides their picnics, they also chewed the air lines, so you had to do some repairs before you could move the truck.

Most of the trucks were cab-overs, so the door to check the oil and water were on the front of the cab, and the door flipped down to open. You can see the thought process for a good practical joke. One night when no one was around, I unsnapped one of the animals from this collar and put it inside the small door on one of the trucks so it would fall down when the drivers opened it in the morning. In a dimly lit garage I hoped it would have a good effect. The next morning I was long gone before the other drivers came to work. Did my practical joke work? Well, it must have because three hours later I got a call from my answering service asking me questions about some fox I had caught. Later that day I heard that when they opened that little door and that fox fell out, they nearly ran out the garage door without bothering to open it. I was on guard a long time after that for the foxes to reappear, and the fox did make appearances on various parts of my truck, but never to any effect. I had aced the surprise element on the other drivers.

I think my joke was probably the best one—so good, in fact, that David, one of the owners of the garage, even wanted to claim it as his own. As recently as six months ago David's daughter told this story back to me, but according to her, it was her father who played the joke on me.

Nation, owned by Rick Hatterus, had acquired an afternoon-night route, and one of his trucks would leave at four in the afternoon to go downtown and pick up the work in the evening after stores closed. This truck would be on the road till about 2 a.m. depending on conditions. It would return in time for the day shift to take it over and do the conventional early morning operation. Nation would continue to grow from a one-truck operation, and the owner guided that growth till it became part of the Ally conglomerate. Rick could see the future of this business and was able to steer the operation through all the new competition in the trash hauling business. He gave good service, his pricings were fair, and his was one of the first of the upstarts to pay union wages, and overtime. He showed us it could be done, even with stiff competition. His equipment was clean and new, and he paid attention to every detail. Many of us would copy his example for years to come.

Warner and David, the owners of Action Disposal, were also very aggressive and also gave very good service, charged fair prices, and were able to build route after route. Warner had a knack for hustling work. He had a very good gift of gab and was able to bring in many new accounts every month. This presented a dilemma. The garage originally would house eight trucks comfortably. But Warner and David were putting on one new route per year, and Nation was acquiring routes at the same rate. The garage, originally built for eight trucks, suddenly had twelve, and there were some growing pains. Nation decided to build a brand new garage for himself about a mile away from the existing structure. Warner and David kept their trucks in the original garage, while Nation moved to the new building, and I moved down the street from Nation to a warehouse, which later became an unmitigated nightmare.

The Anchor company that I had started did not remain dormant either. The neighborhood I was operating in was being hauled by old-line Association members, who even though the Association had fallen by the way side, still adhered to the principles of "I scratch your back, you scratch mine." I had been dealt almost a death knell by competition, so I did not want any part of this Association type behavior. I figured those days were over, and with the wounds of my Mercury days still fresh in my mind, I figured that way to run a business was in the past. I had watched Warner and David build a few routes by aggressively seeking out new accounts, and I had watched Nation do the same. To me this was a new day dawning.

Before I went to park at Hamster's garage, down the street from Nation, I had acquired a second truck and a helper who was laid off at Nation, who did not want to pay two men on their truck. This guy, Hoagie, came to work for me, and I taught him to drive. He was my first employee. Hoagie worked for me for eight years, but I could never get him to go past thirty-six hours a week, as much as I tried. But what I got out of him in the thirty-six hours was a fast, efficient, but crabby employee. He had no patience with rude drivers, and he blocked alleys and customers who got in his way. There were several times I had to explain to a customer, "You're getting your trash picked up in a timely efficient manner. I suggest you stay out of his way, and let him do his job. I could send you a driver who is polite and tips his hat, but does not do the job as well as Hoagie."

When I started Anchor the second time, (Yes, there is a another chapter for Anchor) David, who had old Action, informed me that Hoagie was dying in the hospital. On a Sunday morning, I went up to see him. He was 52 years old, was riddled with cancer and at first did not recognize me. We talked for about an hour, catching up on old times. I asked him if he missed his days of hauling trash. He said, "No, not in the least." Not the sub-zero mornings, the frozen containers, the drafty trucks. When his folks arrived at his hospital room, I said my goodbyes and left. Exactly one week later Hoagie passed away.

While writing this book, I saw an article in the Chicago Sun-Times, and it was about a movie called *All Things Must Pass*. The film is about the rise and fall of Tower Records, a nationwide chain back in the 70s that sold record albums, how it had grown from basically a drugstore to a nationwide chain. The article went on to talk about some of the people that had worked there. It was a place where a hippie with long hair could get a job and become an expert on things like music just by doing his job. Hoagie was just such a person. He had long blonde hair, and the outward trappings of life, such as a fancy car, a large home, etc., were not part of Hoagie's DNA. He had a wife, a comfortable home and a degree which allowed him to teach school, which is what he did after completing college. But teaching school was not his cup of tea, and after a very short time he decided he did not want to be a babysitter for young teenage ruffians. So he quit and went to work as a helper for Nation, on a night route. His friend Whelan was the driver. When Whelan left, Hoagie had not learned to drive, and Nation no longer used helpers, and I needed a helper and he fit the bill. Later, I did teach him to drive and he served me very well for those ten years, but it was impossible to get him to work past thirty-six hours. At first this was okay. That's all I had work for. But after teaching him to drive and him getting a chauffeur's license, I wanted to implement him more because he did such an excellent job. As I said before I had to come between him and a customer several times. But as I told one guy who ran a tavern, "When Hoagie leaves here, everything is taken, and he will be back at the appropriate time when your next pickup is due, so I'm not going to get rid of him. I'd rather get rid of you." Not the best way to handle customer relations, but this guy had a knack for aggravating even the most patient person, and Hoagie had no patience with stupid people. This guy was really only the boyfriend of the woman who owned the tavern, so I knew I could get away with it. I told him, "Just put your stuff out, take in your dogs, and get out of his way."

I had to stay out of his way too. I would check his truck out, check his tires and leave, knowing full well that his route would be complete, and it would be done in a timely manner, with very little mistakes. As I said, it worked great for ten years, and I always had to make sure that we did not go longer than thirty-six hours because he also worked at a place called Hagewich Records. Hagewich had started in a very small store on the far South Side of Chicago, and had opened a second location in Calumet City, and a third in Merriville, Indiana. Hoagie was the manager of the Merriville location, and he knew everything about vinyl that anyone could know. In fact, in his basement he had over 6000 albums, all neatly stacked in milk crates, all unopened and many had become very valuable. Over the years he amassed quite a collection, and one of the final conversations we had before he died was the fact that his record collection was paying for his medical care during his last days.

Some time earlier, when Martin and Norbert acquired Anchor from me, Hoagie went to work for them. But shortly thereafter, he had an appendix burst and was out of commission for about six months. When he returned, he put in his notice and left, claiming he was not physically able to do this job anymore. I think he had had enough of the exertion that goes with pulling containers. And even though he never told me what he made at Hegewich, I think that was his first love.

The coal companies, now in the garbage business, the biggest one being Cook County Disposal, an offshoot of J. W. Peterson Coal and the one that had put twenty-five trucks and routes on the street overnight, had developed chinks in their armor, as I had predicted they would. At first I was told I would lose stops to Cook County Disposal, and the one I remember very vividly was a building at 7000

South Shore Drive. This was a fourteen-story high-rise, facing the South Shore Country Club, a nine-hole golf course, which when the trees were not in bloom, you could see the lake. If you lived on the top floor, you could see the lake anyway over the trees. This was a rather complicated stop because on Mondays, Wednesdays and Fridays I would pull down five containers of house trash, and on Wednesdays I would crank up the lift from the basement. Remember the story of Deacon and the Fisher building? This was similar to it, only I did not have to shovel the ashes into the cans in the basement. They had about eight cans of their own, which had hooks on them, and a guy named Poncho would operate the lift from the basement. When it hit the top, it would stop automatically, and I would swing the can over and dump it into the hopper of the garbage truck. Then Poncho would lowered it to the basement and give me the next one. When all eight were dumped, Poncho would crank the sky-hook down into the basement again, and I would go on my way.

 The real estate company informed me that the building was being sold, and did I have a way to empty the contents of the basement? I looked down there, and it was a collection of old stoves, screens, bicycles, an assortment of junk that people collect over the years. Fortunately, my brother Glenn, and my cousin Clarence—Uncle Deck's youngest son—had both dropped out of school, and both were looking for something to do. So I took Glenn and Clarence and a couple of hand dollies, and we corralled the elevator. I told Glenn and Clary to bring the contents of the basement to where the containers were. I would go and finish part of the route and return about 10 o'clock, and we would load the packer truck with the stuff they had put on the driveway. I told him them to repeat the process, breaking for lunch, and I would return in the afternoon, and they could take their car back home. When I came back at 2 o'clock, they helped me load, and I said, "Your day is complete. See you here tomorrow." And I went to the dump. They repeated this process, and by the end of the week we had the basement all cleaned. Never again did I hear any rumor about me losing this particular building to Cook County Disposal. I had a similar situation, where I did the negotiations with the woman on the spot, said if she would keep my service, I would give her the next two months free. That account stayed on my route for many years.

The new owners of the high rise did take over, and I was introduced to a stately woman, who seemed to be in charge. She did not appear bossy, just asked me a few questions, like could I acquire five-mill plastic bags capable of holding fifty-five gallons of trash? I told her I would see what I could do, and I would give her a price before I did anything. I called several restaurant supply houses, and they said yes, for about 40 cents a bag, they had just what I needed. I reported this back to Pamela, and she gave me the authorization to order several cases. I then noticed that these bags would contain the apartment garbage when I dumped the containers.

I began to notice something else: when I got there, there would be a car and an old pickup in the driveway, the car being hers, the pickup belonging to a guy name Frank King. I would move her car and double park it in the street, then do the same with Frank King's pickup. One time when I went to move his pickup, Frank informed me that the pickup was for sale for 150 bucks. I said, "Sold." I needed a beat-up truck to haul containers with because the work was coming in at quite an amazing clip. Each time a new account was signed up, it required maybe one or two additional containers. I also began to notice that the driveway was being used as a staging area for old rugs, wooden trim, drywall and other assorted construction material. One afternoon when I was late, I discovered what was being done after the day's work stripping those apartments. A man would come with a small dump truck and a tractor similar to the one that Uncle Pete used many years prior to plow snow. And the guy would use the tractor to load the dump truck so that the next morning the driveway was clean and they could reload it in much the same way that my brother Glenn, Clary and I had done when we cleaned the basement.

I suggested to Pamela, "Why not use a roll-off to save the added labor of picking it up off the ground?" Once again she said, "Can you get them?" "Of course," I answered. So I called Jim Lytle and he put, not one, but two of them in, and the workers proceeded to strip the apartments and load them directly into the roll-off. What I found out later was, when the top seven floors were done, they moved the bottom seven floor residents to the top new apartments, which had been totally refurbished. Then they repeated the rehab project on the bottom seven floors. So the roll-off boxes remained in the driveway at 7000 South Shore Drive for quite some time. Little did I know that this was the beginning of a relationship with one of the most influential developers in the City of Chicago.

Chicago had just elected its first black mayor, Harold Washington. What usually happens in those cases is certain neighborhoods undergo quite a transition. It's called "white flight," and many white owners were eager to sell apartment buildings at a cut-rate price, and many newcomers were eager to buy them and try their hand at apartment rentals and building ownership. Many were not qualified, or lacked the funding necessary, to upgrade those buildings into a viable enterprise. And like a lot of people who jump into quicksand, they hasten to get out as fast as they got in. So, many buildings fell into disarray in a very short time. A footnote to this: it's the same as getting into the trash hauling business. It looks easy because somebody else is doing it. But when you are put to the test, you find out this is all a lot of work and a lot of headache, and it requires a lot of capital to get started and to keep it going. And if all these various elements are not in the place, you can be on a fast track to failure.

It was two years after I started Anchor Disposal, as I was leaving the building at 7000 South Shore Drive one afternoon, that I mentioned to Pamela that if I was hauling this one, why could I not bid on the other building two blocks away, which I had found out her company also owned? After a few months Pamela informed me that I was to start hauling the building at 6900 Crandon Avenue, effective the first of the month. This presented a problem, because the guy that was hauling it was a guy I had grown up with, who had lived about a half a block away from me when we were kids. We had both grown up and got into the garbage business, and I should have looked at this like my grandfather did, and said, "I will scratch your back if you will scratch mine." But times had changed, which is no excuse for my bad behavior. Sometimes greed gets the best of us, and we do things which we later regret. Warden, the previous hauler, came to me, and with a hurt look called me out on it, and I could offer no reasonable explanation for my action. I can only offer the excuse that it was meant to be.

One afternoon I exited 7000 South Shore, only to find a Cadillac parked in the driveway. This was a common occurrence. The driveway was wide enough for two cars parked side-by-side, and a chain across the mouth of the driveway kept cars from going all the way into the driveway. Normally I would have voiced my opinion very vocally about parking in this driveway, but on this particular afternoon something held me back from engaging my big mouth and telling this man who was walking toward the Cadillac, in no uncertain terms, that he could not park there. What helped me keep my mouth in check was the fact that he uttered my name in saying, "My car is not in your way, is it, Owen?" And with that, I stopped myself from saying anything. He stuck out his hand and said, "My name is Elmer Higgins."

Elmer Higgins was somebody I had heard about from the office girl at 7000, and from Pamela herself. He was the brains behind the transformation of this high-rise from a dowdy building to a jewel on the Chicago lakefront. The building at 6900 Crandon had undergone a similar transformation, and because I knew all of his work, by the grapevine, I was certainly impressed and stuck out my hand and said, "It is a pleasure to meet you." My relationship with this man continues to this day (40 years), and I am proud, and, at the same time, humbled that on that afternoon I did not engage my big mouth, and my small brain, and tell him off about him parking in his own driveway. You can apologize for your words afterward, but once they have leave your mouth, the damage is done.

    6900 Crandon turned out to be the tip of the iceberg. I don't know how much later I was informed by Pamela to go to 6101 S. Vernon, and see what was needed to begin hauling this building. Now this address was not a prime location. At that time many of the buildings seemed to be held together with bailing wire, or abandoned, and left for the street people to invade and tear apart. So I drove over there, and not knowing what I would find when I arrived, I found another Higgins jewel, newly-renovated, with an elevated parking structure, and right across the street from a park. I just shook my head. Who would build such a nice, tall, elaborate building in this area, which was in such decay. Then the light went on in my head, and I said to myself, "This guy certainly has a long term vision. And a lot a guts."

Ever so slowly, Pamela would tell me to begin service on a number of their other properties, and I would issue the price, get the okay and begin to service the accounts. If it was not Pamela, it was Elmer himself who gave the okay on several Westside structures. With his approval, I sublet some of them to Regal Disposal, which was operating in that neighborhood and could do it much more efficiently than I could. Before long a good part of the Anchor operation was focused on the properties that Elmer Higgins owned, and it showed me that good service, fair pricing, and a one-on-one relationship with the customer himself went a long way. In the old Association days, many scavenger contractors, did not even know what some of their customers looked like. But at that time, this was not a bad thing because they didn't have to know their customers. They could concentrate on taking care of business. But in the new era of open competition, "taking care of business" required that there be a little PR, and a lot of communication, between customer and hauler. And of course, it helps if your price is cheaper than the next guy.

Unfortunately, Elmer's wife Pamela passed away in, I think, 1989, much too young. I never really was able to thank her for her help. In the mid- 90s, one of Elmer's properties had a serious fire when one of its resident fell asleep with a lit cigarette and caught his apartment on fire. In the closet was a set of tires, which made the fire burn even hotter. Pictures in the paper showed a young girl jumping out of an upper story window of that building and being caught in mid-air by a fireman on an extended ladder. The press had a field day, calling Elmer Higgins a slumlord. I knew his history and wrote to many papers telling them to quit shooting from the hip, that a little investigation would show that he really was a top-notch property manager, who knew how to build and take care of both large and small buildings, and that his track record was almost perfect. These many years later, I will still say the same, and I'm proud to have known him and Pamela.

The next several years, the Anchor logo represented a departure from the old days of the Association. Because many of the old-timers were still clinging to that Association model, I received the reputation of being a …. Well, you can hang any adjective you want on that. A bad guy. If a potential customer would call, I would definitely look into it and, most of the time, give him a price. And if I didn't want the account, I would tell him why. There were times when a customer had had an argument with his present hauler, and I knew that if I took the stop, I would be subject to the same type of treatment if that customer ever had a falling out with me. So I told those potential customers that it would be in all of our best interests if they would work out their differences and leave me out of the middle. But the fact was, this was no longer a good-old-boys' network. You had to operate your business in a very efficient manner. And Pat helped me to do that.

I had married Pat on December 28, 1974, and we purchased a house and proceeded to put "hers, mine," and eventually "ours" together. To her credit, she was directly opposite of me, personality-wise. My personality was quick to react, sometimes with little thought as to what the consequences down the road would be. She was more a thinker, and slow to react, weighing out both cause and effect of certain actions.

Because I wanted to expand the business, I had to pay a visit to the bank, and when you pay a visit to the bank, you better put knee pads on, because they are going to ask first for a financial statement, profit and loss, and they are going to ask you for collateral. I was never a paperwork type person. My financial statements looked like something a third-grader would present. Trucks and containers were not the type of collateral that bankers were looking for.
But Pat was what bankers, and lawyers alike, would call a stickler for detail, somebody who went to great lengths to make sure that every penny was accounted for. When she made up a financial statement, she would present it in a dignified, legitimate way. Bankers like this, and the vault of the bank suddenly started to creak open just a little bit. Expansion required new containers, so every two months I would present the bills from the container purchase, take out a ninety-day note, and then after ninety days would present more bills from the container purchase and incorporate them into one loan. (Thanks, Tim, for the tip.) My desk drawer started to look like a collection of Sears catalogues, with my loan payments books. This is

usually what happens when a company starts from scratch and proceeds to grow. The more growth, the harder it is to control. In the old days, a one-truck route was fairly easy to manage. You were always around the truck, so you could see the things that would happen to it in your daily operation. If you did not see the truck or you were not very observant, you could miss things. Also, drivers were of different personalities. Some would take care of things very delicately. Others were like bulls in a china shop; every time they left the garage, something bad would happen.

This is something I began to notice with employees. The first guy I hired (Hoagie) was very good with the equipment. Yes, I would have to check things out to make sure he didn't have any flat tires, and change them if they were flat, then send him on his way. Most of the time he would come back without trouble. But there were others I hired who could not go a week without destroying somebody's property or something on the truck. One in particular, named Dilbert, was always hitting something, always asking when he was going to be put in the union, and always had me thinking, "When am I going to fire his guy?" Finally, one day, he backed into a huge tractor at SID, and then lied about it, saying the tractor had backed into him. But while we were on our way to the office of SID to straighten this out, he admitted to me that, indeed, the tractor had been stationary and he had backed into it. My mind made up, I fired him. But his replacement was just as bad, and I fired him. That guy's replacement with also bad. What I began to notice was that the companies with some degree of success were those that hired union drivers lured away from existing companies. They did this by paying union wages and benefits, making sure the equipment was always in good shape, and giving them pretty close to whatever they wanted in the way of working conditions and hours.

I hired one guy at the beginning of a particularly brutal winter, and he worked about sixty-five hours a week, and I could not wait for spring to come so I could get a break from the astronomical cost of overtime. But when the overtime ended, he gave me his two-weeks' notice. So I was getting a baptism by fire: I was learning that it takes a special touch to navigate a business with more than one truck. At the time, Anchor had grown from one partial route to three very large routes and four trucks.

The minority contractors who had started up in the early 70s were now starting to crumble under the same pressure that I was feeling, and sometimes it was hard to sidestep the increased work that coming my way because those companies were crumbling. You might tell somebody you could not handle hauling his garbage when you were picking up next-door, and he would say, "Well, you're picking up my next-door neighbor's. Why can't you pick up mine?" And you could tell a customer only so often that it's impossible to find good help, help that would not destroy the equipment. The scavenger contractors who had been around a while knew how to finesse their employees and keep them on board, and knew when to fire them before they did any major damage. I, on the other hand, was the training ground for somebody who wanted to do this for a living but had not learn the tricks of the trade. I taught them, they would learn on my equipment, and then jump ship, taking their knowledge of what I had taught them to somebody who would pay them more money. Another problem was: if you brought somebody on board, you would have to take quite a bit of time to teach him, so you could not do a full route while you were teaching him. You were between a rock and a hard place.

In 1981, as a way of alleviating some of the pressure of a growing operation, I offered to sell to a driver named Danny a part of my route, with a truck and the containers on the route. This proved to be a good move because Danny took the small operation and ran with it for the next twenty-five years. He did very well with it, made a good living, and for some strange reason, was able to keep it contained to one route, one truck, by himself. The expense of expansion never was a problem for him, and in the twenty-five years he only had to buy two more used trucks, besides the one I sold him, which he sold because it was too small. And after those twenty-five years, he sold the operation for a tidy profit. So, looking back, I often say he probably had a better idea than I did. But I'm still trying to figure out how in the world he kept it to one truck, and by himself? He used the name Quality, which came to belong to me again, as I will explain in the next few pages.

I started Anchor and was in business this time for about a year and a half. Then one night, I received a call from my cousin Rusty. He informed me that his father, Uncle Al, who had bought Quality Disposal from me, after I had bought it from him (sounds confusing, but it wasn't; just a back-and-forth situation), was no longer going to get up and haul garbage. Uncle Al was tired of the day-to-day grind, of the buying and maintaining of trucks, and like many others was going to join the 9 to 5 crowd and get a paid vacation as well as health benefits. Rusty said, "You know which customers are worth keeping, and you might as well go after them because you have the trucks and know how to do it." Rusty was right. There were several accounts that were worth keeping. Not hard to haul. You could just back up to the container—no ashes to haul out of the basement on your back—and you would get paid in a very timely manner. So I went to the stops late in the afternoon and informed the janitors that I was going to clean them up. I knew that I could contact the real estate or management companies at a later date and make the proper arrangements. After cleaning them up, I went to the management company with the biggest building of the group at the time. I walked in the door and introduced myself, making sure that the truck was visible from the inside of the office. I said I was interested in doing business with them. They did not know who I was, except that a janitor had told them that some guy had come around and cleaned everything up. The man behind the desk replied, "What if I don't give it to you?" I answered, "I came in that door, and I can walk out that door. I will only bill for the amount of trash I cleaned up." His reply was, "Well, go ahead and do it for now until we find somebody else." I thanked him and started to walk out the door. He called out, "Come on back here." Then he said, "Go ahead and haul the building. You cleaned it up." He added, "Here are three more that are also part of the same group. I will make the cancellation of the other hauler's service on those three, effective the first of the month. Scope them out and put in your containers, and begin hauling the first of the coming month." The other two real estate management companies had three buildings each, so I was given a total of six more.

Once I folded these into the route, I saw I could still use my uncle's containers, which he had left there. A month later my aunt called me and asked if we could sit down and talk this situation over. When we got together, my uncle, my aunt and I were able to work out a mutually satisfying agreement.

By selling one of my newer trucks to Quality, that left me with two older trucks. So I purchased a third, slightly-used Packer. In the meantime, I also had acquired from Uncle Pete Lindemulder a used roll-off. I had been around roll-offs. I knew how they worked: throw the hook on the front of the box and draw it up on the truck. In theory, this is easy, should work without a hitch. But I had never worked on a roll-off route. Different ballgame. And, as I began to find out, the only way to learn something is to actually do it. Don't grease your truck and in time it will break down. Buy really old trucks and that's exactly what you got. Somebody else got rid of it before it "hit the wall."

Uncle Al had told me many years prior. He said, "The only difference between you and starvation is the condition of your equipment. Do not take care of it and it will fail you. If it fails you, either you fix it and continue on your way or you quit."

The additional roll-off component was something I misjudged also. I thought I could do handle it in addition to running a small route. The problem was: as mistake-prone as I was, the roll-offs turned into a full time enterprise. After hauling a few boxes, I would have to go all the way back to South Holland, change trucks there, then come back with the packer truck to finish a route. When I got to some of the stops to pick up the roll-off boxes, I would have to round-trip the box because I did not have a switch box to give them. But for the Higgins' stop I *did* have a switch box, and his men would stop what they were doing just to watch the circus of me picking up a box and making a switch. Years down the road, I still was not a big fan of roll-offs, even though I had done quite a bit of it. It's easy physically since you do not have to push containers, especially with the snow on the ground. The truck and its hydraulics are all you need to move, lift and transport those containers. But many a time you would come to round-trip one box, and by the time you came back, they would have another one full. So you would round-trip that one and…Well, you get the picture. So a task that was only allotted two hours suddenly became a complete day. I had jumped into the quicksand and was looking for a way to get out without drowning. Hire more help, and you would add to your problems because help had to be paid. And to pay them, you had to generate revenue. So I became like the hamster in the cage, chasing his tail.

In 1982 Martin (the guy I mentioned earlier, who pushed the pallets off my flatbed truck with his bull dozer) approached me several times, asking if I would be interested in selling my total operation to him and his brother Norton. My response was I would sell part, in order to get it down to something that I could manage by myself, but I was not interested in selling it entirely. His response was the reverse: "You know we're not going to buy part of you, and have you come back and attack us once you catch your breath." Each of us had valid points. I could understand why he was apprehensive; he could understand why I was apprehensive. So for about two years we kind of left this offer out on the table.

Owen - Lost & Found

Grandma Laning circa 1943 in cab of trash truck. Grandpa would take us on picnics by putting benches in the body of the truck.
(Photo courtesy of Peter Laning)

Uncle Murph (top), Uncle Slim (bottom left), and Grandpa Laning (right), Circa 1940.
(Photo courtesy of Peter Laning)

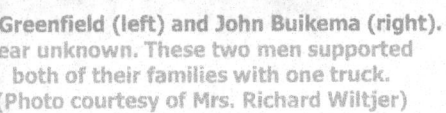

Greenfield (left) and John Buikema (right). Year unknown. These two men supported both of their families with one truck.
(Photo courtesy of Mrs. Richard Wiltjer)

Two views of the Big O in his 20s with his second truck (first solo venture). Note long hair and dirty clothes

Second Anchor1 truck (bought from the Coop). First time to run two trucks at once

Some early Anchor1 trucks

The NEW way to SAVE MONEY

No Investment Needed
containers ready for delivery.

USE
OUR NEW AND MODERN PICK-UP SERVICE

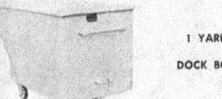
1 YARD DOCK BOX

4 YARD CONTAINER

Phone: PR 9-0853

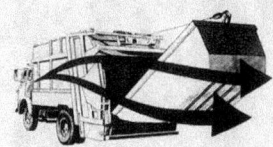

2 YARD DOCK BOX

6 YARD CONTAINER

1 OR 2 YARD CONTAINER

8 YARD CONTAINER

Peter Laning Sons
Scavenger Contractors
7113 DEMPSTER STREET   NILES, ILLINOIS 60648

Rubbish, Ashes and Garbage
Promptly Removed

15 TO 40 YARD ROLL-OFF CONTAINER

15 TO 40 YARD STATIONARY PACKER CONTAINER

MORE PAYLOADS PER DAY PER TRUCK

News to Delight You!

Here's how you benefit
FROM THIS MODERN NEW PICK-UP SERVICE...

FREE CONTAINERS
1 to 40 Yard Capacity

Our new Container has a large, 1-cubic yard capacity. This means you will replace many smaller and less sanitary containers.

YOU PROTECT YOUR ESTABLISHMENT AGAINST THE HAZARDS OF FIRE

IT'S ECONOMICAL!

IT'S CONVENIENT!

IT'S SANITARY!

HOLDS EQUIVALENT OF 4 FIFTY-FIVE GALLON DRUMS

YOU DRESS UP PREMISES AND ELIMINATE MANY UGLY GARBAGE CANS

YOU ELIMINATE A SERIOUS HEALTH HAZARD

Improperly stored refuse attracts rodents—is a breeding place for flys and other disease-bearing insects. Subscribers to our new service eliminate this problem because we provide them with a sanitary Container.

Sales brochure from Uncle Slim's business, Peter Laning Sons. Note the North Side location. Uncle Slim was always willing to go into new territory. (Brochure courtesy of Matt Lytle)

This truck was bought from Uncle Pete. He liked green; I hated green. Owen Jr and his friend repainted it for $200. This was my first—and last—venture into roll-offs.

Owen, Carol Lindemulder (Peter Jr's widow), and Auntie Ruth Lindemulder (Uncle Pete's widow). Circa 2007.

Peter III, Uncle Pete's grandson (in white shirt) was my boss for one year (2007-08). He later was active in starting a medical waste company. (Photo courtesy John Deckinga)

Backside of the Pres. Hospital, being torn down.
Many hours were spent picking up trash at this location.

GIFT CERTIFICATE
To: Owen Deckinga Sr.
From: Owen Deckinga Jr.

Redeem for:
    Two Weeks Garbage Service Next Summer

This very good gift from my oldest son was well received.

My first Kenworth. This photo proves that a trash truck can also be a work or art.

Last day of service before retirement. Brother John was filming while I was working.
(Photo courtesy John Deckinga)

CHAPTER 14 – CHICAGO COLD

Despite Al Gore's worries about global warming, the winters of 1976-1983 convinced me we were going to freeze to death. We had winters that were consistently below zero, weeks on an end. We had snow that fell the first week in November, 1977, and did not melt till April 1978. During this time we had four feet of total accumulation. Steel becomes very brittle in subzero weather, and things would break without explanation. Airlines on the trucks would freeze and diesel fuel would gell because it was so cold. Drivers would call in sick without reasonable explanations, and you knew why they were staying home.

My older son, Owen Junior, graduated from high school, even though, like his father, he was not a very good student. Did not mind the socializing, but book learning was not his cup of tea. He showed an interest in going into the Army. I had noticed from past experiences with my uncles and their sons, that not everyone had a liking for the trash hauling business. Some of the sons liked to read books, dream dreams, and do other things. College education was becoming a very fashionable thing to do, and when somebody graduated from high school, they usually went on to college. Go away from home for a while. Learn how to live on your own without father and mother looking over your shoulder. Some sons went into the family business, either concrete trucking, or trash hauling. I did not want to put this on my son and say, "Well, you gotta go into your father's business." Like I said, some sons were not suited for following in their father's footsteps. And putting a square peg in a round hole was almost criminal. Some sons left and later realized that maybe coming back and helping Pop out was not such a bad idea. My son enlisted in the Army. His basic training was going to be in South Carolina, but he hadn't left yet.

On one particular day, the weather was subzero, and the trucks would not start. So O Jr. and I tried to pull-start them, and in the process, one of them slid off the road into a ditch and punched a hole in the fuel tank. Now we had double trouble: a truck that wouldn't start, and fuel pouring on the ground. Back inside the garage, my son witnessed a total meltdown of his father, in which I went completely berserk, throwing wrenches across the garage, yelling at the top of my lungs that going into the trash business was the biggest mistake of my life. So, even if I *had* wanted to convince my son that hauling trash was a golden opportunity, my display of temperament that day shot it down. Even now we talk about that defining moment in his life. I am glad he made the choice that he did.

Owen Jr. did quite well in the military. His choice led him down the path of world travel, where after thirteen years of service and dedication to the Army, he was asked if he would like to go to the White House. Yes, the one where the president lives. My son was first assigned to the basement there, to make sure that the calls to the White House were routed in the proper channels. Later he got to travel with George Bush Sr., and was an advance communication man for him as he traveled around the world. Owen Jr. met his wife while working for the President, since she was on the same assignment. They now reside in Florida, both retired from the military (Owen after 25 years), and are raising two sons. Am I a proud father? Yes, especially after I received a letter from George Bush Sr. at the end of his term of office, praising my son's service. (For a while, my son Owen's voice was on the Bushes' answering machine at their summer home in Kennebunkport Me. It certainly would have been a tragedy for my son to follow in his father's footsteps. I had always told my sons, "Travel the world, see the sights, and when you get older, then you can settle down and put your feet up and say, 'Been there, done that.'" Also, the bigger picture is that if my son Owen had stayed home to follow in the family business, he would not have met his very precious wife Veronica. When I am around the both of them, I see God's eternal hand on his children. They are matched for each other. I said it after they were married, and now some twenty-five years later, I say it again: they are matched for each other.

Did things get any better for me? No. Unfortunately, when you start down a path of mistakes, you seem to compound them by making more mistakes. The more mistakes you make, like the hamster chasing his tail, the faster you go, and the more worn out you get. So it seemed that I would take one step forward and three steps back. In January 1983, with 12 inches of snow on the ground—not soft, fluffy kind, but the wet, heavy kind—I laid in an alley with two feet of this snow, putting a truck suspension back together so I could drive it home. I then went home, got in a hot bath and decided that my time had come to end this three ring circus I had found myself in. I contacted Martin and Norton, and said, "Let's hash out these details and make a deal so that you can acquire Anchor Disposal.

So on April 1, 1983, with the temperature about zero, I packed up all the equipment that belong to Anchor Disposal Inc. and drove over to Martin and Norton's garage, which was at 118th and Avenue O in Chicago, and they became the proud owners of my business. It was agreed that I would go to work for them. No guarantees, other than they would pay me what the next guy was making (union scale). If they were not satisfied with my work, they could tell me where the door was. I would get a two week vacation, without pay, the first summer. I asked them if they wanted to keep name "Anchor Disposal." And their response was, "No, you can keep that." The problem that exists when you're by yourself is that it is very hard to get away, to take a vacation, to completely sever your mind from the day-to-day operation. You go to bed at night thinking about it. You get up in the morning thinking about it. And the only way to purge your mind of business concerns is to completely sever your ties from the company.

This is something that drivers who do not own the company have no concept of. Punching in, doing your work, and punching out are a big part of the job, yes, but it does not include the after-hour things that go on. And sometimes the after-hour things hold the biggest problems. Did I regret selling the business? I knew at the time it was the only way to go. Now, looking back, I've come to realize I have about an eight-year span of patience, then it seems like I run out of gas. My days driving for Martin and Norton lasted eighteen years, as long as they remained in business. And with the exception of a few incidents which I will unfold in the next few chapters, it was a very good, exciting relationship. These two guys were cutting edge, as I had tried to be. So it was good to be around them and watch them go forward. In the final analysis, I am glad that the business was as successful as it was.

CHAPTER 15 – MEMORABLE PEOPLE

Henry

While I was parked at Hamster's garage, I met several interesting people. The first one was Henry Tori, who was a good example of a self-made man. Henry had a large family. He had been a farmer most of his life in the area around South Highland. I don't know if he owned the land or if he just farmed it for somebody, but when I met him, he had just stopped selling eggs in the inner-city. He had been held up and could see the handwriting on the wall, that it was not safe for a man to sell things on a cash-and-carry basis in the city. So Henry teamed up with a large printer, who made quite a bit of trash every day. This printer pitched the idea to Henry to go into the garbage business. This was the case of a lot of people who went into trash hauling. Somebody who generated a lot of trash was able to get you started by providing you with work and thus, income. So Henry decided to go into business with an acquaintance, Elmo Katzheimer. Henry was a soft-spoken guy, about forty-five, quite old for a start-up guy. Henry bought a truck and hauled his first load of garbage. He took advice from other people who had done it before him, and from time to time Henry would call me and asked me a question about trash hauling. Henry was mildly successful. He managed to fill that truck up very quickly, was able to dump at a landfill on 138th and Cottage Grove, and kind of minded his own business.

But before him, the printing company had been hauled by two brothers who went under the name of West Suburban Disposal. They felt Henry had taken their stop, and being of the mindset of the old-school, Association days, they went to the Association for retribution. When they failed to get that, they went directly to one of the Christian Reformed churches in the South Holland area. There is a part in the Bible where it says: if you have a dispute with your Christian brothers, you have to take it up with the church council. I don't recall the outcome of that particular council meeting, and I don't know the members who were sitting in attendance. I just know there were two brothers on one side, and Henry by himself on the other. As it turned out, the proceedings backfired on the two brothers, and Henry kept his business. The two brothers never hauled the printing company again and later sold out to Trash Management. They obtained jobs with Trash Management, since these jobs were frequently given to people who sold out, as a pacifier when the transition occurred. (More about Trash Management in future chapters, as this became a very important part of the transition of trash hauling from little companies to world-wide conglomerates.)

Henry worked that business for roughly twelve years. He bought a much larger truck, with the bells and whistles, and hired a driver. That driver, Carl, is still part of the same company that acquired New Way, the original company I had worked for. He has worked for one company his entire adult life, and I assume he is ready for retirement. I know he has enough time in to get a retirement pension. But some guys don't want to retire, so they continue on.

Mexican Soap Brothers

One day I was standing around, waiting for my truck to be fixed at a repair station in South Holland. A Hispanic guy came in and asked the guy fixing my truck if he knew of a good trash hauler. Chuck pointed to me and Ray, of Regal Disposal, who was also there, and said, "Either one of these two guys will fit the bill. Ray looked at me and said, "You take it." The old saying, "You snooze, you loose," holds true, and on that day I was introduced to the factory we'll call Max's, owned by four brothers. What they did was fill bottles and boxes with soap and cleaners for major corporations. They supplied the labor, the warehousing and all the components that go into some well-known products on supermarket shelves.

The reason they were asking for a new trash hauler was they were moving to a very large warehouse at 91st and Halsted. They had were leasing it, and had contracts to fill things like windshield washer fluid, anti-freeze bottles, dish soap and laundry soap boxes. The next day I went over there to scope it out, see what I needed to set the stop up, and found out there were ten containers belonging to another hauler already in that location. So began my war with Crosstown Bill. He was bound and determined that I was not going to muscle him out of this large warehouse, and I was equally determined not to let him stay in this large warehouse. He did his best, appealing to the brothers and working one brother up against the other. I did my part by shrugging my shoulders and letting the chips fall where they might. Eventually I won out and began to haul this large factory three times a week.

But this was only the tip of the iceberg. Hispanic people love big celebrations, and every Christmas and one time during the summer, I was invited, along with my wife and children to one of their many celebrations. Mariachi music and piñatas were the order of the day, and to this day, my two oldest sons talk about the days of going to the Max's Corporation's family picnics.

They had started this company in one of the brother's garages, filling small numbers of orders at a time, and like other small businesses, they did a very good job, and the large soap companies eventually gave them more and more responsibilities and bigger orders to fill. Their original 89th St. location was expanded many times. A sad commentary was that, later on, one of the brothers, the one with controlling interest, went to prison and left his wife to call the shots. She hired someone she shouldn't have, and basically he stole the company out from under the three remaining brothers. The last time I talked to one of the brothers, they were trying to start up a new company. But it only had limited success. This is another case where I hope someday to cross paths with them again, and we can break bread and talk about things that happened in the past, and what we have would have done to improve the future. (The youngest brother died in March of 2016.)

Cowboy Jim

At Hamsters warehouse there was a guy named Jim with one Packer truck parked next to mine. Jim always had a pistol strapped to his leg. This was highly unusual because most of us of Dutch extraction felt we did not need armed guards to conduct our business. We were capable of doing it honestly and without the fear of violence.

Although Henry had been robbed selling eggs, and I had been robbed about three times—once with a gun, twice at knife point—of a grand total of $65 or $70, I felt that a gun would probably do me more harm than good. I would probably get shot because the perpetrator would notice I had a gun. The first time I got robbed, I was walking out of the basement which I had just walked into, and two guys were sitting on the stoop. As I walked out with a can of ashes on my back, I felt a gun poked in my ribs from behind. The perpetrator asked for my money. I replied, "It's in my left rear pocket. But please let me set this can down because it's heavy. I kept my head bowed, so as not to catch a glimpse of the perpetrator. He reached into my rear pocket and took my wallet, emptied the contents and threw the wallet in front of me.

The next two times was at knifepoint, and let me tell you, you have a tendency to cooperate if a knife is shoved up your nose. I couldn't imagine how I could breathe with three nostrils. So once again, I cooperated and emptied my pockets of $20 each time. Later when I had help again, I told the help, "Do not carry more than $15. If you are robbed of that, I will replace it. But if it is more than $15, you're going to eat the difference. Fifteen dollars will satisfy them, so they won't shoot you. But you have no business carrying anything more." One night I found a pistol, and put it in my pocket, feeling quite confident that I now had protection. The chamber was empty, but I felt that was okay. I would get ammunition and walk around with a pistol strapped to my side. When I stopped at a gas station at 6 o'clock that night, I noticed this guy back away from me quite rapidly and I wondered why? Only then did I realize that the outline of that pistol was visible in my pants pocket. When I got to the garage, I hid the pistol so that I would not have to carry it. To this day, I don't know what happened to it.

But back to Jim. He could not operate without having his pistol strapped to his leg, and I suppose there had been times when he got into an argument where he waved it around. Then one day when I was working at City Disposal, I got word that Jim had been assassinated gangland style from someone jumping out of the hopper of his garbage truck and pulling the trigger of a shotgun. I don't have to go in graphic detail of what a shotgun at close range will do to a human body. But I accompanied another guy who knew Jim to his funeral, and that was the scariest wake I have ever been to. People I did not know, looking at each other, or hugging each other, like a scene out of *The Godfather*. My sidekick and I agreed that it would be best if we paid our respects to the widow and left as fast as we got there. I will not get preachy about carrying a gun. This is our right, and we now see just how far these rights have got us.

Early Employees

Some of the memorable employees I've had, besides Hoagie, were Hubert Princeton and James R Knight. Both had been in the trash hauling business as owner operators. I never asked them straightforward what happened with their businesses, but when each of them came to me they were looking for a job, not at the same time, but at different intervals. Hubert was not a bad driver, but he tended not to pick up the drums that were alongside of a container. What I used to do was give the customer a container, and if it wasn't enough, I would add a few drums to catch the overflow, thereby avoiding a mess around the container. Hubert would dump the container and leave the drums. When I asked him about it he said, "All okay. I'll take care of it." Which he would do for a while, but then he would fall back into his old habits. The reason I eventually let him go was—and I felt bad afterward, bad enough to rehire him—he could not read or write. Now in the late 70s and early 80s this seemed almost like an impossibility, that a grown man would not be able to read or write. But what happened was, I had dead-bolted the garage door, and I put a note over the tumbler keylock not to open the door from the outside but to go through the service store and remove the dead bolt. When I got there the next morning, here was the huge overhead door halfway up waving in the breeze. The note I had left had been torn loose and the key had been inserted to raise the door. Needless to say, I was going to have to get the door fixed at about $500. So I was fuming mad when he came in that night, and I read him the riot act saying, "What's the matter? Can't you read?," not knowing that he could not. Only later did I realize that the reason he asked that small decals be put up at each of our stops (in accordance with the city ordinance) was that this allowed him go down the alley and look from side to side to identify each stop. He had made quite an adjustment for his inability to read., and had done a much better job than some of the other guys I had who were able to read and write but hit everything.

James R. Knight was a different story. Before I hired him, he had been in business for himself with one truck. He lived on his route, and many times during the course of the morning hours, I would see his truck parked for several hours near his home. Didn't give it much thought, thinking maybe he had a night route. But then I asked somebody for a driver, and James R. Knight showed up. I asked if he could read a route book. "Oh yeah, no problem." I handed him a route book and a ring of keys, and every morning I would see James R. Knight coming down toward the garage to pick up the truck. He did the job flawlessly, and I was waiting for him to ask for a raise to bring his salary up to scale. And then one morning as I was leaving, headed for the expressway, I did not see James R. Knight. Something told me I better not start on my route. Better make sure something had not happened to him. After about an hour, I had not reached him on the phone number he had given me, and I decided I had better do two routes that day. At the end of the day I received a phone call from one of his sons informing me that his father would no longer be returning to work. The keys and route book had been placed on the truck seat while I was doing his route.

This is part of the problem that you run into being the owner of a small business. You have no clue that these things are about to happen. When they do hit you, you have to put two hats on and do both routes. I would give guys time off for rule infractions, only to find out later that they were at the beach, or enjoying time off with their wives. And I had to do both routes. Larger companies have much more flexibility because they hire people called "swing men," who are capable of filling in at short notice, and everything does not all fall on one person's shoulder. Several months later I get a call from the Unemployment Compensation Board telling me that James R. Knight was applying for unemployment compensation. My response was, "How can this be? I did not fire him. I did not tell him to leave."

So, when I went down to the Unemployment Compensation Board at 63rd and Cottage Grove, I walked up to the man there and he said, "Here, take a number, and we will hear your complaint." And you guessed it. I was Number 62, starting with Number 1, so I estimated at the rate they were going, this would take all day. So I dismissed the matter as one of those lost causes.

But there we go again: the working people supplying tax dollars for the people who are fully capable of working but have figured out a way to scam the system so that they can stay home and do nothing, or do things on the side to earn cash money which generates no tax dollars. And you wonder why Donald Trump garners so much interest when he throws his hat in the political arena?

So this is an example of the government, in its infinite wisdom, once again totally screwing something up. They gave James R. Knight a reason not to come to work: they paid him. They also paid me a tax credit of $2500 when I hired him off the unemployment compensation roles initially. I did not know this, but when he started to receive paychecks with the proper withholding tax, they sent me a notice and said, "Okay, you're entitled to this money." But James R. Knight knew the system, and when he had enough time in to once again receive unemployment, he was ready for the free money.

There were several others who did basically the same thing: work a while, then take the government handout. Find a hustle on the side to supplement their income from the government, and they had a comfortable living. Those who don't believe in this scam are always roundly criticized as lacking compassion. But then they sound like Rush Limbaugh or the other conservative people, and what does it gain.? But I did find out one thing: as time went on, you were less likely to hire somebody who "needed a job," or some greenhorn you had to break in, and more likely to hire somebody who was experienced. If you read any ad for drivers, most prefer experience—some even demand it, because it's very expensive to take a total greenhorn and turn him into an experienced driver. So the best way is to pay union scale up front and give your driver the benefits afforded by the union.

CHAPTER 16 – GARBIO TRUCK STOPS

On the corner of 75th and Exchange there was a restaurant called Milo's. You know the kind: counter, booths, waitresses, and a collection of people that you could write a book about. In the morning the janitors of the nearby buildings would gather for morning coffee, and talk shop. In the afternoon another collection of colorful people would gather after lunch. The owner of Regal Disposal, Ray Vander Aa, hauled Milo's, and he and I would meet there for lunch. We would shut the trucks off, and for about an hour we'd talk shop over lunch and watch the colorful people come and go. Sometimes our wives would drop off the kids, and we would fire up our trucks and show our kids the ins and outs of the big city. There were several restaurants like Milo's throughout the city, each with a line of trucks parked outside. Drivers from various companies, a lot of them trash haulers, would come inside, high-five each other, and then have coffee or lunch. We would chew the fat, finding out who was hiring, who was firing, what stops were gained, what stops were lost. All the latest scuttlebutt.

In my earlier days with Uncle Slim and his drivers, there was a similar restaurant on Franklin Street, run by Jim, a skinny guy with a motor-mouth. His partner was Frank, a rather rotund fella, who would cook your eggs while smoking his cigarette, and would never say a word. Everyone would watch to see whether he would lose his ash in your eggs. But Frank was an artist. Just about the time you think, "It's going to fall into my bacon," he would flip it in the ashtray and continue smoking and cooking at the same time. Not the most healthy breakfast, but it sure was colorful. Jim would go on chattering about how he was going to teach you to ride the range, and I don't mean herding cattle, but cleaning the huge flat surface that was used to cook the bacon eggs and hash brown potatoes. This meant that you would learn how to clean it. Never got that privilege. Did not want that privilege. But if you wanted a cheeseburger at nine in the morning, or bacon and eggs, it was fast, it was cheap, and it always tasted good with High Q orange soda. Every time I see the bit in *Saturday Night Live* with John Belushi yelling, "Cheeseburger! Cheeseburger! Cheeseburger!", I'm not reminded of the Billy Goat Tavern in the show as much as I am reminded of Frank and Jim's diner. And if you talk to trash truck drivers, they all have a favorite restaurant story. Mine, of course, is the time Jack Ter Mitt ordered a steak with two shots, and proceeded to down them in short order, illustrating the principle that you can't do this job on an empty stomach.

    If I analyze why I sold my business so many times, I would probably say that in order to do this right I had to take a vacation. As time goes by, the pressures of running a business get greater and greater. That's probably the only excuse I can offer for selling each time. This business became a passion, a way to succeed, and the opportunity to do something to the best of my ability. The problem is that it takes all of your physical, as well as your mental, capacity to stay on top of the game. If you snooze, you lose, and the minute you don't aggressively go after something, you regret not going after it. The obsession to compete takes almost complete control of you, and when it does, it tires you both physically and mentally. And to avoid total burnout or meltdown, you have to step away from it every once in a while.

When my brothers John, Peter, Glenn, and Mark were younger, I could turn some of the work over to them and maybe get a brief vacation. But as they got older and went into their own professions, it was harder and harder to do. Now you may say, "Well, you got to learn not to micro-manage." That's the truth. But I found out that if you didn't micro-manage, things would get away from you. And I used to have a saying: "stay at one truck, or jump to twenty-one." The rationale, for me, was that at one truck, it was easier to catch somebody who had a seasonal job and could fill in for a couple weeks while you took a much-needed vacation. But it was always the middle ground that was so tricky, the area between two and twenty-one trucks. You had to hire people who were able to run the show, make decisions, and not break the bank while you were gone on your vacation. I never seemed to get a good handle on that after my brothers went on to their own careers. Oh, yeah, there were some employees I had who were totally capable of taking the reins while I was gone. But my mind still would circle back to what was happening while I was away.

CHAPTER 17 – FIRE

One time when Pat and I were just getting home from a trip to Acapulco, the phone rang, and I was informed me that my truck garage was on fire. Anybody who has been in this business will tell you horror stories about fire. One minute you have a fleet of totally functional trucks housed in a garage, and the next instant there is total devastation.

You cannot begin to imagine the desperation and emptiness that comes with watching everything you worked for go up in smoke. The seven miles from my house to the garage was probably one of the longest journeys I have ever taken, and when I arrived the array of South Holland fire equipment was out in front of the garage, lights flashing. They had ripped the overhead doors down to access the three trucks inside. It was too late to save the one truck where the fire had started in its load, but the other two trucks were still operational. They had been empty and only suffered smoke damage.

The next day they were on the road, doing their routes. But many companies that have faced similar disasters have had eight or ten trucks wiped out in one morning or afternoon. Many of the larger corporations have the luxury of watchmen, who keep an eye on things and know what to do in the event something like that happens. If you notice the fire right away, you can pull the truck whose load is on fire outside, open the tailgate, push out the trash that's burning inside the truck and pull the truck away from the burning garbage. But the problem arises when no one knows what to do, other than yell "Help!"

Trucks now come with automatic shut-offs to prevent electrical fires caused by shorts in the twenty-four-volt battery systems, and this safety measure has saved many a truck, and many a building.

CHAPTER 18 – BRICK TO THE FACE

In the late 70s my father had open-heart surgery. When he was on the mend, I kind of wanted to show him what I had accomplished on my own after starting in business the third time. One day, he and my youngest brother Mark came with me on the route after meeting me at Milo's. I had to go back to 71st and Stewart to pick up a stop that was missed that morning. No big deal. Or so I thought.

When we got there, my father was in his car, and my brother was in the truck with me. He was going to help me. Out of nowhere, this guy came up to me and asked, "Where's your crib?" At first I didn't understand what he was trying to ask me, so he repeated it. What I didn't see was the brick in his hand, which he slapped me in the face with, sending me to my knees. I was stunned, trying to keep from losing consciousness, while my dad and brother were yelling, "Leave him alone!"

About this time the owner of the building came and started yelling at the perpetrator, calling him by name. "Holmes," he said, "leave my garbageman alone." The man dropped the brick and walked away, and I struggled to my feet to regain some form of composure, with large scratches on my face.

I sent my brother away with my father, and I picked up one more stop by myself. The scratches weren't that bad, but later I had to listen to my father once again as he told me how dumb I was for working in that kind of environment.

Much of the 70s were a racial tinderbox, and harsh words easily escalated into violence. So this Mr. Holmes, who happened to be a black man, had decided that he would resort to violence and pick on the next white guys he encountered. But the guy who came to my rescue, the owner of the building, was also a black man.

Did I give up hauling garbage in that neighborhood? Not at all. I used to recite the 23rd Psalm quite a bit as I worked. Besides being held up three times, there were several other minor skirmishes, but, well, I read the 23rd Psalm, and this is something that you can take to the bank.

I had a similar instance several years prior, when Martin Luther King Jr. was assassinated, and someone threw a large cinderblock at me from the overpass on the Dan Ryan Expressway at 35th St. It missed my windshield, but caught and broke the mirror on the right side.

At the time I thought, *Maybe we can work the steam out and get along peacefully*. But I am saddened when I see that close to fifty years later we still have this same glaring problem. Did I take my father's advice and abandon ship? No, not right away, and not for that reason. But he did make sure that my younger brother found a different line of employment. So Mark took a job driving a cartage truck, only to find after the first week's check came in from the cartage company, that he was not paid for the time he was parked at the dock, waiting to be loaded. This resulted in about a six-hour gift to the company every day. I know he didn't last at that job very long. The excuse can always be given that he was only doing it in the summertime and was going back to college.

CHAPTER 19 – KINGDOM COME

So after a while, this business of trash hauling becomes like a Chinese water torture for the little guy, not a big gush that will drown you all at once, but a little drip, drip, drip, that eventually begs the question: what am I doing this for? And when you look at what someone else is making per hour, and what benefits he is receiving per month, and how many paid days of vacation he's allowed in a year, the temptation to sell to a larger company and go to work for them sometimes is overwhelming. So in January 1983 after lying in two feet of snow in an alley on the south side of Chicago, putting my truck back together, I did the deal. Anchor 1 was sold.

Part of the water torture process comes from your competition. And with open competition you have a tendency to hustle work from people, and they can become very irate. If it happens more than once, you take the chance of waking up a sleeping lion. This is what I did when I took on Kingdom Disposal. I was threatened, not so much with physical violence, but was told I would regret tangling with them. Their first attempt at intimidation was through legal channels. No, not lawyer to lawyer, but the backhanded use of city inspectors, which is a common trick to make sure all your legal i's are dotted and your t's are crossed. I forget the bozo's name now, but I was later informed by one of Kingdom's employees that this inspector used to come by their garage quite often, so, I guess, he was on a friendly basis with them. But this inspector approached me, and I could see him coming across the street as I was about to pick up a federally inspected meat company at 66th and Wentworth. It took me about twenty minutes to pick up the garbage inside, and when I came out, I noticed an ambulance. This is not an unusual occurrence, and most of the time you're not so curious that you go over and see what has happened. But I was later informed that the city inspector had gotten hit by a car while crossing the street.

Not knowing what really happened, I didn't give it much thought, and it was about six months later I rounded the corner with my truck and noticed the same bozo walking toward my other truck, driven by Hoagie, who was about to pick up some containers at 71st and Stewart. Bozo had his ticket book in hand, ready to issue us a ticket for starting too early in a residential district. (The start time in residential districts is 7 a.m., and we were early.) I walked over and shut the truck off and told Hoagie, "Go to your next stop and don't pick it up before 7 a.m." Well, now Bozo couldn't write a ticket.

But a week later Bozo approached me at the same meat company, and informed me that I was in violation of the law by picking up before 7 a.m. I informed him that this was not the case because federal statues override city ordinances, and in this case, the federal guidelines say that the meat company has to be picked up before they can begin operations. His argument was, "No, they do not." My second prong of attack was to say, "I am also within the guidelines because there is no residence within 500 feet," and he said, "Yes, there is, right over there," and pointed to a very small house between a gas station and a large garage housing trucks. He wrote me a ticket.

The ticket was not so bad in itself, but the problem had to be resolved because every day this meat company had to be picked up by 6 a.m. I could walk away from the stop and be done with it, or I could fight. Those were my two options. I choose to fight thinking that I could very easily explain to an understanding judge that the federal law would certainly supercede the city law.

But, of course, in Chicago nothing is easy. The very simple procedure of explaining has to be done on a grander scale because nobody seems to want to take the initiative to make a decision. A decision may sometimes mean political death for some hack who has a job dependent on who they know and what they know. So at my first court appearance I requested a continuance allowing me to obtain a permit for such an early-pickup operation. By my second appearance I still was no closer to getting a permit because nobody ever heard of issuing such a permit, even though the statue allowed for such permits to be given.

The question remained: how do I get a permit? After chasing around downtown, from lower Wacker Drive to a few floors of City Hall, I was making no headway, with my third court date that afternoon. So in desperation, I called an insurance agent acquaintance who I thought might know "the right people." He said, "Stay by the phone." (Cellular phones were not invented yet.) I received a return call within twenty minutes and was given the name of a person to mention to the judge and to the prosecutor when I returned to court that afternoon. I did as I was instructed, and when I returned to court, it was like the doors of City Hall had opened, and the judge said, "I will grant you a continuance while a permit is being processed. Please return here in two months at such-and-such a time."

I walked out not knowing what would happen, and within one month I received a phone call and was told to meet at a certain person at a popular watering hole on the near North Side for lunch, on a given date at a given time. I did so, and was handed a nice shiny plaque with all the necessary stamps and symbols which would allow me to haul a meat company at 66th and Wentworth before the hour of seven in the morning.

On the given court date, I walked into the courtroom, and Bozo and the prosecutor were standing there. My name was called, and I slapped the metal permit on the judge's rail, and I swear, they almost had to call the ambulance again to come to Bozo's aid, because he turned beet red, and I was afraid he was going to have an aneurysm. While he was stammering and stuttering and yelling at the prosecutor, who replied, "There's not a thing I can do. He did this legally." So with an inward smile, I walked out of the courtroom.

Chalk one up for the Big O.

But the Kingdom was not done with me yet, and this is where I go berserk, because I don't think the IRS should do the bidding of a particular business because of some assumed infraction one of their competitors is committing. One year I was called in for an audit and had no problem explaining my books to the IRS agent, and six months later I was called back in for another audit. This is no accident, but is being done by somebody dropping a dime on some perceived infraction. I did not do a complete meltdown, and informed the owner of Kingdom Disposal and the owner, Jack Van Writer, that I would continue to fight his back-stabbing ways.

Ironically, a funny thing happened some years later. Several of Jack's friends, who were, you might say, "on the side," made his life miserable. So, in the words of Earl (*My Name Is Earl*): "Karma will get you every time."

Did Jack Van Writer stop? No. One Christmas morning, Hoagie was picking up a building at 71st and Bennett, and another city inspector bozo comes out of nowhere and is going to write a ticket for an early start. (This time, a holiday start, which is 9:30.) That was until a Ms. Perkins, who lived in that building, let ole Bozo 2 have a piece of her mind, about how low can you go, giving a hard working man a ticket on Christmas morning. She did not mince word with Bozo 2.

Good old Ms. Perkins later approached me for a charitable donation, and I was more than happy to show my appreciation with something of monetary value.

But the days spent chasing through the maze of City Hall and getting quick audits by the IRS, all add up to days that you're not accomplishing your main activity of picking up trash. These are the things that make up the drips of the Chinese water torture. But they also add some interest to what makes a small business a small business. Large corporations have a legal staff, which handle this every day. To them it's their cup of tea, and they could probably do it in their sleep. But to some greenhorn like me, this is a new set of problems. But every problem has some kind of solution, and whether you like it or not, you have to deal with it, and often very quickly.

CHAPTER 20 – BACK TO HOURLY

So on April 1, 1983, the assets of Anchor Disposal were moved to the facilities of City Disposal. Martin and Norbert, the owners, were very aggressive, not letting any moss grow under their feet. They were forceful competitors. They knew how to acquire work, both on a large and a small scale, and they knew how to keep it. They were not afraid of the large corporations, which were capable of putting large roadblocks in the way of smaller companies, and bringing on the Chinese water torture that has forced many smaller companies to throw up their hands and say, "Well, what's the use?"

By turning everything over to City Disposal, I had to admit some small defeats, had to adjust my thinking that I was no longer in charge of making decisions for the business. I had to stop myself from trying to impose my will on somebody else, but it didn't take long for me to adjust my thinking into saying, "Okay, I'm an employee now, not the boss. These are not the type of decisions I can make." Sometimes the boss would ask me to make a decision, and then I did.

But the upside was that I had days off and the weight of the business did not all fall on this man's shoulders. People at the company were given a certain job to do and they did it. A mechanic would fix the trucks, and I would not have to lay under them after hours. I could concentrate on twelve hours a day of doing a route and I got amazingly efficient at it. The bosses had personnel to do the Mickey Mouse stuff, to go to court to argue and plead, to do what it took to get the wrinkles ironed out of the legal stuff. I could see the validity of getting bigger. While the personal touch of a small operation was nice, it was something that I could see was going to fall by the wayside. Or so I thought. In the next eighteen years I watched Martin and Norbert's operation grow from a dozen trucks, to about seventy-two, I think, when they sold. And they would take over two or three routes and combine them into one. No longer did we have large gaps in the amount of travel between stops. Most stops were next to each other, or within a baseball throw of the last one. This increases productivity, with very little wasted motion.

    I had gone from running the show to being a route man, which to me was good. I could concentrate on picking up trash, driving and making sure the route was in order. I had no desire to go to an easier type of hauling, such as driving a roll-off or dump truck. I realized that doing a route would keep me physically fit. Because of the hard work, I could eat what I wanted, when I wanted and would not have to worry about waist size or diets. Also, even though the days were long, most of the time if I made an appointment to be somewhere, I could usually fulfill that commitment.

    By doing a route I had a certain framework, and rarely did I exceed the allotted time it took to do that route. I would work one out of three Saturdays, so it was easy to be involved with the kids' baseball, basketball or volleyball. So the experience working for somebody else was so not bad. They made arrangements when I went on vacation, and I could usually horse trade with another driver to get a Saturday off if I needed to.

    On occasion, I would ask myself if I'd made a mistake by selling out to Martin and Norbert, and, of course I said "no." I savored the time I had with my last two children. I participated in my son's baseball games till he got to be a teenager, and I got a schedule of my daughter's basketball and volleyball games and was able to attend almost all of them, both home and away. This was something that I had hoped I would be able to do, to be given a second chance with my family. And I got it with the boy and girl God blessed Pat and me with. Did I ever savor those moments!

CHAPTER 21 – CRUSHED

March 11, 1987, 5:50 a.m., Franklin School, East Chicago, Indiana, changed my life. The truck I was driving was Number 52, a DM 600 Mack with a 25-yard Leach body. I had opened the gate at the school and backed up to a 4-yard container. On each side of the container were eleven boiler plates, standing on end and weighing 1100 pounds each, twenty-two plates in all. I backed up to the container in order to dump it, walked to the back of the truck and observed that I had missed the trunnion of the container by a couple of inches. I turned my back and walked toward the cab of the truck.

A boilerplate, standing too vertically, fell over and just caught the back of my foot. The weight of the boilerplate caused my foot to explode inside my shoe, completely breaking the shoelaces apart. I fell to the ground, not knowing what exactly had happened or how bad my injury was. Got up off the ground, and on one foot hopped to the cab of the truck, where I grabbed the truck microphone and tried to talk to the other truck that was out on the street on this Saturday morning. We had two brands of two-way radios, Johnson and Motorola, and I was not sure what brand the other truck was using.

But at that moment, I noticed a squad car in the parking lot of the school. In order to reduce my chance of being left there alone in agony I figured the best way to get help was to hop over to the squad car. After receiving no response on the radio, I slid out of the cab and hopped over to the squad car, where I fell on the hood. When the officer exited his car, I explained what had happened and that I was hurt and would he take me to St. Catherine's Hospital, which was about a mile away? He opened the back of the squad, and I dove in, in much the same fashion as I had done at Jay's Potato Chips many years prior.

A short ride to St. Catherine's and I was in the emergency room. They removed my shoe, cut my pants off and asked me for all the important information: Who owned the truck? Where had the accident happened? What was my doctor's name? And, of course, who was my next of kin?

For the next ninety days and eight surgeries, except for two brief visits home, I remained in the hospital while they attempted to put my foot back together. No broken bones, but that boilerplate had raked the back of my foot, exposing my Achilles tendon. Two of the surgeries involved pig skin grafts, which were only mildly successful, and it was determined that I would have to have a Cross Legged Pedicle Graft.

If you don't know what that is, they cut part of one leg away and sew your opposite, injured foot to it. Then they put you in a cast from the tip of your toes to halfway up your chest. This is to allow the skin from your left leg to grow onto your right foot, and to do this you cannot move either your leg or your foot. You remain in this position for twenty-one days.

So for those twenty-one days I laid in the bed in St. Catherine's Hospital and waited for this miracle to occur. Thanks to Dr. Santos and Dr. Goldenberg for their expertise. The foot has healed, but to the day, just shy of thirty years later, I still have to be very careful with my right foot and make sure that I don't do anything to disturb the very fragile skin covering that heel. No longer can I wear $20 shoes. It took me a while to find just what shoes would work and not wear my foot out. In fact, it's funny. I now have to pay $300 for a pair shoes, but the right foot is the only one that needs the $300 shoes, and when I began working again, I noticed that the left boot was the one that was getting torn up.

So today I wear one right shoe that cost $300 a pair and one left shoe that cost 40 bucks. What happens when I wear $40 shoes on that right foot? The material in the shoes causes abrasions on the right heel, and I am afraid of wearing through that skin and having to repeat that long hospitalization again.

Now the question arises: what's the company going to do with a driver with one good foot and one very questionable foot? Well, they can always stick you in the office. But after several months of being in the office doing sales, I could see that this was not my cup of tea. The company did have one possible fit for me in the form of a front loader, which they used in hauling two of the steel mills they acquired from a company called Laidlaw.

Laidlaw was a trucking company from Canada that had looked at the trash hauling business and said that anybody could do it, especially if you had a background in trucking, which they did. And if you know anything about Laidlaw, they do know how to run school buses and a trucking fleet. So in the 80s they decided to put their expertise to work in the trash hauling business. They went on a buying spree, setting up headquarters, I think, in Naperville, Illinois.

But in a short time they realized trash hauling was certainly different than taking a box from Point A to Point Z and dropping it off. This was a whole different ballgame. So as fast as they acquired the trash hauling work, they began to shed parts of it, Martin and Norbert acquiring the Indiana part, with the steel mills and surrounding areas. And eventually, Ally took control of the rest of the Laidlaw operation. Another example of someone who looked at trash hauling and said, "Aw, that looks easy," until they really got into it.

Well, how did I fit in this? The driver on the front loader quit, and I was informed that I would be taking it over. So I went one

Saturday and practiced. I had seen these things before, but thought there were halfway useless, so didn't pay much attention to them. A front loader is the kind of truck where the forks pick up the box in front of the truck and dump it in the opening right behind the cab. Then it puts the box back down, all without the driver leaving the cab of the truck. And while in transit, the driver can activate the compaction panel, and the truck will pack the garbage before he gets to the next stop. Instead of packing from back to front, it reverses the procedure, packing from front to back. The reason they were not used very much was that the compaction was not as much as the trucks that went from back to front, and because most companies were paying dump fees based on volume not weight, they got rid of most front loaders.

When I got on the front loader, I could see that it was considerably faster to haul trash that way. Most containers were exposed, so you did not have to move them, and in a matter of seconds you had completely dumped and returned the container to the spot where you picked it up and you were on your way. If you used a rear load container, it took you half a minute just to get the back of the truck positioned near the container. Then you had to hook up the container and dump it, and then it took you half a minute to get back in the truck. As much as five minutes were involved in this whole process, and that's only one stop. Do the math for a whole day's worth of stops and you can see out how much time is involved.

At the mill most of the containers were located where you could easily access them. This is a big plus. Drive up, lift container, dump it, lower it and move on. You didn't have to get out of the truck. But I had a selfish reason: I wanted to stay in the truck, not in the office. I had to get more hours than that front load route was giving me at the time. So I talked Martin and Norbert into extending that route by another eight hours a week. How? By talking them into putting front load boxes in several stops that were not part of the mill. Some were grocery stores, some were fruit markets and some were apartment buildings. These were are already our accounts, being hauled by a different truck of ours.

It also helped that Laidlaw called and offered a hundred front load boxes for $35 apiece. Martin sent me to look at them, and after seeing them, I told him he would be a fool not to buy them. Some of those boxes were made at a cost of $500 per container. So I got my wish, got my extra ten hours a week and also noticed that I could work almost fifty hours with less exertion than on a rear load truck.

Not only did I not have to wear my foot out, I did not have to freeze to death in the winter, standing behind the truck, waiting for the container to dump. No, now my work was done in the comfort of a warm cab, while listening to the radio/tape player, which I made good use of. I recorded my favorite radio shows at home while I was sleeping, and I could eliminate the commercials very easily by fast-forwarding past them on the truck tape player. As a lay preacher, I also was able to make up sermons while doing this job.

I tell guys that haul now, "You could take college courses while making a living, or learn to speak a foreign language while dumping garbage." Will the corporations eliminate the players in the trucks? Why should they? Look at the productivity they get. In my highest producing 12-hour days, I was able to pick up and dump five loads. Yes, these loads were dumped on site- transfer stations, but still, five loads is a lot of volume to pick up in a single day. You would not get this kind of production on a suburban route, where you only had one or two containers at a particular stop. But you get the idea. And now I see these trucks out twelve hours a day, and if I talk to the drivers in confidence, they tell me they are not as tired as they were doing ten hours a day on the rear load style trucks they used to drive.

So I was sitting in the catbird seat. I had the job I wanted, and was happy working for Martin and Norbert. Life was good. I had told the guy that broke me in on the front loader: when you go to work for somebody, don't get too excited if you get a good job and if you like your job. If you like starting at midnight, don't tell anybody. Just moan and groan about it, especially if you're working for a large corporation. I don't know what there is about it, but if you like something, they'll change it on you. If you don't like starting at 5 a.m., jump for joy when they tell you have to start at 5 a.m. Then they'll, hopefully to something you like better. You get my drift. So Norbert tells me, "We're building you another front loader. You see, they realized the validity of what I had told them, that while they might lose some compaction by not using a rear loader, but they were gaining because the driver hauling more volume on his same shift. And if the trucks were allowed to use transfer stations close by, this would also make up for the loss of compaction.

CHAPTER 22 – WILD WILL AND THE MILL

The rules had also changed at the landfills. Why? Because the compaction technology had advanced to the point that there was virtually no airspace in the trash. Trash was being compacted almost into bricks. So if you owned a landfill, it was now to your advantage to charge by tonnage rather than volume. Because of this, many of the companies that had been switching from front loaders to rear loaders suddenly stopped what they were doing and re-assessed, switching back to front loaders. Not only did this increase the volume that each truck was able to haul, but it also reduced the number of drivers that were needed to clean up a particular area. The driver who had been doing a hundred stops a day, could very easily go up to a hundred fifty. So for every three trucks, one was being eliminated.

Again, what's this got to do with me? Well, Norbert and Martin said they were going to build a truck with a combined front load/roll-off type arrangement. And what were they going to do with that new truck? Well, one day Norbert informed me that I was to haul the mill in Burns Harbor with another driver, just the two of us. So they moved me further south and gave me George D. Fry to help me out. I had originally got George a job at City Disposal. George was a real go getter, and he and I worked real well together. The new truck, however, proved to be a nightmare. It was way too heavy and just did not have what was needed to do the job effectively, and I was not happy being there.

So now I was faced with a choice: do I do as I'm told and accept my new responsibility? Or do I look for another job? Seeking employment was something I had not been forced to do in quite a while. But there really was no hurry because I was still gainfully employed. So when you're in that position, you can do your job, collect a paycheck, keep your ear to the ground and casually send out feelers. Which is what I did.

But two incidents changed my mind. First, one day in 1992 I left the mill about noontime, my work having been shifted around so I could leave and go downtown Chicago to run an errand. It didn't take me long to go from Burns Harbor to Ohio Street on the North Side of Chicago. But the return from Ohio Street home was a nightmare. I was stuck in traffic, and fuming because of it. I had just been thinking I might like to do some job other than hauling garbage. Shed my work clothes for something a little cleaner. But would that mean a daily commute like this? The longer I sat in traffic, the more I realized that maybe it wasn't the worst thing in the world to go to work at 2 a.m. and leave at 2 p.m., and miss most of the traffic to and from work.

The second incident was when a cement truck driver approached several of us trash haulers and said if we were looking for jobs, his company was hiring. He claimed they paid good with lots of hours. He repeated his offer several times, and I finally asked him point blank what he made a year. "Between $13- and $15,000," he responded. Less per year than I was making. And so the idea of making a job change was quickly put out of my mind. No sense poking a hornets' nest and getting stung.

So George and I grabbed the bull by the horns, and took care of the business that was put before us. We divided the mill in half; George took one side, I took the other. I would do the front load part of it, and he would assist me if I needed help. This worked fantastic for a long time. It's called "teamwork," something that was mentioned in the first couple of pages of the Association's directory that I used to page through when I was in my pre-teens. George eventually got married and bought a house close to the mill. Life was good.

Then George got a little restless. He had gotten job offers from other people, and the mill work, like home routes, can be somewhat mundane, same old same old everyday. As much as I tried to talk George out of it, he left and went to work for another company.

That's when the nightmare really began. Norbert hired a guy named Will Parr, and at first, it wasn't bad. He took care of his business, and I took care what I had to do.

But as time went on, I began to see that there was a reason he had bounced around so much in the last several years. Will had worked it City Disposal before and I didn't not have much contact with him at the time, since he started and finished at different hours than me in his route, and our paths very seldom would cross. But now we were working side-by-side, and the friction began to increase.

The two sides of the mill which George and I had divided up, but would cross to help each other out, became a hard line. No longer would we cross over if something would come up. His excuse was, "Well, it's your side. You take care of it," not realizing that my day involved a couple more hours on the front loader then his did.

So a minor war ensued between him and me, and my days got longer because he refused to help. He started at a different time than I did, and finished up earlier than I did, and went home. For a long time we did not talk to each other, and that suited me fine because this was an hourly job. You're paid for the time you spend doing the work, and what's the difference if you are hauling trash on the east side of the mill, or the west side of the mill? The boxes look the same, the trucks look the same, the road looks the same. So what's the big deal?

As I mentioned earlier, fires are the trash hauler's nightmare. In a matter of hours, things which may have taken months to build, trucks that were acquired over many years, and even your jobs can be removed if a fire occurs. City Disposal had already had a serious fire at their main garage on 118th St. They were using the wash bay as a paint booth, with a big exhaust fan sending fumes into the repair shop. Whether it was a torch or sparks from a grinding wheel, I'm not entirely sure, but it caught the fumes from the spray booth and ignited the garage on fire. Fortunately, only one truck was in the garage at the time, but before the fire was put out, it had completely burned a steel structure halfway to the ground. That is a weird occurrence when the only thing fueling the flames is something you cannot see. So, after many months of wrangling with the insurance company and all the parties that were involved, they rebuilt the structure with restrictions on what they could and couldn't do inside the building.

At the steel mill they had a similar situation. As any steel maker will tell you, to increase the heat of a blast furnace, there's a product called magnesium lime (mag lime) put into the burning process. The problem with mag lime is, it ignites at the craziest times, and I was introduced to this as a teenager when my Uncle Pete dumped his load at 95th and Crawford in an open field, and it burned for a week. The fire department attempted to put it out with water, which is one of the crazy characteristics of mag lime: water only makes it burn hotter. At the time, I thought my uncle was pulling my chain when he said water won't put it out, but makes it burn hotter.

But one weekend we got a call that a Butler-type structure made of wood and sheeting had completely burned to the ground over the weekend. I won't blame mag lime on that, but I'm almost positive that's what happened. The owner, Martin, decided to make the new structure fireproof and much larger. So they moved it several feet to the south and built concrete walls a foot thick and ten feet in the air, and on top of the concrete wall they put up a chain-link fence and sheeting on top of the chain-link. This was done professionally, not in a makeshift manner.

But one morning a driver dumped a load in the transfer, and before he could put the body back down, the load had burst into flames. He quickly drove half a block to get the loader driver to drag the burning load out of the transfer. But by the time they got back, the mag lime had caught the rest of the transfer station on fire. Mag lime burns hot, and on this particular day there was a lot of trash in the transfer station. The fire melted the sheeting roof, the chain-link fence and the steel girders that held up this top structure. Attempts to put water on this inferno only made matters worse. So as a last resort, they dragged the burning garbage into a nearby field, and as my uncle had done years earlier, they let it burn itself out. I think it took about a week for it to completely burn out. But to Martin's credit, the structure he had specially built withstood most of the damage the fire caused. They didn't have lights for a while, and they had to repair the sheeting on the roof and replace the chain-link fence around the perimeter of the concrete wall.

On another occasion, there was mag lime in a front load box I had picked up earlier, and I heard it explode in the body of my truck on my way to the transfer station. I knew what had happened because I could see the smoke coming out the gaps in the body, so I raced to an open field in back of the transfer and pushed the load onto the ground before the fire destroyed the hydraulic hoses needed to raise the tailgate and push the load off.

In previous chapters I mentioned why experience is so important. Lessons like these cannot be taught in a classroom. You learn what fire will do by standing there and watching it burn.

Will got even madder at me when I was able to get my daughter, who was only sixteen years old at the time, hired as my assistant. You're probably asking yourself right now, "How can a sixteen-year-old be Big O's assistant driver on a roll-off/front loader? Any fool knows that's a one-man job." Aha! That's where it gets real interesting. Martin and Norbert were toying with the idea of selling. Ally was on a buying spree, looking at any operation that was available and, most of the time, buying it. Trash Management was in a kind of limbo: their acquisition days were over, for the time being, and they themselves were in the process of being acquired by a smaller company in Houston. My wife Pat said to me, "I don't want my daughter flipping hamburgers." So I said, "Well, okay, I can get her to haul garbage." She exclaimed, "You're nuts!" So I presented the idea to Norbert, telling him I needed the help. His response was, "How are you going to do this?" I told him, "Let me worry about it." He said, "How much is this going to cost me?" So we agreed on an hourly wage, and in June 1998 my daughter Tricia and I drove to the mill.

Sometimes you get a driver that is a good route man, but hard on the truck, especially the clutch and transmission. So over the years, automatic transmissions have greatly helped, and now are almost automatically—excuse the pun—put in trash trucks. We were no exception, and that greatly helped in my training in Tricia. She and I would get our roll-off trucks started. Wild Will was already working. I would say to her, "Push the yellow button in to release the brakes, put the selector in Drive and follow my truck, but don't you dare hit me." When we got to a certain door, I would go in, pull the full box up on the truck, come out the door and switch trucks with her. Then I would tell her once again, "Follow me." We would go to the next door and repeat the process.

In this way, we would go to the transfer station on the mill property, not with just one loaded roll-off, but with two. I would dump both loads and say once again, "Follow me," and this process would be repeated till about 7 a.m. Much can be done when you have two trucks moving at the same time. That's why when you see doubles and triples on the highway, there's a good reason for it. One truck, two loads. Not a bad deal.

Then at 7 o'clock I would fire up the front load truck and tell her she could go in the air-conditioned office trailer, which we had parked at the mill, make herself a Hot Pocket for her 7 a.m. "lunch," and I would be back in about two hours. In two hours I would have completed making my rounds of picking up and dumping the front end boxes (120 of them), that were located at various parts of the mill. After this was done, I would return, and we would repeat the process of the early morning till it was time to go home.

For a while, I was able to disguise the fact that she was a girl, and that she was quite young. On many occasions, Tricia would not take a nap, but would take the pickup I had purchased used from somebody that worked in the mill. It had a standard transmission, and she would practice driving around the transfer station till she got her clutch-accelerator coordination. After several attempts, which it's best if you do it yourself, with nobody barking in your ear, I told her, "Now go around the mill, stopping at all the stop signs and signals, and be able to drive a stick shift like a real truck driver. You will not be restricted to automatic transmissions." It's kinda comical to see somebody who has been driving for several years jump in the truck and say, "I can't do this. It's not automatic." But my daughter Tricia mastered the stick.

I can spend several years teaching a son or daughter to play baseball, basketball, or some other sport, and not be as instructional as one summer showing a young teenage son or daughter the ins and outs of what their father does for a living. I am proud of my daughter as well as my sons, and I am glad I fudged a little to get her in for a summer of instruction. She worked the months of June, July and two weeks in August. This was the cut-off point, one week before she returned to high school, and it tickles the daylights out of me that Norbert allowed me to run with this harebrained idea.

But it drove Wild Will crazy. He had been trying to get his daughter's boyfriend a job somewhat along the same lines as I got my daughter hired. The kid eventually got a job for one of the sewer sucking companies that had a contract at the mill. But the fact that I aced him out on this one was something that made him really mad, but I didn't care. Will could stay on his side of the mill and I could stay on min. So this is how we dealt with each other in a civilized manner.

But on the second-to-the-last day a curious thing happened—and I don't know if Will had anything to do with it or not. As we pulled up to the gate at the mill (Tricia hidden behind the driver's seat in my Suburban as usual), I stuck my hand out to wave to the security guard, who usually just waved back. But this time he stopped me and said, "We have to search your car." I couldn't refuse because that was part of our agreement with the mill. I said, "Okay" to the guard, and told my daughter that she had better get up because the Suburban was about to be searched. But when the guy opened the door to the second seat, no daughter! She was between the second and third seat. She poked her head up and said, "Here I am," and the guard looked and said, "Okay, you guys are all right," and Tricia and I proceeded out the gate.

To this day, I don't know what was going on there, but Tricia and I still laugh about it.

I have a middle son and his name is Edward. When he was a junior in high school, my wife said to him, "No, you are not going to sit around the whole all summer. You are going to find a job." She looked at me and I knew what that meant: find something at City

Disposal to keep him busy for the summer. They were very helpful in this respect. If you had family members who needed employment, as long as they did not demand top dollar, they were welcome aboard.

One day I was dumping in the transfer station located next to the garage. It was about 2 o'clock in the afternoon, and I heard somebody say, "HEY!" I looked around, but couldn't see anybody. And then I heard it again, and there under a piece of equipment I saw two eyes and some grinning teeth. Ed had been assigned to the pit crew. No, he did not have to change tires on a race car or add fuel, but he had to take a shovel and dig out the crap that was underneath the compaction unit. If it was a hot day, this was work that would tax any man, and Ed was sure earning his money—which was a few bucks over minimum wage—the hard way.

The next summer I asked Ed, "Do you want me to put your name in the hat for summer work?" and his reply was, "No! I have already secured an internship at a computer company." Ed, like my oldest son, had been cured of a future in the trash hauling industry, and years later he told me that being assigned to the pit crew was something that had changed his mind about a future in that business.

Some people gravitate toward this industry, while others want absolutely no part of it. Ed was in that second group. He has done quite well in the computer industry, and at age forty-five he has worked for three different companies in the computer field.

CHAPTER 23 – UNION MAN

Another thing that had a profound impact on my life—and I have to thank Norbert for that too—is one day he came up to me and asked me if I wanted to join the union. Now you need to understand that I had always been afforded a close parallel to what the union scale was. I received a check at the end the year to make up for my IRA, and health and welfare were paid by the company. So my incentive to join the union was not very high. My question to him was, "Why, after all these years of working for you, do you want to make that offer?" He did not give me a response but turned his head, and I could see he was chuckling a little bit. But he did say, "Well, you had almost five years with New Way/Alter, and after five years you're vested, and you're eligible to receive that pension money back when you retire."

He went on to say, "I don't know what your plans are in your future employment, but if you're going to keep doing this, you might as well join the union and have your employer contribute to the pension fund." In addition, a former employee of City Disposal had told me that the pension fund was now under governmental control, and that any money put in was money you would receive.

My father and I use to argue constantly about the merits of being a member of the Teamsters Union. When he retired at age sixty-two and went to draw his pension from three locals of the Teamsters Union, he was rudely awakened to the fact that he could receive only from one of them. And even though he had saved all his pay stubs from twenty-three years driving a laundry truck, his eligibility remained at ten years driving for a bakery supply corporation. And during my almost eighteen years with City, I had refrained from joining the union based on his experience.

During my uncles' days I had seen the abuses of the pension system, which required a man to work till he was sixty-five and have put at least twenty-five years into that pension fund. And I could hold up one hand…well, maybe both my hands with one finger missing…and count the number of people that had retired from that pension fund. Most guys that worked in trash hauling were burnt out at age forty-five, not ever hoping to make it to sixty-five, twenty years away, so the money that was put in during their working years remained in the pension fund coffers. I remember Uncle Slim carrying a couple guys, who had lost their jobs at sixty or sixty-two, and were driving to get to the sixty-five mark. Slim, being a compassionate man, was able to employ them at a diminished capacity and paid their pension demands, so that at age sixty-five they were able to retire with a pension.

I know of others who went to claim their pension upon reaching the required age/ employment, only to find out that several of the years that they thought were being paid to the pension, had not been paid. And the union, which should have made it their job to make sure the employer was paying into the fund, turned a blind eye. The government clamping down hard on pension funds was something that should have been done sooner, and I hope in the future they will continue to do so.

So when Norbert informed me that I had five years from New Way/Alter days, my mind began to roll, and I said, "Well, if I do this for ten more years as a union man, that will give me fifteen, and let me find out what fifteen will give me." Norbert already knew the answer. So I said, "Okay, let me sign up. I will be come a union man again." And all I can say about that is: The Lord moves in mysterious ways, his wonders to perform. What Norbert's motivation was, I don't know, but I thank him and the Lord. I guess for every story about guys like my father, there's one that is about me. Oh yeah, I contributed for the next ten years, but I am thankful that the fund is there, and I am now able to tap into it.

Today, I tell guys in the trash business, "Make sure your union dues are paid because twenty-five years goes by in a big hurry, and there will come a time when you have to, or want to, retire, and at least you can do it with a little bit of a nest egg."

CHAPTER 24 – MORE CHANGES

    Like I said, there had been rumors of Martin and Norbert selling to Action, which at that time was not part of Ally. As it turned out, in August 1998 Martin and Norbert sold out to Action, and we were informed that City Disposal, their old business, was now to be known as Action Waste Corporation. Later in the year AWC was sold to Ally. Very slowly at first, the wheels in my head began to turn: could I make one more serious attempt at running my own business as I had done eighteen years earlier? Or was this some kind of pipe dream I had in the back of my head? Just some wishful thinking of a rapidly-aging has-been?
    An interesting side note to this sale was that when City Disposal was officially turned over to Ally, they brushed Norbert aside. But the Burns Harbor mill made it known that the contract with them would have to be in the existing hauler's name, that is, City Disposal. Norbert had offered to facilitate this transition with the mill, but had been rebuffed by the Ally Corporation, which allowed a Chesterton, Indiana, hauler named Arby to get their foot in the door once again.
    Arby had tried on two occasions to outbid Martin, Norbert and City Disposal, and failed each time. The salesman for Arby approached me at 5 a.m. one morning, looking for information, but I said, "I cannot tell you much because Ally/Action still signs my check, and I know you're free to look around because they gave you access to these grounds. So you do your job and I will do mine." Still fishing for information, the salesman then approached Will Parr,

my despised co-worker, and our man Will got diarrhea of the mouth, and spilled the ins and outs of what every truck did, and which ones were being used, and which ones were not. For two hours he just kept babbling on and on, with the salesman taking mental notes.

That salesman was no greenhorn. He knew exactly the sum total of the information he was getting from this nitwit, and how much value it would be during contract negotiations with this mill. At the same time the office kept calling Will on the radio, and normally he would have answered within five seconds because he did not want to miss anything. But this time he was standing about twenty feet from his truck and he was too busy listening to himself babble to hear his name being called. It took someone coming from the Chicago office and stuffing a sock into his mouth, to shut him up.

Needless to say, the damage had been done, and several months later Arby began to put their equipment in this mill. To this day I shake my head at the incompetent decisions that are made at the corporate level. A simple "yes" from Ally, and Norbert would've facilitated the transition in Ally's favor at the mill. Later on that day, Will Parr kept telling me how this new company was going to take over and both of us were promised jobs. Little did this ding-dong know that I wanted to distance myself far enough from him to never see him again, which I hope is what has happened. (He never did get that job with Arby.)

CHAPTER 25 – ELMER HIGGINS

Some years prior, I had been informed that Pamela, Elmer Higgins' wife, had passed away at a very young age. Elmer had gone on to become quite successful. Mayor Daley, the Second, was in power, and Elmer had continued to transform many rough buildings into diamonds. It's always nice to say, "Hey I know that guy," when you read a newspaper article about someone's success, even someone being blindsided by the press. I did not have his personal phone number, but I did have his office number, and I placed a call to Gracie, the office manager, who had been working there since my Anchor One days. She informed me that she could not help me, but it was worth trying to get ahold of Elmer himself.

Not wanting to appear too aggressive and asking for his private number, I felt the best way to contact him was as I had done in the past, once when his wife had passed away, and another time when the press were taking pot shots at him: I composed a letter. In it I related to him that I would like to try it one more time (hauling trash as head of my own company) if I could receive his blessing, and I sent him the letter. (Remember letters? That's what the Post Office delivers sometimes.)

About a month went by, and one night I received a phone call from him, and he said if I could find suitable dumping arrangements and come up with a truck, then he would be able to provide me with some work. The rusty old train was beginning to roll, and once again I am grateful to the people that have, in the course of my life's excursion, come to my aid, and Elmer Higgins is one I will be eternally grateful to for providing me with a exciting adult career. How can you express gratitude? I don't have the proper words to express it the way I would like to. Now, as I sit back in retirement and do my little side things and think how much God has blessed me, I am so thankful that God has steered me in the right direction and let me cross paths with some very special people. And I think of the words that Fred, my childhood friend, said when we were teenagers: "It's not what you know, but who you know." How true this is. Thanks again, Elmer.

CHAPTER 26 – ANCHOR TWO

But back in October 1998, I burned up the phone lines, trying not to show my cards to my employer. After all, if it fell through for me at age fifty-five, I did not want to be out on the street, looking for a job. Especially not hauling garbage. Because there was an unwritten rule, a rule in place when I went to work at Alter many, many years ago, and still in place today in many of the larger companies: don't hire anyone over thirty unless it's a special need, but if you're over thirty and still working here, we won't mess with you. You will hear corporations deny it, but I know it was in place before, and I know it still exists. And of course, in one way it makes a lot of sense because the human body is a very important ingredient in trash hauling. Who can push or pull containers to the back of the truck, and how fast? Also, the longevity of a worker enters the equation. If you have ten employees with four weeks' vacation, that's forty weeks a year that you have to make room for their vacations. Because of this, the incentive to eliminate workers with the most longevity is very much in the forefront an employer's mind, and most employees are aware that it is an unwritten rule.

So I made phone calls all across the country to find a truck. Cell phones were just coming into their own, but they were big and clunky. So the pay phones in the mall were my office. I called Tennessee, I called Texas, I called Louisiana, and I called New Jersey. I should've flipped over a few cards locally here, because it would've saved me a couple of trips. I arranged to go to New Jersey to purchase a truck to the tune of $35,000. The seller on the phone said, "Yes, this truck is primo, top-of-the-line, nothing wrong with it." Boy, don't trust somebody selling used cars and used trucks over the phone. Was that an eye-opener!

I took a flight from Chicago to Philadelphia with the understanding that someone would pick me up the next morning at a certain motel in Philadelphia. My daughter called me the night before and wished me well. (She was just starting her first year in college.) The next morning I was picked up by a guy who, if you went to central casting for a mob enforcer, he would be the one. His father owned the company, and when I arrived there, I could see what they were up to. They would take a tailgate from one piece of junk and put it on a different shell, and put the complete body on this junk of a chassis. The only thing that was new was the hundred-dollar paint job that they had put on the body.

It took me about five minutes to decide that this thing was, well, let's say if you had put $35,000 into it, you would have a truck that might do one route. I had to humor him a little bit because I needed a ride back to the airport, so I put my disposable coverall and crawled underneath. I noticed that the clutch had been doctored to get it to move and that there were cracks in the cross-members. The body was a similar disaster. All the welds on the roof were broke, the carrier was broke, and the tailgate would not go up, meaning the pump was shot. So an inspection of the inside of the body was impossible.

He asked me if I wanted to drive it. "Of course," I said to humor him because I still needed that ride to the airport. It was a ten-speed Road Ranger with no low range. It smoked, which meant the engine was almost gone. To this day, I don't know what he was thinking about when he said I could drive it back to Chicago. I was lucky to get in the three-mile test run and come back. His last response was, "Well, we can adjust the price a little." My answer to that was, "I don't have time to fix everything that is wrong with the truck. Did I say $35,000 in repairs? Let's make that $50,000, and that's if I'm lucky." No deal. But I did get him to take me back to the airport.

Before this trip, I had called my second son, Sean, who was a road driver for a company covering northern Minnesota/northern Wisconsin and knew what I was about to do (start up my own business). He had located a Mack conventional with a 20-yard Leach body in Minnesota, which he said probably could be driven to Chicago without too much trouble. I called Sean from Atlanta, (the flight went from Philadelphia to Atlanta, then to Chicago), and told him I would fly up to Minnesota to check out that truck and make sure it was roadworthy. The following weekend I was in Duluth, looking at that 1989 Mack, this time with three certified checks for considerably less than $35,000. This truck was in fairly good shape, and seemed to me, a good buy for the money.

So I paid the man, grabbed the title and with minor alterations drove home on a late Saturday night/early Sunday morning in November. I had made arrangements with my friend Fred (more about him in later chapters) to take the body off, reinforce the frame, and make it route worthy in a little over two months. I needed to be ready by my target date of January 1, 1999. Then the floodgates of not having a spare truck hit me. The complexion of trash hauling had changed so much in the past twenty years, and most of my former acquaintances who were also in the business had either sold out, were working for somebody else, had moved away, or were part of what had now become the corporate competition, and I knew I would not be able to get my hands on a spare truck.

So I mentioned to Fred that if he knew somebody who could get me a truck that would suffice as a spare, to let me know. He lined me up with Albert Clegg, who had sold trucks professionally and was now in business for himself (not trash hauling), but brokered truck deals on the side. On a Saturday morning Clegg admonished me for going all the way to New Jersey before contacting him, saying, "You're not gonna find nothing but junk in New York or New Jersey on the used truck market." His explanation was that those two states are not too fussy about weight restrictions, and those trucks are allowed to haul as heavy as they can, with long trips to get rid of their loads. So when they do hit the market, they're pretty well used up. "In fact," he said, "it's coin toss whether they go straight to the junkyard or somebody tries to resurrect them and sell them to an unsuspecting customer."

Clegg located a couple of prospects for me closer to home, and he and I went to a yard in a suburb of Chicago that sells…well, let's just say Larry, the owner, had a whole yard full of used, ugly (paint and cosmetics) trucks. But they definitely were not junk. So after looking the whole field over, and getting prices, Larry started one truck up (a Crane Carrier), raised the tailgate, looked at it and said, "Well, for $5500 this certainly will do." There was a second truck (another Crane Carrier), and I agreed that if he got that one started, I would take it also and be back on Thursday to pick the first one up, check in hand.

My question to Clegg: "Why didn't you tell me you had access to these trucks before I went all the way to Minnesota to pick up the one I got?" His response was: "I thought you guys were Mack and Ford men, so I didn't even bother letting you know these were available." I was kicking myself because at the price I paid for the one in Minnesota, I could've bought more of these ugly, but very usable, trucks in the Chicago area. Like I said, I probably should have flipped a few more cards over about what my intentions were and maybe I would've got some help here locally.

You see what was happening: the big corporations in the past were eager to sell surplus equipment. Most required major overhauls, both in the chassis and in the body. So, to make them route worthy, they decided to go with new equipment, rather than put good money after bad. But what had happened was that many of their competitors, or even upstarts, had resurrected the used, but not totally junk, trucks. They were using their surplus equipment to compete with them. So the big boys adopted a new tack, and that was to strip the valuable parts off and send the rest to the scrap yard with no chance of being resold to a third party. So the used truck market dried up very fast.

My meeting with Elmer Higgins was postponed several times, and I began to wonder if it was going to happen. But on December 3, 1998, a day which I will go to my grave remembering, Elmer's secretary called me and said he could not make a lunch date, but could I come by the office at two in the afternoon? "Of course," was my reply. So that afternoon, two days prior to Christmas, Elmer, his secretary Grace and myself agreed that I would begin hauling eight accounts on February 1, 1999. A flood of relief came over me. I was now on my way to begin Anchor2. Prices were agreed upon, number of days of service, and the number of containers I needed to buy were all hashed out on that afternoon. The reason I was given one particular account was I knew that the building owned the containers that were in that building. (Each compactor unit is sold with two boxes.) So this eliminated the need for me to buy several very expensive boxes. My Christmas present had arrived! The truck was almost ready, and I was itching to restart Anchor for the second time. Martin and Norbert had not laid claim to the Anchor trademark and name, so I was free to use it.

CHAPTER 27 – LEARNING THE ROPES...AGAIN

When a trash hauling company is acquired, whether a large company acquiring a small company, or equals acquiring equals, there is a window of about six months where you can get your foot in the door, and try to out-hustle your opponent. Most companies today use the contract, which forces the customer to remain loyal for whatever the length of the contract is. If the customer had signed one for two years and the acquisition occurs three months into the birth of the contract, then that customer is on the hook for another year and nine months. So today's companies are sold with an eye for how many of the accounts are under contract.

It is funny how hard the customer fought to shake the shackles of the Association many years ago, only to find out that they're still caught. There are ways to get out of that contract, but the question remains how much are you going to spend trying to get out of it? Pricing has been scrutinized so long by so many people that any customer paying a ridiculously high price has, by now, figured out how to get it reduced.

In the far south suburbs, where the licenses had been restricted, I signed up a new account and was immediately informed that I could not operate without the proper licenses. *Okay*, I thought, *here we go again*. A competing company salesman had informed the town that I did not have a license and should not be allowed to operate in the village limits. So I visited the city hall and was informed that it was a closed license, and I explained to the village clerk that yes, five of the licenses were held by one corporation, but in fairness to the business owners, I felt that some of those licenses should be removed from the giant corporation and issued to smaller companies like mine. The clerk agreed with me, and I was issued a village license and allowed to compete against the giant corporations.

You see, when the big boys think they got the ball game sewed up, they can raise their prices, but if somebody cracks the code, he does quite well. I had cracked the code. And in very short order, one of my days each week was spent servicing the accounts of this very small village. This kind of stuff is fun for me. Others might think it too much hassle, but to be David and go against Goliath is satisfying for me. I was developing a thick skin to the tricks of the trade which people use to trip you up. I can thank Jack Van Writer and Kingdom Disposal for teaching me how to navigate this maze of competition. In some villages, all that's required is that you go in, pay your money and sign your name, and you're allowed to operate within the village limits.

The acquisition process by large corporations opens the door for upstarts like me, and as a result, within about a year's span, maybe eight or ten new trash hauling companies all over Chicago and its suburbs started up. Large corporations try to keep their pricing and corporate strategy a secret, but because they need to hire so many bodies to keep the machine rolling, the risk of somebody starting up, or going to work for a competitor, is always present. They can make you sign a non-compete agreement when you're hired, stating that you will not go to work for a competitor within a certain length of time, but most of these have been struck down in the court of law. The problem is that sometimes it requires high-priced attorneys to get you to where you need that legal definition proven. And this is what corporations will do: they will bare their teeth, and the minute you bring it to a lawyer, you find out just how pricey that can be. But what they can't make you stop is your earning a living, and what you retain in your head—unless you get amnesia or Alzheimer's—stuff like what this company was paying, who runs that company, or who to see if you want to get your foot in the door for that company? This knowledge that comes from experience cannot be purged from your brain. I had envisioned about a hundred different companies in the Chicago area, all competing with each other on a friendly basis. This was not to be. The big corporations were making their footprint in this industry, and once they adjusted their style and got their act together, it was hard to shake anything of significant value loose from their corporate tree.

The decision to start Anchor for the second time was a risky one for me. My only daughter, Tricia, was just entering college, and while I was deciding whether I should or should not start up the new business, I started to ask around, thinking maybe there was an easier way to make a living, like buying a tractor/trailer rig and hauling steel coils. But a trucker at the steel mill said, "I wouldn't do it if you got kids going to college. Income's too irregular." So I decided that running my own company, with control of the pricing, would be a better idea. And that is the route I took, thankfully. I figured maybe I had ten more years of working in me, which would be to bring me close to retirement, which I was definitely looking forward to.

Anchor Number Two was fun. The earlier years of owning and growing a business were still fresh in my mind. The lessons I had learned were also fresh in my mind. The knowledge I had gained while working for Martin and Norbert were also part of my portfolio, as well as the rest of the benefits, both mental and physical, which I enjoyed while working there. Now, don't get me wrong. I worked hard physically, and but that's sure a lot easier than working hard both physically and mentally. I was fresh and eager to go, but I wanted to stay small. I had learned a valuable lesson from my old acquaintance Quality Dale, and that was: you could make a real good living if you did most of the work yourself. Some companies would get bigger just impress somebody. I say, do it yourself with the money in your own pocket. Nothing wrong with that theory.

So every morning, I got up, fired the truck up and went to work. But that Mack I had bought in Minnesota was not all that good. One lesson I should have learned from the Mercury days was that you can't take a tractor made for the road, with a big engine and light frame, and put a heavy garbage body on it. After about a year and several thousands of dollars in repairs, I could see the handwriting on the wall. In fact, the ugly truck that I had bought from Larry had been painted company colors and was doing a far better job than the one I bought in Minnesota. It was not fast and it was cold in the winter time, but it would start and do a route. And like I've repeated, over and over again: this was the important ingredient. The truck stood between you and starvation. I took the body off that truck and put it on a 1992 chassis, later changing it to a third chassis, a 2004 Kenworth, which was brand-new. I did this several times with two other trucks in my last days at Anchor2. Bodies are basically steel and cylinders. The modern rear-load body contains seven cylinders, all of which can be bought on the aftermarket rebuilt, and the rest is steel, which can be welded in place so that a very old body becomes like new.

As I said, Anchor Number Two was fun. It seemed like I had learned my lessons well. Did I still make mistakes? Of course. Some were repeats of old mistakes, but this time I knew how to change course because I understood cause and effect. This time I had also put some of our own (Pat's and my) money into it. Pat was now what you might call a seasoned veteran of hauling trash. No, I don't mean she drove the truck. But she was able to keep tidy books, and present this company in a much more civilized fashion than when I started Anchor the first time.

Also, an interesting thing was happening in the banking industry: it had begun its total meltdown. We do not have to go to college and take a course in economics to figure out what precipitated the mortgage crisis. All I know was, you could put the kneepads away because this time it seemed like the bankers were looking for you. For a short period of time, I would receive one call a week from somebody that was more than happy to lend the money for equipment/containers/expansion. The terms "mortgage banker" and "investment banking" were now part of people's everyday lingo. I began to hear of things like fifty-year home mortgages, no income verification mortgages, and even mortgages given to people that didn't have jobs. Economics course at my alma mater, Chicago Christian High, told me that all money lent out has to be paid back, and it seemed like the so-called experts had forgotten that last part. Not only banks had lost their mind, credit card companies, thinking they were smarter than most people, were giving credit cards with no interest for six months, and I figured this was a nice way of getting free money.

Now, I knew I had a pay it back, so what I would do is when five months would come due, I would go to the next credit card company and pay the last one with fresh money. If you had a stack of six no-interest, six-month loans, just think of how many containers I could buy without paying any interest. Eventually they all got paid back, but like I said, there was a lot of free money floating around. My son Chris and I have had many a discussion about the fact that one day the piper is going to have to be paid, and if the piper doesn't get paid, somebody's going to be left holding the bag. And so we had the recession that began in 2007 and continued for several years afterward.

CHAPTER 28 – HUBERT AND ERIC

As Anchor2 began to grow, I could see that it was not going to stay a one-truck, one-route operation. So the question arose: how do I handle expansion? One day while I was making a left turn on 57th St., this guy jumps out of nowhere and introduces himself, and at first I could barely understand him. Turns out to be Hubert Princeton, the driver who could not read and had worked for me prior. I did not recognize him, but he recognized me. He needed work.

So I decided, "Well, let's give this a try again." I did not want him as a driver, but I said, "I can drive and you can do the work. I'll pick you up one a.m. Monday morning." I went on to explain that we would make two loads together, and I would drop him off at the end of the day and use him sparingly throughout the week. This worked for a while, but as time went on, I could see that either I had to make him a driver or something else would had to be done. Then as quickly as he had re-appeared, he disappeared and for six months I did not hear from him.

Tommy Captian had approached me about putting his son to work. His son was seventeen, a sophomore in high school, and made a very good helper. I used him throughout the summer, and just as the cold weather approached Hubert showed up again. Perfect timing. The next summer Eric got a job on a construction crew and was not available for summer, so Hubert was the helper that summer. When Eric graduated from high school, the construction job fell through, and Hubert disappeared again, only this time I was informed that he'd had a heart attack and passed away.

I used Eric another summer, and then he enrolled in college locally and lived on campus for the first semester. The second semester he decided that since it was a short commute, he would live at home. This turned out to be a perfect fit once again, and I started to teach him how to drive a garbage truck. Eric got his CDL, and he would meet me early Monday morning and take the first loaded truck to the transfer station, dump it, park it, jump in his car and go to class.

As time went on, I said, "Well, let's extend this a little more." The far south suburban area, which I had obtained a license for, suddenly had grown to about a three-hour route, mostly once-a-week pickups, and I said to Eric, "This is perfect for you on a Saturday morning. Three hours of pickups, dump what you have on, park the truck and go home."

The advent of paying by weight and not by volume made things a lot easier as far as warehousing trucks. You could dump a part of a load and park in the garage totally empty, thus reducing the chance of fire in the garage. This setup worked for Eric throughout his college days: work in the summertime, on Saturdays and early Monday mornings, thereby giving me a chance to catch my breath, do maintenance and all the side issues that go with running a business.

When Eric graduated from college, this time I was little more pro-active. I asked him what his future plans were. And the response I got was, "Well, I'll look for a job." I offered him one as a full-time driver if this was what he was looking for. It has worked very well. More than ten years later he is still doing it, has gotten married, has a lovely wife and a couple of precious children, and, oh yeah, if you run into him, I guess he'll complain about how hard it is picking up trash. But at this point, he's got about eleven years into the pension plan of two Teamster Locals, and I hope someday that I can see him retire with his full twenty-five years.

But then, who knows what the Lord has in store for each one of us? There were two more cases where someone came to work for me, and I did not need somebody full time but they were willing to learn how to drive a truck, how to run a route and I was willing to teach them, thinking that I could build a route as they were learning. One was able to find employment with a large corporation before I could get a large enough route for him to come aboard full-time. The work came in just fast enough for him to proceed with his learning curve and morph into full-time employment. Both are still involved in trash hauling.

CHAPTER 29 – JOB SECURITY

If you have a conversation with drivers who have been doing this for quite a while, the talk always gets back to what used to be referred to as the farm system in trash hauling. Many guys got their start, not by jumping into a truck and being handed a route book, but by starting in high school as a helper for either a father or grandfather or uncle, or even a total stranger. They may have lived near a garage, and run errands for somebody, much in the fashion that I did as a kid, and eventually they were pressed into service to either wash trucks or paint containers or work as helpers.

The large corporations eliminated these type of entry-level jobs. Oh yes, they do exist, but many who take these entry-level jobs do not rise above the rank of helper to driver or mid-management. They are taught to do one thing, whatever that may be, and no longer are they pressed into service in an emergency to do a route, drive a truck, or something on that order. You cannot entirely blame the corporations. Many fathers, grandfathers, or uncles assumed their children would want to go on to bigger and better things, so they urged them to go to college. When those sons (or grandsons, or nephews) finished college, they went into fields that were new to them, and many succeeded, to the delight of their parents, who paid for their college tuition. Some got out and had no clue what to do, then tried to claw their way up the ladder of some corporation, only to find out that the pay scale is not nearly as not nearly as good as gripping a steering wheel and hauling trash.

The corporations are doing their best to cut back on their drivers' pay scale. In small markets they have been able to do this, but in larger cities they have not been as successful yet, thanks, in large part, to a strong union and the fact that there is no longer a farm system in place. I remember when I walked into Alter and asked if they needed a list of recommendations to show them I was competent to pilot one of their trucks? Their reply was, "No, we know exactly where you came from." And today, whether they admit it or not, despite having tried their own farm system, the new crop of drivers is very thin. Some companies start drivers on recycling routes, which are fairly simple: "Go down this alley and pick up every blue cart you see. When you get to the next street, make a right turn and go down the next alley and do the same thing." But only two companies in the City of Chicago have contracts with the city to pick up blue carts, so there aren't many drivers coming up through the ranks.

During my early years of working in a union, employers and employees had a pretty good deal. There were very few grievances, and the Union would pretty much say, "Why don't you guys work this out yourself?" Most of the time it could be done, because it was usually over the important ingredient of money. Many times in the early days, a deal would be struck where somebody would collect a few cash stops, and that would be his pay for working on Saturday for a few hours. Or the boss would turn a blind eye on a cleanup that the employee did, while pocketing the money and charging the dump fee to the employer, along with the fuel, truck and insurance. Many drivers had several side stops. In fact, "several" would be putting it mildly. Greed can get the best of any of us. If the differences could not be worked out between the two parties and the employee had to be let go because of the insurance problems, or bad blood, then many times he could be employed by the time he got home. The new employer probably had a different insurance company, and was not diligent in checking out his driving record. Now, once a person knew that you were capable of doing a route and reading a route book, you had very little to worry about if you left one place of employment.

But the rules were starting to change. Large corporations did not want you to the haul tons of side stops, and put the money in your pocket. To prevent this, they decided to wean this type of behavior out. They hired either employees of the company with video cameras, or in some cases, private investigating companies, with no ties to either employees or employer, other than billing for services rendered. And so the practice of work/accounts on the side slowly came to a halt. In the book *Waste Management: An American Success Story,* author Timothy C. Jacobson says, "Any driver that cannot make his lunch is not very good." This quote was used later on to save some employee's job who was making money on the side. I'm don't know the driver's name or who he worked for, but I heard he won the grievance based on this particular quote. But the practice definitely was coming to a halt.

So if you're an employee and this frosting on the cake begins to melt away, and the corporations begin to show you just who is in charge, the employee/employer relationship takes on an air of hostility. No longer did you receive a letter from the employer every three years stating what the new contract would pay, and how much more the employer was paying into the health and welfare/pension fund, and how much the dues were being raised. But also the rules of the Union were changing. It became necessary to have a grievance committee to prevent the dismissal of employees just because the boss did not like his looks, or like the way he ran a route. Many drivers had gone through three or four employers for the same route.

Also, it was not unusual for some guy to come in from a trucking company, or some other remote outpost, and begin wholesale firing of people he did not think were doing a good job, employees who had been doing this job for many years and knew every crack in the sidewalk and when school got out and when it got in, so as to avoid problems with children or other safety concerns. Many times there were problems with wage differences, and the person from the corporation calling the shots may not have been making quite as much as the guy driving a truck.

So in 2003 the Chicago area experienced its first countywide trash hauling work stoppage, otherwise known as "The Strike." I had heard of strikes in the trash hauling business before, the most famous one was when Dr. Martin Luther King Jr. was assassinated in Memphis. The strike lasted eleven days, but had no violence. Now, in 2003, I was still at the early stages of Anchor2, and the picket lines were set up around all of the transfer stations, many of the main corporate garages, and even some of the smaller ones. I agreed verbally with the Union that I would definitely abide by the terms of the contract, which meant I was going to have to pay myself whatever raise those guys got because I was by myself. The Union basically said to me, "Do what you have to do." So I picked up at night, loaded both trucks, and in the daytime went to East Chicago, Indiana, via the Skyway/Indiana Toll Road to a transfer station in East Chicago.

A few other companies were doing the same thing. But you can imagine what happened when people saw a garbage truck picking up trash. My phone began to ring off the hook. No, not threats from the Union or other companies. Just people wanting me to come and get their garbage. Of course, I couldn't bite the hand that was feeding me. I had to remember that this strike probably would not last forever. But it gave the union quite a bit of muscle, because the corporations could see that they could not provide thirty-five competent drivers at the shake of a hat to cover for the striking drivers. After the strike was settled, about a week went by before most of the trash was picked up and things began to get back to normal. But it was a real eye-opener for all of us, the corporations, the employees and myself, that this big city called Chicago generates a lot of trash.

CHAPTER 30 – REHABS

Early on when Anchor2 was just getting started, I received a call from Manny Silvio, and he said he would like to talk to me about service on a few buildings he had in Hyde Park. So I went to see him in his office, in a nice tall building, and after talking to him, said, "Definitely. I sure would appreciate the business." Then he asked me if I was opposed to hauling broken drywall. No, of course not. Trash is trash. And we agreed on a price per container to haul broken drywall. He instructed me to put one container for the conventional house garbage and four more for the drywall, and these were to be picked up when he called me. Well, this was fun and games for a while. At first, most of them were full in the morning, and I dumped them and kept track and billed Manny. He paid me on time, but there were times when I noticed the containers were empty, and I wondered, *what's going on here?*

Well, I did a little snooping and found out that one of the drivers from one of the big corporations was dumping them for Manny and receiving payment in cash. I knew the driver and figured, *he's going to get caught*. And that is exactly what happened. The corporation had one of their employees with a video camera, and he was recording several of the drivers in the area doing side work. Let's just say, changes were made. So it became my responsibility once again to make sure that these containers were empty in the morning, so they could refill them again. Sometimes there would be a second pick up in the early afternoon, or I would get a call from Manny, and he would have a crew of his guys load me while I was standing there.

Many times I could not run the blade fast enough to get this stuff in the truck, and one of the best stories I like to tell is the day I backed up to a two-car garage with the overhead door already removed, and in forty-five minutes we tore down the garage and nothing was left but the concrete pad. The whole garage was in the truck, and I was on my way to the dump in under an hour. I really like doing that stuff. The names of the customers were Porch John, Porch Dave, Porch John Number Two and Casey the Bricklayer (I kid you not!). Their nicknames spell out what they did, and many times, beside doing a small route, I could made a load a day just on construction material.

You might ask yourself: why take down a perfectly good two-car garage? Nothing wrong with it. But a two-car garage will only hold two cars. By taking it down, Manny could pave the lot, mark off ten or eleven parking spaces, blacktop the whole yard, and charge so much per space per month, thereby increasing the revenue of the building whose yard it was. Manny was a real go getter, and I didn't mind going in behind him and picking up whatever he decided to change. One building needed two pickups per day. Each time the five containers were half full of sand, and I had to pull them out of the backyard, through a garage, and dump them. After putting the containers back in place, I had to close the garage door, and in the afternoon I had to return and repeat the process. He was dropping the basement down 2½ more feet so he could convert a two flat into a three flat. One more unit, one more rent. Made sense to me, and I was glad to help him out.

Manny would buy a building, fix it up, and then turn around and sell it. One of the buildings he sold was to a corporation based in New Jersey, and they too were doing the same thing: buying a building, and rehabbing both exterior and interior. But instead of selling it, they would manage the rental units. The Hyde Park area is around the University of Chicago, and housing is always in demand.

Every semester students move out, the building is vacant for a couple of months and they can do rehab or cleanup to each unit during the summertime. I got my foot in the door of hauling these rehabs, thanks to Manny. He told the New Jersey firm that I was willing to go the extra mile and do the oddball stuff, like put in containers for construction material and pick them up either once a day or twice a day, whatever was needed.

Makow, the NJ company, bought a twelve-story building, with no space on the street to put a roll-off box. The street was very narrow, and the city of Chicago charges $120 per month per box for space on the street. The building had a very steep driveway off the street, which went into an underground garage, and the driver who used to pick the trash up before I did, called it "the driveway from hell." The brakes of the truck had to be adjusted tight so the truck would not creep backwards into the building, and in winter the driveway had to be heavily salted so the truck would not slide backwards. In fact, one truck did not have enough power, when fully loaded, to get back up that steep driveway.

My method when I had finished loading, was to put the truck in gear, gun the engine, release the brake and hope for the best. Makow asked me to put nine containers in the building, and empty them up every morning. Like Manny, they would call if they needed a second pick up. So at approximate 5 a.m. every morning I would back on down the driveway from hell, open the door with the garage door opener and load nine containers, plus whatever was around them, into the truck and be on my way. At first, most of it was trash from people moving out, but as time went on, it became things like doors and broken countertops and sometimes broken drywall, all the stuff that would be taken out of a building that was being rehabbed. This was a lot like the old days with Anchor1 and 7000 South Shore, only this time I did not have to pay a roll-off company to haul the boxes.

This time the money went into Anchor2's bank account. This made Big O a happy trash hauler.

But there was a small downside to this: I remember once going to this Makow building on a Saturday afternoon, because I think the crew was going to work on Sunday and needed all nine of those containers to be empty for Sunday morning. I got into a brief argument with the guy that lived next-door, because he said the smoke was blowing in his window, and when I told him to close the window he looked at me like I was an idiot. Just before the building was completely rehabbed, I got a call from some irate neighbor, who was in charge of a block club, and said, "I hate to inform you, but you're in violation of the law by picking that building up at 5 a.m. I informed him that I would refrain from doing it in the future, but I had dodged a major bullet because the building was just about complete and ready for occupancy, and after that, I could put it on a regular route without any complications.

My relationship with Makow remained very upbeat all the days of Anchor2. I sold my business to Prescott Disposal in 2007 and worked for them till September 2008, when I retired.

CHAPTER 31 – THE NOISE ORDINANCE

From time to time, I have referred to early work starts and how, in a few instances, it caused problems. To this day it is still an issue. The Chicago noise ordinance was inaugurated back in the early 70s. Basically, it says that no garbage may be picked up before 7 a.m. outside the boundaries of Illinois St. on the north, Halsted on the west and Roosevelt on the south and Lake Michigan on the east, unless it's in an industrial area with no residential houses/buildings within 100 feet unless a special permit is issued. Remember the meat company at 66th and Wentworth? Exactly one year after that permit was given to me, that little house that forced me to obtain that permit burned completely to the ground, leaving an empty lot. No permit needed after that.

After retiring, when I volunteered for hurricane disaster relief work in Louisiana, six travel trailers provided housing for volunteer couples, and at breakfast one morning a man and his wife who were living in the one trailer began to complain about the noise that the front load driver made at 2 a.m. when he picked up the two 8-yard containers which were about thirty feet from where they were trying to sleep. My response was, "Kenneth, I want you to look at the number of children who are getting out of school when we return at 3:30-4:00 in the afternoon. Then you can realize why the driver feels a lot more comfortable waking you up at 2 a.m. than trying to put that truck, with all its wheels and blind spots, in place to pick up the trash at two or three in the afternoon." Couple days later Kenneth said to me, "Well, yeah, that makes a lot of sense."

So that Chicago ordinance was the brainchild of an alderman who got woke up one morning (and I know who it was that told him to shut his big yapping mouth and go back to sleep). That alderman enacted legislation which gave penalties for starting early outside of those boundaries. I'll let you be to judge whether it's a good piece of legislation or not.

What used to be slums east of Halsted Street, till you get into the Loop proper, now have several high-rise residential buildings. The same is true south of Roosevelt Road and north of Illinois Street. In fact, the whole Fulton Market, which was supposed to remain exempt from this ordinance, is now predominantly residential. Since the noise ordinance is still in existence, once people find out about it, depending on who's the block captain, or how much time residents got on their hands, or how pissed off they are at the world, they're going to push for enforcing that ordinance.

CHAPTER 32 - CARLOTTA

Anchor2 days, Saturday morning, 8 a.m., traffic was very light, and I was blocking the street in order to do this cleanup in back of a building. All of a sudden, this woman came screaming out of the building. Let me preface this by saying, if you had to get a witch from Central Casting, this one would fit the bill. Not only did she have gravy stains on her white chenille bathrobe, her shrill voice pierced the air while she fumbled to put on her coke bottle glasses.

Her complaint was, "You cannot be out here this early in the morning." (Saturdays, Sundays and holidays were a 9:30 start.) Her shrill voice woke up the sleepy janitor that the building had supplied to help me clean this mess up, and the two of them began to argue. I held the janitor back because I knew she knew what she was talking about. I also knew the longer we argued, the longer the street would remain blocked, and then I would have another argument because some irate motorist would be laying on his horn. So in order to avoid a potential riot, I agreed with her, saying that this was a one-shot deal and I would not repeat my actions by being there at 8 a.m. on a Saturday morning. She agreed to let me finish, which I did, and in less than half an hour, I was on my way, my hope being that I would never have to see this woman again.

You guessed it. The building owner gave me the stop twice a week. Then, as if to rub salt in the wounds, the building across the street called me up, so that I had two stops on this block that had to be picked up around 7 a.m. I did not put this on a regular route because I knew it was a potential explosion if the driver got there at five minutes before 7, and it was best to abide by the exact 7 o'clock restriction. But during the week you block the street while you dump a total of five containers.

So I devised a plan where I would back down the street the wrong way and utilize a driveway which would barely let traffic pass in front of the truck while I was dumping the three on the north side of the street. Then I would walk across the street and bring both containers from the south side to the curb. I would pull up to the two containers, dump them, and if I did not have any cars waiting to go by, I would return the two containers to the south building and drive the wrong way down a one-way street and be on my way.

This plan worked good for several months. Always on Mondays and Thursdays would I do this, with no complaint. In the meantime I found out from somebody on another part of the route that this wild woman's name was Carlotta, and she made a practice of harassing people for minor infractions of city ordinances. Seems she did not have to work full time (or I'm not exactly sure what the story was from this guy), but she evidently had time to pour over the city rulebooks and search out people who did not abide by the law. One day, many months after my first encounter with her, about ten after seven in the morning, she came out waving this piece of paper, yelling at me again. My response, "What is your problem now?"

Waving her piece of paper, she shouted, "This is the rule and you have to abide by it." I took her piece of paper and read it, and now it was my turn to yell. "Carlotta, get back in the house and don't you dare pester me again, especially when you don't know one rule from another." She had taken the page out of the construction ordinance, not realizing that I was totally familiar with the ins and outs of this particular rule. I was at City Hall when they wrote that stupid ordinance, so I knew exactly what I was talking about. I handed her back her piece of paper, and she knew I had caught her in this attempted deception.

Some time after that encounter with Carlotta, my wife and I were at a family reunion in Bemidji, Minnesota. It was a Sunday afternoon, and my wife had decided to stay in Bemidji an extra day with her sister and an aunt who was in from California. I decided to take an afternoon flight from Bemidji to St. Paul, and then from St. Paul to Chicago. My flight was for 2 p.m., and I arrived at the Bemidji airport at 12:30. The security lines in Bemidji are next to nothing compared to major airports, so in a matter of five minutes I was through that line. I checked the flight schedule, hoping that maybe I could get on an earlier flight and be home an hour earlier (they fly out every hour).

I went to the counter and inquired about a departure at 1 o'clock. The lady agreed to put me on standby in the event that somebody canceled, and as I was leaving the counter in this small town in northern Minnesota, who should be within shouting distance of me but Carlotta. Did I want to introduce myself? Of course not, but I thought maybe I could have some fun with her and mess with her like she tried to do with me. So I kept an eye on her, and she went to the counter and I came within earshot and noticed that she was asking for a later flight. About ten minutes later I was called to the desk and informed that I would be able to board the 1 o'clock flight, so I put two and two together and figured that Carlotta had canceled her 1 o'clock flight for a 2 o'clock flight, and I was going home earlier thanks to Carlotta.

About fifteen minutes before I went to the security line, I casually walked over to Carlotta and pretended that I had supernatural power. I thanked her for changing her flight and said that I knew where she lived by telling her the address and the fact she lived on the third floor. When I mentioned these last two facts, her eyes got wide. Then she looked at me for a moment and finally recognized me, pointing her bony finger at me as she searched for my name. "Oscar...Omar...(and finally)...Owen!" Chuckling, I asked her, "What in the world are you doing up here?" "I came to visit friends," was her reply. My response: "You mean you actually have friends?" And then I walked to the security line and got aboard the plane.

But Carlotta was not done with her complaints. After I retired, my replacement, Eric, informed me that she actually called a cop, and he had written him a ticket. But Eric said the company paid it. This fine was not that heavy just irritating. What Carlotta did not know was that a Makow property building that I had hauled all the construction material out of—twelve floors worth—was just around the corner from her apartment, and that for several months I had done this at 5 a.m. without her knowledge. Ha, ha, Carlotta. The joke is on you. In fact, I thought very seriously about climbing the back stairs to her apartment and lighting a string of fireworks at four in the morning after I retired. But I'm glad I didn't, because poor Eric would have never had peace with her.

CHAPTER 33 – Ms LeMAY

While I was picking up a stop one afternoon—the location is of little importance—a lady came out of a back yard across the alley, walking with the aid of two canes. She was with a man, about forty, who she later identified as her son. She was not very polite, and I forget the exact words she spoke to me, but they were in a very sharp tone. I had no dealing with her, since she wasn't my customer, so the discourtesy was handed right back at her. But after a moment, she asked me how much I would charge to pick up her trash. I gave her a price and told her I would replace the drums with a container.

Her tone was not much better after our negotiations, and I was not very interested in doing business with her, but I gave her a business card and said I would set it up for the first of the month. I told her to call me if she changed her mind, hoping the present hauler would be able to talk her out of switching service. I was not too keen on doing business with her.

But about a week later she called and told me to put a container in place at the beginning of the month. I was informed by a driver from the other company that she was a real pain in the behind, and they were glad to get rid of her. (Even her son said that he would break out in a sweat when she was around.) I began to pick up the trash and did so for about two months, while listening to her gripe about the former hauler whenever I would have the misfortune of seeing her while doing my pickups.

After those two months, she called me and asked if I would be willing to haul three more buildings that she had interests in. My thought was: *how can this woman, who looked like she was another Central Casting witch, have her hands on a total of four buildings?* I couldn't answer that, but my real question was: how is she going to pay? So I began to haul three more buildings, which, I might add, were very decent stops with a nice return.

From time to time a very old Dodge K-Car station wagon would come flying down the alley with her at the wheel, surrounded by an array of junk inside the car. It only had room for one person and that was her. She would stop by my truck, break open a package of Little Debbie Donuts and offer me one. At first I was not so sure that she wasn't trying to poison me. But the cellophane wrapper on the package was not opened, so what the heck! I loved donuts.

Every month she would call me and say, "Long arms (her name for me), the check is in the mail." Then she would go on to complain about the shabby service of the Post Office, and whatever else she could fit in, before I would cut off the phone conversation. I found out that she taught school, but not much else about her life. One time I was at a light at 87th and Stony Island, and I felt someone hit the back of the truck. When I went out to investigate, there she was, not in the shabby K-Car, but in a newer model minivan. I asked her why she had run into me, and she answered, "Just wanted to get your attention." I said, "Well, you scratched your car." Her reply was, "So what? It's only a scratch." Kind of a strange way to get my attention.

Then one day the phone calls stopped, and I did not run into her in her beat-up K-Car or her minivan. In addition, I noticed that the invoices on the four buildings were not being paid. So the question was: *do I discontinue her service?* My phone calls to her kept going to voice mail or went unanswered. While picking up at one of the buildings, I noticed a memo on the front door of the building. That's when I discovered that she had just passed away, and the funeral arrangements were being handled by a Jackson Funeral Home. There were two Jackson Funeral Homes on my travels. I checked, and one was closed, the other had never heard of her. A third Jackson Funeral Home said, yes, she was the same person. I thanked the man and ordered flowers, knowing that the Crazy Lady would no longer be part of my cast of characters. I hope that she believed in the Lord so I might meet her in heaven, because after she was gone I sure did miss the craziness.

CHAPTER 34 – ON THE CLOCK AGAIN

By 2007 I was once again starting to run out of gas. As I mentioned, I have about an eight year span where I can run at a good pace, and then I have to step back and re-evaluate what is going on. My target date for retirement was August 31, 2008, and I was bound and determined that I would not go past that date. I had been hauling trash for over half a century, and I felt that this was a perfect time to go out with a smile on my face. Prescott Disposal was a startup company that began its operation two months before I did.

The owners, Mick and Will had worked for Martin and Norbert during the City Disposal days, and in the time that both of us (Prescott and Anchor2) were in business, running parallel to each other, they had amassed a fleet of some fifty trucks, both packers and roll-offs. Some of their growth was done by acquisition; other by outright hustle. They were several years younger than I was and were out to conquer the world. They had found an investment banker, and the idea was to expand and see where it would lead them.

They had approached me several times to buy me out, but each time I had rebuffed their offer because I was not ready, the time was not right. Beside holding a full-time job, my wife Pat also had to take care of the finances and secretarial items of my growing company, and to bring someone else in at this late stage was not part of my plan. Remember, I had said I wanted to stay small, and so as not to incur any more debt, Pat and I both decided that July 2007 it would be the appropriate time to sell my business to Prescott and spend the last year working for somebody else prior to my retirement.

    As it turned out, this worked rather well. The terms of the agreement were that I would remain a union employee with payments to the Teamster pension fund for the duration of my time with them. All parties agreed, we did the deal, and I brought all three of my trucks over to their yard in Chicago, changed my uniform from black (my company color) to red (their color), and after a two-week unpaid vacation, grabbed one of my former trucks and began to work for them. In this way I made the transition smooth, and I began to see the shores of Alligator Lake, Florida, on the horizon.

CHAPTER 35 – EQUIPMENT, PART TWO

Rear Loaders

As I've discussed throughout the book, trash hauling equipment has evolved quite a bit. The first exposure I had to the equipment used to haul trash and garbage was a basic dump truck and a ladder. You had to climb up the ladder while carrying a barrel on your back, throw the barrel into the load, wrestle the barrel till it was empty, then put it on your back and carry it back to where you got it. Very time-consuming and labor-intensive. Of course, necessity is the mother of invention, and so the side loader was invented.

This made way for the rear loader, which still involved hand dumping, but was a little neater than the side loader. (Today we walk around with cell phones that have built-in cameras. But in those days cameras were something you left at home because they were likely to get broken, so very few pictures were taken of that procedure. I am sure someone, somewhere, has a picture of their father or grandfather or even great-grandfather using one of these trucks. I have asked around my family with very little success.)

The rear load packer made a lot a sense. In the days of barrels, you could throw a barrel in a hopper, roll it around a little bit and the trash would come out, and you could put the barrel back on your back without going through the up-the-truck-across-the-truck process. And eventually, along came the 1-yard container, the brainchild of Herman Mulder, who worked on his process and then turned it over to the Leach Corporation, where they patented the 1-yard container, and the process used to dump it. And I remember in the early days every container that you bought had a metal label on the front listing the number of that container, and the patent number, and that it was made by the Leach Corporation of Oshkosh, Wisconsin.

But, as it's been said: necessity is the mother of invention, and a company in Franklin Park named Bynal decided to get around the patent on this idea. How did they do it? They made the container bigger, and when you bought a 1½-yard Tripsaver container, they would hand you a set of trunnions, which would slide into the front of the box and you could slip a bolt in for permanent attachment.

They also did away with the stupid tailgate that Leach incorporated in dumping the container to hold the garbage and the silly sleeves that would slide up over the trunnion and the cables, which never seemed to stay on the box. Bynal used the elephant ear, which had a slot in it that would allow the trunnion to follow the slot, and would remain in place while the container was in the up position. They also made 2-yard containers with the same design. Their three-yard containers were also a little different than the style that Leach had come out with. Their 4-yard up to 10-yard containers incorporated a hydraulic cylinder which laid on the roof of the truck. I am still a little fuzzy about whether Bynal got caught up in a patent infringement lawsuit, but shortly after I came to work at New Way, Bynal went out of business, and I'm not really sure why.

Heil Corporation used a different style rear load compaction truck. They incorporated a bucket into which the operator would dump the trash, then activate a switch and the bucket would raise up and a blade would scoop the contents into the truck. The bucket helped the contents into the bed of the truck and did not allow it to come back down into the hopper, as would happen when you used a Leach, which had a sloping hopper. This Heil hopper was very effective for a long time, and very popular with routes that were predominantly made up of coal ash and incineration. Nothing more frustrating than your hopper being full before the ashes being dumped had a place to go. Many was the time a Leach would go out on a demonstration and be sent back for this reason. It was something Leach did not advertise, but certain routes were much better suited for the Heil Mark3 than the Leach Packmaster.

The drawback of the Heil Mark3 was when containers were incorporated as part of the route. The hopper would smash the container unless the container was lowered completely to the ground. Heil got around that by using a set of arms which would swing out and lift the container. The arms were lifted by two small cylinders mounted on the side of the helper steps, and these arms would grab the handles of the container. A crossbar would lift the container in the air, and the operator would then lower the container so that the bucket would not smash the container when the bucket was raising up. You can imagine how many operators had to make the phone call to the office, that they had forgotten to lower the box and had smashed the container.

Another drawback of the Heil Mark3 was with 4-, 6- and 10-yard containers, where it was almost totally useless. The overhead winch would have to let the box down while the bucket went up, and the hopper only having a 1 yard capacity, the box would then have to be raised up again each time. If the box was left in the up position, the trash would fall into the street underneath the bucket. I can only remember one company installing an overhead winch and tailgate capable of dumping the larger containers because of this reason. Many companies went from the Heil Mark3 to the Leach or Loadmaster brand strictly for this reason. Heil Corporation came out with a Mark4 and 5 model, which did away with the bucket, and went to a different blade operation (a packer/carrier type). Later on, Leach sued Heil Corporation, successfully, and Heil was forced to discontinue the Mark5 version, or pay a royalty for every unit sold.

If you look in the archives of Garwood and Roto Pac, you will find pictures and a history of both manufacturers of rear load trucks. Neither was very practical once the use of coal was discontinued and trash was no longer being burned. Garwood used a chain driven swing blade, which would stop at the height of the body floor and a packer blade would sweep the trash into the body. Not many of them were sold because they could not handle large bulky items. So Garwood invented a packer/carrier style sytem that Heil eventually bought, and it is still being used today.

E-Z Pack

This rear-load packer was invented by Hercules Gallion, based in Ohio. The design was good, but they put it on the market too soon in order to compete with Leach, Heil and Loadmaster, and let their customers (the haulers) do the research and development, at the customer's expense. The truck is a major expense for the trash hauler, and all it takes is one bad product, and the hauler will drop that product forever. I think E-Z Pack made these mistakes: letting their customers do their R&D.

Another part of this process is listening to your customers. For example, in the late 80s Leach was riding the crest of success with a major portion of the rear load packer market, but they started listening to their customers at more of a distance and making changes that weren't necessarily improvements. Heil was better. They listened and made a major change by buying the Garwood patent, thereby making them a serious player in the trash hauling business. McNeilus, who I will talk about later with a particular story, made cement mixers back in the 60s and had not yet entered the rear load packer market. But when they did, they were all ears, not talking to their own salesman, but touching base with the drivers, helpers, mechanics and the owners, who had to work with and fix these things. We can always look back with perfect hindsight, but I think E Z Pack would have had a large footprint in this market if they had been a little slower putting this on the street with some feedback from the guy who bought it, the guy who fixed it, and the guy who drove it. So they did not sell too many, and anyone who has manufactured large equipment will tell you it has to be made right the first time[, with no serious design flaws which would torpedo your product from the start.

There are basically three manufacturers of today's modern packer trucks: Leach, Heil and McNeilus. Each has undergone changes over my lifetime, but this is to be expected, and one thing that remains in my mind is an interview that *60 Minutes* did with the chairman of the board of Amazon, in which he said that every company seems to have a shelf life of about forty years. Some remain much longer, and some fall by the wayside much sooner.

The Roll-Off

In the early part of my story I talked about Jack Ter Mitt and how I thought he had invented the roll-off. Now I don't want to get into a big debate about it because Heil will say they invented it and Dempster will say they did. The fact is, it is not important who did what. The fact is, it was done. I'm only talking about what I saw as I was growing up. This product was begging to be invented, re-invented and expanded, and it was. Today we have semis that are capable of picking up and hauling two boxes at one time, and this was beyond my wildest dreams as a kid growing up. Much like the shipping containers that now are loaded in China, shipped across the ocean, unloaded in ports like New Jersey/Florida/California, and the same container that was loaded in China now winds up in somebody's factory in Nebraska. The need for loading and unloading at each port of entry is no longer in the shipping program. So, in my business, the trash that was once thrown in a burn pile, burned, then later hauled away by a private scavenger, who would come with a tractor and clean up the burnt residue, now never even hits the ground till it winds up in the landfill. It is put in a trash container by one person and many times never touched again by another human. The days of carrying one barrel at a time have gone by the wayside. Now we have one load at a time.

Several versions of the roll-off came out, but basically in this industry the idea was the same: pull the box onto the bed of a truck after first tarping the load down so the contents won't blow all over, drive to the transfer station or landfill, and dump it. Much like the freight box, it allows a person to move a lotta stuff from point A to point C with relatively little labor. The roll-off idea is great! The roll-off market today is dominated by four manufacturers: Heil, Galbreath, Benlee and Ampliroll, Heil being the best seller with its dead lift design. As companies were acquired by other companies and the boxes began to wear out , the parent company would replace them with the brand of boxes they were familiar with, unless there was a major reason to switch.

As I've mentioned, the various brands of containers were similar. The sizes ranged from one cubic yard to ten cubic yards, and today I will still see containers that were purchased in the early 60s on the street, and when I do it's fun for me to try to guess where they originally came from. Not only who manufactured them, but then, digging deeper, try to find out who originally bought it. For a period of time, during the Wild West days of this business during the 60s and 70s and part of the 80s, container theft was a big thing, sort of like cattle rustling. If you needed ten new containers, it would be quite a bit of savings if you bought five of them and stole the other five, and this happened quite a bit. So, what changed was, when the containers were built, the manufacturer would ask you what stamp you wanted on your new containers—sort of like branding cattle—and some guys would make interesting designs, others would simply use their first names, and others would just put the initials of the company on the containers. And it is not unusual to run into a container where the "brand" has been left on. So, when I stumble across one of those, the game is on. From my knowledge of the business I run the board on what happened to the original owner, who he sold to, and who that company might have sold to.

Most major container companies have fabricating shops, where they take the old boxes off the street once the bottom wears out and put new bottoms on them. Many containers on the streets may have had three or four bottoms put on them. My son-in-law Kurt does this welding work for a living, and it is his cup of tea. Neither of us knew he had a talent for doing this type of work. In fact, when he applied for work at the company he is working for now—I knew a driving job was open at the time—I recommended that he apply for that position…as a driver. Remember: to err is human. Not only does he weld new bottoms on old containers, thus extending their life, but he can build, from scratch, compactor boxes, and if need be, roll-off boxes. I tip my hat to him also.

Front Loader

The front loader is not a new way of hauling trash. Many companies who were outside of large city limits used this type of truck quite extensively since back in the 50s. It was easier, faster and less tiring on the driver to haul trash with the forks sticking out in front of the truck and the box going over the cab to dump in the hopper behind him. One downside to this was that if you had multiple stops with limited access, where you couldn't approach a box with the forks, it was easier to use a rear loader. Another downside was that on city streets and alleys, the driver risked bringing down overhead wires or obstructions if he wasn't paying attention. But the advent of the transfer station brought a dumpsite closer to the route, and there you paid by weight not volume. So, a front load truck made much more sense, and many routes, after being converted from front load to rear, were re-converted from rear to front. Once again progress allowed us to haul much more with less manpower. Now money is being spent on the equipment side rather than on the labor side, and it's easy to get preachy here about jobs being eliminated. But in this business very few people get laid off if they're any good. Today there's much more opportunity for them to get moved laterally, which makes this business even more appealing if you're looking for longevity. A person might actually retire and collect his pension.

Mechanized arms were also utilized in residential routes. The idea of walking thirty feet to the back of the truck to dump a couple of toters, then walking the same thirty feet to the front of the truck, pulling ahead to the next house—maybe seventy-five feet—and then repeating this process, is now being eliminated by trucks which use a "better mousetrap" process. A truck is equipped with a mechanical arm, which the driver operates from the right-hand side of the truck.

He extends the arm and grabs a toter, brings it to the truck and dumps it right behind the cab, then returns the toter to its original position. If there are more than one toter, the driver pulls ahead slightly to dump each of the others.

This requires that the homeowners place their toters with the lids facing the street, and if a house has more than one, that they are spaced so that the arm can grab each one individually. I used to make the comment that you don't see any fat people driving garbage trucks especially on a house route, but this is not the case any more because a rotund person can sit in that cab all day and only get calluses on the fingertips.

Does this faster way of picking up trash benefit only the driver? No. It also benefits the company and the homeowner. The company can now do 1200 homes a day, so I'm told. A driver, after doing 1200 homes, is not any more tired than when he was doing 500. Probably less so. And the homeowner is probably not paying a hundred times more for the service than he was in the 60s, but maybe only twenty times as much, even though wages have gone up significantly.

As you can see, the amount of capital needed to enter this field and survive is much greater than it was in the 60s, 70s and part of the 80s. A new front load/side load residential truck now costs about $225,000, as opposed to a truck in the 60s that would run you about $60,000 brand new, chassis and body.

Compaction Units

The compaction unit has also made a big change in the collection of trash. If you go back to the Merchandise Mart and Jack Ter Mitt leaving a box at a dock, today's compaction unit has increased the capacity of that roll-off box three times. A person dumps trash in the chute, and when the hopper is full, an electric eye triggers the compaction automatically. This is done not only at factories, but also in apartment buildings, where each floor might have a trash chute at the end of the hall, and the trash will go down to the basement. There the same procedure happens: an electric eye compacts the garbage into a small container, and when that container is full, it is removed and an empty one is put in its place, whether a complete body or just a small container.

The need for high compaction trucks is not as critical as it was years ago because the compaction units can do it for you. Some of these units are self-contained, that is, the compaction is built into the box. You open a door, throw the trash in, close the door and manually hit a switch. When the unit is full, a truck will come in and either dump it, or replace it with an empty one. Gone are the days of a garbage room or a trash storage area. These have been replaced by compaction units and their equipment.

Transfer Stations

Boy, if anything, transfer stations have been a game changer. As landfills began to move further and further away from the big cities, the need to have a place to dump near the city was the same, if not more, than it was in the mid-70s. The idea of a transfer station was born: a place to dump trash on a large concrete floor and reload it into semi trailers, to be hauled to those now-faraway landfills. A one-hundred-yard trailer is capable of holding the contents of two and a half 25-yard rear load compactor trucks. "Capable of," but most of the time not legally allowed, unless the load is mixed with the fluff from various roll-off loads. But Nation, the company I parked by years ago, was able to buy a piece of property in the city, a run-down warehouse, and convert it into a transfer station.

This idea caught on very quickly, and many companies followed suit. But the problem with that was: you had to do it right. And there were several cases of people who took in, let's say, ten loads and would only ship out only five, thereby saving the dumping fee and transportation cost of those five. The extra trash was stored in a huge building or out in a field. Self governing doesn't always work. There were also a few cases of guys going out of business and leaving a big empty lot in some obscure part of the city, full of trash that never found its way to a landfill. Well, you know what happens when the city and the state intervene. They draw up a list of rules and regulations, and also require these sites to get a permit, and you know what happens when you need a governmental permit: not everyone who applies gets them, and you have to jump through many legal hoops in order to get the permits. Many tried unsuccessfully to get them, but those who *did* get them were in the catbird seat.

All this makes trash hauling much more expensive. No longer does a truck go from its route to dump in a landfill maybe ten miles down the road. Now he has to dump at a transfer station at a much higher cost because it is being reloaded—big machines cost money and labor—and trucked sometimes as much as seventy-five miles to a landfill. For a while, transfer stations and landfills existed side by side, but in Chicago two of the landfills closed, and the need for transfer stations became more and more important.

The use of transfer stations also eliminated another big problem, and that was overweight. This existed since about… Well, let's just say it always existed. The bond for overweight is astronomical, and for a while it was not unheard of to have bonds for getting your truck back at $5,000 or $10,000. No checks, only certified funds or cash. It made a lot of people rethink this whole idea of being self-employed. To law enforcement it was a gravy train: pull the truck over, ticket it and put $5,000 on your commander's desk. Do two in a day and you just brought in 10,000 bucks on one shift. So the incentive for cops to do this was quite high. When the law was finally changed, there was some relief, but for a long time you can imagine just how fast your heart would beat when you went through towns which knew the drill, and also knew you were loaded and on your way to the dump. It sure was a lot easier to dump half a load at a transfer station and start back on the second load. And when you felt you were getting too heavy, dump that, and even at the end of the day, dump a third time.

When I got started with Anchor2, I got lucky with the truck I bought a truck in Minnesota, a 20-yard Leach, not the big heavy model, but a lighter version. After being stopped several times on the way to the dump, I could almost... Well, let's just say, I would make wagers with the cops: my 10 bucks to their one that I was legal. Most time I was right. I was always cognizant of what stuff would weigh, and I had one officer who was intent on making my life miserable, and when he could not hit me with an overweight ticket, he gave me a Mickey Mouse ticket, you know, like no insurance card, or improper display of license plate. I think he has since retired.

But they were still out there, still trying, and every once in a while the flashing lights will come on, and I have to explain things to them, or follow them to the scale. But what has really changed is you no longer have to come up with cash because the number of companies has been reduced significantly in the Chicagoland area, and most law enforcement know that the companies aren't going anywhere and are good for the money. So, they now bond you and let you go for a later court appearance. But as I used to say: you could probably get a cheaper bond by committing murder than you could by having an overweight truck. In my last nine years at

Anchor2 the total cost of overweight was about $1800, so I cannot complain too much.

CHAPTER 36 – A COUPLE OF RANTS

To Burn or Not to Burn

As I mentioned in earlier chapters, when my uncles and grandfather were active in this industry, everybody would burn their trash. This was the way to do it, and it did two things: it reduced trash to ash, and it also provided heat in some cases. But, obviously, it was not very good for the air quality, so in the very early 70s severe restrictions were put on the burning of trash and the use of coal as a primary source of heat. And as I have stated a couple of times, every discussion has two sides. You can present the one side: yes, we have cleaner, much cleaner, air, which of course is true. But there is the other side: we have also probably quadrupled the volume of trash that is put out every day. The industry has adapted over the years to the demand for removing that trash.

When I was thirteen or fourteen, while picking up the at the Cook County School of Nursing, a building engineer there made this comment: "When you get to be a grownup, they will have invented a way to throw this stuff in a big pit and it will dissolve." Boy, was that guy wrong! Now, with four times the amount of trash, we have to keep inventing the wheel. Trucks are now three times the size of what my Uncle Deck used. Landfills are no longer a few miles away, and extensive transportation is required to get to the landfills. No longer can a husband and wife run a one- or two-truck operation and support five or six children. They have to work for a large corporation. The cost of startup is astronomical, and most people cannot see a good reason to start a business. The big get bigger, and the small just stand by and watch.

Many years ago Uncle Murph invested in the incinerator, thinking this was a fantastically good idea. At that time air pollution was not even a concern for most people. Even without EPA restrictions on air quality, the incinerator made absolutely no sense, and four years later Uncle Murph went around saying, "You want to buy my stock?" That incinerator has since been closed. But as recently as fifteen years ago, in order to preserve the landfill space—I always laugh at this one—the State of Illinois decided to help fund an incinerator in the suburbs south of Chicago. It was an engineering nightmare, dreamed up on a drawing board and built at an astronomical cost, only to be shuttered after the state refused to subsidize it anymore.

Anyone who puts their faith in the subsidy of our government better be very careful. Politicians need votes to stay in office, and votes are necessary for the future of their ideas, and when the truth comes out that an idea was really harebrained (such as an incinerator as the way of the future), then they will withdraw the funding and say, "Sorry, Charlie. You're on your own." No private industry would touch this incinerator with a 50-foot pole, and while the incinerator was still open, I attended a breakfast meeting in the incinerator conference room and looked over the vast array of people that were sitting in the office, who were employees of this incinerator, and said to myself, "This place has nowhere to go but in the crapper." Which it did a few months later.

The advent of governmental regulations in the trash hauling business is a mixed bag, as it is with any business. Remove the regulations, and the industry turns into the Wild West, so that anything goes. Put too many restrictions on an industry, and people will only circumvent the maze of restrictions that are required. Example: in 1970 there were over 300 private haulers in the City of Chicago and its surrounding areas that hauled trash within the city limits. As of January 1, 2016, the City of Chicago has about a dozen licensed trash haulers within the city limits. No longer is this a mom-and-pop operation, but the restrictions and cost have made it so that small private haulers will ask, "Who needs these headaches?" And the remaining few that are still standing will eventually dictate the rules and the prices of this business. Look around at other industries which have gone the same route: airlines, cable companies, the cell phone industry, not to mention automobiles, washing machines and many other products.

So getting back to the question of to burn or not to burn, do you ever wonder why big cities have such a big rat problem? On any given day in downtown streets and alleys of up-and-coming re-habbed neighborhoods, the pride neighborhoods, the rats are big enough…well, you got to look at them to see if they're rats or cats. We are supplying them with full course meals and desserts on a daily basis, and we are fortunate enough that they hide in the daytime, so that we do not see them. When we burned, we destroyed most of their food supply, and most of them simply starved, or migrated to a place where food was more plentiful and we could eliminate them all at once. Many factories had full-time employees who burned their trash in incinerators, and even grocery stores, at one time, had a similar operation. The factories also had places in the back where much of the bulky material was burned on an overcast day. I'm not advocating that we go back to incinerators and burn pits, but it is something to think about when we enact legislation to cure one ill, only to find out that we have created an equally troublesome problem elsewhere.

Now don't get me wrong. If legislation had not been in acted, we would still be dumping dangerous chemicals in open fields and pouring dirt on top of them, only to reap what we sowed some twenty years down the road. There is a delicate balance between government and business, and we all want clean air and clean water. We need a balance between legislation and common sense.

This was very apparent in 2008. The EPA had declared that trucks would have to comply with a certain standard of exhaust emissions. We had come a long way from the 60s when diesel engines became popular in almost every truck. The law which made us burn low sulfur fuel was a very good idea, as it forced the refineries to produce such a product. The first Kenworth I purchased, which was compliant with the new standards, burned so clean that I could run the truck inside the garage for twenty minutes and it would not even bother anyone. In the past, if you chose to run a truck inside a garage, you would definitely have to route the exhaust outside. But the EPA wanted the standards to be higher, and after 2008 the engine manufacturers and truck builders put out some of the biggest pieces of junk that ever hit the engine market. Why junk? Most truck buyers were aware that there would be problems in the next several years. Caterpillar was smart with their truck engines. They quit making them till they got the technology down pat, and made sure that the engines would operate under all types of applications. International did what Volkswagen has done recently: ran their engines slightly dirty and paid the $5000 penalty. Till they were forced to remedy that situation. The head honcho at International was ousted because of this non-compliance policy.

One manufacturer put this junk out without, I don't think, even testing it, and it was nothing for me to shuttle the same truck back to the dealer five or six times in a month because they would not run properly. Imagine what it was like to have a garage full of these pieces of crap, where you paid in excess of $125,000 per unit

($185,000 if you include the body), only to not be able to use them 50% of the time. The whole idea behind buying new equipment is to lower your repair bills, but now the apple cart had been turned completely upside down. The salesman would always tell you the warranty is 36 months, or 100,000 miles, but they left out the other two fine-print facts: engine hours, and the fact that trash trucks have a multiplier of three on the mileage. Three times 35,000 miles = 115,000 miles. Warranty over, and then you were on your own, sucker. I once commented to the service manager that he was very fortunate that the buyers of these pieces of crap were big corporations, because, I said, if it was twenty years ago, in the day of one- and two-truck operators, he would have to wear a bulletproof vest and hide behind bulletproof glass. Many small guys who bought this junk had to park them and buy the old-style engines, which were in trucks five to ten years old, and remount the bodies to continue in business. It was the only way to survive.

Many bought into a different bill of goods: the use of natural gas, which was pitched very heavily. It would burn clean, pass the exhaust emissions standards, and it was touted as being cheaper than diesel fuel, which was close to four dollars per gallon around Chicago in the early 2010s, while natural gas was at $2.65 per gallon. This was a big incentive to buy natural gas powered trucks. Now let's turn the page over. Trucks that used natural gas burned more; therefore, they required very large tanks. At first the government would subsidize the additional cost of two tanks—which added an additional $30,000 per truck—under the guise of protecting the environment. But remember what I said about depending on a governmental subsidy? Some lawmaker wakes up one morning and withdraws the subsidy, and this is exactly what the politicians did once the ball got rolling on the natural gas bandwagon.

So, by the time a unit was purchased with a new chassis, new body, the added items for natural gas brought the price tag right up to $300,000. The negative page is still turned over. Calculate the taxes on $300,000, then add interest on the cost of the truck, and this is all added onto the front of the loan. Oh yeah, there's more. In the City of Chicago there are only five places where you can buy natural gas. The cost of adding these fueling stations to a regular gas station that sells diesel fuel? Well, I read the price tag one time, and it was quite high. I know one fueling station has a technician on call because of the size of the fleet, and if the pumps do not work, the fleet stands still. And on more than one occasion, I have heard that the pumps at one station were inoperable, and the trucks had to crisscross the city, hoping that the one on the other side of the city would be able to pump natural gas into their tanks. Also, if the truck runs out of fuel, it is impossible to grab a 5- or 10-gallon bucket and pump fuel into it, then prime the injection pump and start yourself back up. The only thing you can do is to call a tow truck and have him bring you to a station, and pump directly from the station pump to the truck.

  Natural gas has a higher flashpoint, so truck manufacturers have installed several circuit breakers throughout the electrical system that will prevent electricity from causing an explosion. Problem is, these breakers short out and shut the truck down. Many people bought natural gas trucks for the fuel savings, and I asked the question, "What happens if the price of diesel fuel comes down and matches the price of natural gas?" Well, guess what happened? The price of diesel fuel is now about $.25 a gallon below the price of natural gas, and the only thing that the owners of these trucks can do is grin and bear it. One thing's for sure: the used trash truck market is hot. Trucks that are pre-2007 are selling at a premium because they can be rebuilt, and for the price of one complete unit powered by natural gas, you can purchase three pre-2007 units with less aggravation than the truck with the higher price tag. In fact, there are fleets with year 2008 to 2010 units that have been taken out of service and are up for sale. But they lack one thing, and that is buyers. I am totally convinced that this is one area where the government should have left well enough alone. Pre-2008, this industry was at a happy medium. It had found its middle ground.

Recycling

Just above, you witnessed one of my rants about something that should have been left alone and not forced down someone's throat. I will do that again when it comes to recycling. Recycling is a fairly new word, but if you go back to my early accounts, you will see that we were already doing it in the 40s, 50s and later. At Sunbeam Corporation we scooped up handfuls of copper wire, which was easy to do because it was usually on the top of the drum. We would store it in a cardboard box on the truck, and my uncle would trade it in later. My father would collect pop bottles, two cents apiece, five cents for the big ones. Twice a year when I attended Englewood Christian School, we would have a paper drive, and trucks would go around to people's houses where they had collected their newspapers and bundled them, along with their rags, and with volunteer labor we would add to the school's coffer. But then plastic began to replace glass pop bottles, as well as paper shopping bags, and Styrofoam replaced cardboard packaging fillers, and plastic water bottles became part of many people's daily existence.

People began to notice the increase in plastic products, including the tree huggers. The problem of disposing these products fell to the trash haulers, even though they did not invent these products. We, the trash haulers, cannot just throw these things away, we have to sell them, we have to create a market for them, even if one does not exist. Recycling has become almost a religion for some people, so that today if you do not put your plastic bottles in the recycling bin along with your tin cans and your plastic shopping bags, lightning is going to strike you dead. And I have been told many times I am destroying the planet if I do not adhere to the religion of recycling. I hate to be rude, but I do not believe that saving plastic is going to make one hill of beans difference in saving the planet.

Here are two examples which I will use to bring my point across. (I could probably come up with about a dozen more, but two should suffice.)

1 – Peoria Paper Grading

Back in the early 80s, the Mexican soap factory had a contract with a major corporation to re-package bottled products, and in this re-packaging they would remove the bottles from a cardboard carton that needed to be disposed of. They asked me what could be done to dispose of these cardboard cartons without costing them an arm and a leg. I liked these guys and I made them this offer: I would give them a 30-yard roll-off box and would charge them $125 per load to take the cardboard to Peoria Paper Grading. The soap factory people would have to flatten them down, because if they didn't there was no sense in paying that kind of money to go that far with nothing on the load (a 30-yard load to a landfill and back was about $150). Peoria was paying $40 per ton for cardboard, the highest rate in the city, and I agreed to give the check from Peoria to the Mexican soap factory, and I would bill them for the $125 per load cartage. Each load would bring about four tons, or $160 per load, subtract my fee, and they would make about $35 per load. Man, were those guys happy! Instead of paying $150 per load to dispose of the cardboard, they were receiving $35 per load profit. How could you go wrong? Well, this went on for about six months. The checks from Peoria were turned over to them, and they paid the bill at the end of the month for my $125 per load. Both parties were happy. And then one bright sunny day I pulled into Peoria, and when I received the ticket for my load, instead of the usual $160 for that load, the ticket read $40. I said to the girl, "There must be some mistake. This is not the usual amount." Her reply was, "See him," pointing to the boss. He walked me to the window and pointed to about a dozen trailers backed up against the dock, then said, "You know what they are filled with?" He answered his own question. "Baled cardboard. And you know why they are filled with baled cardboard?" "No, I don't," was my reply. "Well, let me tell you. Two days ago I got a notice from the mill I sell to that the price they were paying for cardboard had been cut by three quarters of what I was getting, and do you think I am going to pay you $40 a ton when I have cardboard coming out of my ears? Ten bucks a ton is the best I can do, take it or leave it." The next load I tried a different scrap yard, which was much closer than going to Peoria, and the guy there said, "I will give you $10 for the whole load." I had been down this road before, and I had seen a what happens when guys go into recycling big time. It becomes a feast or famine type of existence. I was forced to go to the Mexican soap factory and said, "Ten dollars a load is the best I can do." Eventually the $10 went to 0, but I still charged them $125 to bring the cardboard to a scrap yard. They were still ahead because they did not have to pay the additional $25 dollars that I would have charged them if I had gone to a landfill.

 Today the same thing has happened with co-mingled recycling. Recycling centers were paying about 10 bucks a ton. Eventually it dropped to zero, and now they are charging 10 bucks a ton to "take it off your hands." This very same thing happened in the scrap iron recycling. On any given day in past years, you would see ten pickup trucks going down the same alley in a few hours time. The Chinese were buying scrap at breakneck speed, and freight boxes were being loaded with scrap iron bound for Asia. At that time the price paid at the scale was about $300 a ton for some types of scrap iron. Scrap yards were actually sifting the dirt to get buried pieces of iron that they had missed. Tires were being shredded to access the steel belts inside them. The predictions were that the market would keep going up, up, up. But guess what? Just like Peoria Paper Grading, the up market collapsed, and the $300-per-ton rate dropped almost overnight to, at best, $50 per ton. The trucks that used to scour the alleys are a rare sight today, and scrap yards are no longer lined with cars and trucks bringing their precious cargo.

Several years ago a reporter from a northern Michigan newspaper called me and wanted to talk about this idea of recycling. He had talked to my brother John, and John had informed him, "You should really talk to my brother." The reporter and I talked for a while, and I made the comment, "I always read how much the check a particular village or township or city has received for their recycling efforts. But what they always leave out of the equation is the cost of obtaining that size check. They represent that check as pure profit, which is a blatant falsehood. They never say what the labor cost were, what the truck/equipment cost, and did they have to store the recycled material, or process it, before it was sold, and if they did store or process it, what did the land cost them to rent or buy?"

The reporter used an example of a woman in northern Michigan who was processing recycled material on her farm, and he claimed she was doing well with it. My question was: did she buy the land to use for recycling, or was that land already in her family? And what did her labor cost? Were they volunteers, or did she pay them the prevailing wage? He did not have an answer for these two questions, and I said that if you were to try and put a recycling center in a large city, you could not even begin to purchase the land. And if you did purchase land, it would have to be many miles from the city, and that would add a lot of dollars to your cost because you would have to truck everything out there.

      I knew what I was talking about because I had bid on some work around a major university in Chicago, and this university asked me if I would bid on the recycling. I knew who was doing it at the time, and I thought he was doing it for the price of the materials, meaning what he collected he sold, and paid his bills with that money. "No," I was informed by the university, "we pay as much, if not more, to have that material be recycled than if we were to just throw it away." I declined to bid on it because who wants to attack the "Godfather of Recycling"? He had made several videos and had won the hearts of the tree huggers, and I did not want to get struck by lightning. But it got me to look at this thing a little closer. The Godfather's license plates for a large truck similar to the one I had was not in the $2000 per year range, which is what I paid for mine.; he was allowed to run with charitable plates, which I don't know what they cost, maybe a few bucks a year. Also, he was not required to house his truck in an enclosed garage, as I was, and many times I observed it parked on a city street for an extended length of time. I'm sure his labor rate was much lower than mine, because when I went to hire one of his drivers, not only did he have a DUI pending, but I'm sure that he didn't even have a CDL. I could probably do some more scratching around on this whole thing, but it wouldn't do much good.

      Recycling can be done, but I'm not so sure that the plastic and co-mingled idea is the way to go. I'm sure most cities and towns have been forced into it by the tree huggers and because they need votes for re-election. They do it to satisfy their constituents, who are convinced they are saving the planet. Where I live, I now have three trucks that pick up at my house, each one employing a union driver and each one of those three trucks is burning fossil fuel. Many years ago, one truck owned by the village had three people on it and picked up everything. So what part of the planet are we saving? I don't think any part of it. But we have passed laws because of the recycling-religious people, who think they are saving the earth with their actions. To me, it's a shell game, more smoke and mirrors to make a certain segment of our population feel good. The trash industry has been forced into it, and they have made a good thing out of bad. When you see those ads with the shiny conveyor belts and the helmeted employees with their safety vests on, pulling plastic and cans and bottles off the conveyor belt, it makes for good press. But the broken glass tears up the very expensive conveyor belts, which then have to be replaced. Eventually, the public will have to pay for it.

2 - S.I.D.

This is the abbreviation for South Industrial Development, otherwise known as a landfill, dump, or what ever term you want to use, depending on your age. For years it was in the perfect spot, about ten miles from the center of downtown Chicago. Most Packer type trucks, as well as roll-offs, could access this place to deposit the load at the end of the day. Ten miles by expressway is not hard to do, and many times you could make two loads from the south side with relative ease. It was also the place where I first met Martin, who helped me unload the skid truck, which did not dump. Little did I know that Martin would later on become my employer, and the relationship would last for more than eighteen years.

It also became a very solid foundation for what was later called Trash Management, and my former boss at Alter was very instrumental in the acquisition of the S.I.D. property and the fulfillment of his dream, to open a huge landfill. It stretches from about 130th up to the Calumet River, which is about 136th Street. The landfill started on the far south end of Chicago and as they went along, they acquired more and more property to the north. As they pushed further north, they came up against a house owned by a guy who refused to sell to them. As time went on, they began to engulf his property, so they were forced to build an access road from the expressway. They also had to leave a large portion down the middle of the landfill, which belonged to the Army Corps of Engineers, as an access road to the lock and dam which raises boats on the Calumet River. It was done with a very well planned design, and I heard rumors that they even hired some guy who had a degree in landfill technology. I never knew such a degree existed, but if you watched how they did it, you knew they had some brains behind it. The dragline, working long days, would dig a very deep hole and pile the clay alongside the hole it was digging. Then they used large machines to move the dirt to a different location. When that hole was deep enough, they would start filling it with the trash that was generated in Chicago and its suburbs. The dragline would then move to the next cell and begin the same process all over again. The concept of transfer trailers and tippers were not even on the horizon at this time, so all of the trash was brought in on packer and roll-off trucks and a few tractor-trailer dumps.

  The landfill operated twenty-four hours a day, and it became the ninth wonder of the world, trucks going in and out all day long and even into the evening. Some companies would load their trucks, park them at their garages and have one or two drivers make trips back and forth to the landfill throughout the evening, so that in the morning when the drivers came to work their trucks would be empty. One night at the landfill, I was making my way to where the trash was being dumped, and my injection pump on the engine broke down. I needed a short length of wire and a connector to get it started again. So I made my way to a maintenance building located on the property, hoping that whoever was working inside would be friendly and would able to help me with my simple request. When I opened the door, who is inside washing equipment with a pressure washer, but a cousin of mine named Clarence Laning. He was as surprised at seeing me as I was seeing him, and he supplied me with my wire and connector. I fixed my truck and was on my way. This practice of helping each other out used to be common in this industry, and for a long time it worked very well. Need a job? Call so-and-so. Need a truck for a day? Call so-and-so. And the list went on.

      S.I.D. was also the very thing that was needed to jumpstart the public trading of companies that work in the trash hauling/landfill business. Factor Brownstone had sprung up in Washington State and Oregon, and was using stock certificates to purchase businesses. Because most trash haulers were a little skeptical of taking a piece of paper (i.e., stock certificates) as something of value, F.B.I. had to also use greenback dollars and the promise of paying off any existing debts as part of the deal. Many small time businessmen were running around like Chicken Little saying, "The sky is falling, the sky is falling!" However, when Trash Management proposed the same concept in the five state area around Chicago, many sellers were less skeptical because it involved people that they had dealt with before. Yes, some of the sellers took quite a lot of persuasion, but the same process that had been done in the past was now being done on a much larger scale, and the apprehension about doing business with stock certificates became a thing of the past. After watching the stock of Trash Management go up, up and split, then go up some more and split, people were made wealthy who had never dreamed that when they sold to Trash Management, every dollar that was promised on paper would result in multiple dollars when they went to cash their stock certificates in. Garbage Services of America was also able to transact buyouts in the same fashion, but their stock performance did not live up to expectations and many who had sold to them didn't get their pot of gold.

So, from about the late 60s well into the 90s, this S.I.D landfill served the greater Chicago area very well for getting rid of their trash. There were three smaller landfills within a few miles of S.I.D., a little cheaper per load, but a little harder to access. If you asked people in the trash hauling business, you might get varying opinions about S.I.D., but to me it was the ninth wonder of the world, and I tell people that on parts of that property you used to be able to look as far down as you now look up, and think how well it served this great metropolitan area all these years. After Trash Management decided not to accept any more trash at S.I.D. because of the restrictions imposed on the height of the mound, they acquired property to the northeast of Chicago with the same goal, but to date they have been blocked from opening this property as a sanitary landfill. This new site only needs the destruction of maybe a half a dozen dilapidated houses—if they do not fall down in the next strong windstorm. But like I said earlier, politicians need votes to remain in office, and before the last governor lost his election, he shoved through a bill that would forbid new landfills from opening up in Cook County. The proposed landfill sites have no potential for development because they are basically unusable, and the state and county sure missed a golden opportunity to put money in their coffers. How, you might ask? Well, you do not have to build casinos to pay your debts. All you have to do is charge what is called a "guest fee" on each ton of trash that is dumped in the landfill—thousands and thousands of tons every day, and if each ton had a guest fee of about two bucks per ton, just envision how much would entered the city coffers.

But like all good politicians, they find a way to screw it up, and now tons and tons of trash are being dumped in counties in Indiana, and counties outside of Cook, and each time a load is dumped, that county receives the guest fee. The round-the-clock operation that once was a very good idea has been reduced to the idea that the trash should be covered at 5 o'clock every day, and I think the excuse given was that the birds can't get at the trash once it's covered. Near election time politicians will use landfills as the big boogey-man, and they convince their constituents that they are acting in their best interest, which is a complete falsehood, in much the same fashion that Greenpeace uses landfills to as whipping boys to promote their agenda and, of course, raise needed funds so they can stay around. And in some of my travels since my retirement, I have seen landfills that, if someone had not taking you into them, you would have never known that they existed. I have often said we need more landfills, but of course, if you say this, you run the risk of the environmentalist lightning striking you.

    The town the Munster, Indiana, decided to take it upon themselves to run their own landfill on an abandoned Brickyard quarry. They learned how to do it, and they did it well, and some of the last loads that I put into a landfill were in Munster. Today that landfill is a shining jewel in the Munster Park system. People walk their dogs, jog, and ride bicycles in this park that used to be a landfill, and many high-end homes have been built only a few miles away without any repercussions. In fact, a few people who have done well in the trash business live only a short distance from this park/landfill. But for years I would hear people complain about the smell, the flames from the methane flares, and my response was, "Quit your bellyaching. It is helping you pay your property taxes." And I'm sure, if Munster could, they would definitely open another one. This is my opinion, and I am sticking to it.

CHAPTER 37 – REMARKABLE PEOPLE

Throughout the years there have been many people who I have come in contact with, who have played a very important part in my participation in this business. They have also made a direct impact on how this industry has shaped up. Some I have mentioned already. Here are some others.

Jack Burns

When I first came to City Disposal back in 1983, there was a broker with six tractors and six dump trailers who was doing work for City Disposal. His name was Jack Burns, and I had met his brother Pete and father Dave several years earlier when they had rebuilt an engine in my garage. So when I met Jack, the natural conversation was, "How are your brother and father doing?" They had started a truck repair business, and because I didn't own any trucks anymore, I did not have cause to use their services again. But Jack and I got to talking about trucks, business and flying airplanes because I was taking flying lessons at the time. I never did get my pilot's license. Not my cup of tea. But Jack went on to get his license and buy several planes. Now he is a licensed to fly a jet, and he does. In fact, at one time he owned an airport.

Early on, our conversations were mostly light and fluffy, like, "Hi. How you doing?" And at that time, we all used the same radio on our trucks, so we heard each other's conversations. From that, I could tell Jack was very knowledgeable about trucks and the trucking business.

He had a falling out with Martin and Norbert, and one day he packed up all six of his trucks and struck out on his own. He bought a garage a few miles from City Disposal and did some semi dump and roll-off work. He had a two-bay truck garage and began to add trucks and trailers to his fleet. I would pay him a visit about twice a year, because when he was still at City Disposal, we had made a deal that I would park my boat in his barn in a far southern suburb. Well, not a suburb. More like the country. In fact, the first time Pat and I went to his place, he was on the roof. From up there he could see that I was lost, and he came and got Pat and me, and led us to the barn. So every spring and fall I would go to his shop and tell him I was going to either pick my boat up or drop it off.

My cousin Peter was on the Board of Directors at Ally, and I didn't realize that he had quite a bit of clout there at one time before his untimely death. Peter is the son of my uncle, Peter Lindemulder, who was my best friend while growing up, even though he had the title of being my uncle. His son Peter was real aggressive and had helped during the growth years of Ally. God called him home very early, while still in his early 50s. As I mentioned in the previous section, the transfer station was becoming the way to go since the government had put severe restrictions on the existing landfills in the Chicago area. No longer could we dump round-the-clock as in previous years. Every day at 5 o'clock p.m. that day's accumulation of trash had to be covered with a layer of dirt, I think about three or four inches thick, and dumping could not resume until 6 a.m. the next morning.

The problem with this, of course, is that the removal of trash in a big metropolitan area like Chicago and its suburbs is a round-the-clock operation, and what to do with the accumulation of trash began to be a problem. Jack Burns, in the meantime, had bought another trucking company and had joined the two operations together. At the same time Ally was having a problem getting the trash from the transfer stations to the landfill, and many times the transfer driver would arrive at the landfill after closing time, so the question became: what do you do with a fully loaded truck that you cannot dump? To return fully loaded to the city was counterproductive, with the transfer stations paying an hourly rate for the driver, and well, you get the picture.

Much of the trash being hauled this way was done with brokers, and I had experienced problems when I was working in the mill, because if you're hourly and there's an hour and a half left in the day, and it takes you two hours to go to a landfill, there's little incentive to get there. Why not save the trip for another day? And I had several shouting matches with both drivers and brokers who knew I wasn't the boss and couldn't order them around.

This problem of inefficiency was coming to the surface at the larger companies also, and cousin Peter thought Jack Burns was just the man to solve it. What did Jack do that was any different than the large corporations? Well, he thought outside the box. For example, he came up with the idea of leaving the back door of the trailer open on the return trip from the dump. We've all experienced the turbulence when a semi passes us, whether alongside or oncoming. Opening the back door allows the movement of air through the trailer, reducing the turbulence of the trailer and decreasing fuel consumption. Today most tractor-trailers are manufactured with a two-part door that swings open when dumped and can be secured to the side of the trailer while in transit.

Another improvement on transfer trailers is what is called a live bottom. This is a series of aluminum slats with about a thousand nylon clips, which make up what is called a "walking floor," using a back-and-forth motion to dump the garbage out the back of the trailer. The problem with this system is that those aluminum slats will bend and twist, and eventually fail, which requires you to take them out and install a thousand new clips and push these 53-foot-long slats back into the bottom of the trailer. It also requires that the trailer have a pump, a hydraulic system and a motor to move these slats back and forth. This adds approximately 5000 additional pounds to the truck, and because it weighs five thousand more pounds, that means less trash that can be hauled.

So, how do you dump a trailer if you do not have these components on it? This is where Jack and the Ally Corporation worked together. A contraption called a tipper had just come on the market. A tipper is a large platform on huge rubber wheels which will lift a 53- foot trailer loaded with garbage. The driver backs onto the platform, unhooks the tractor from the trailer and pulls away. Then two large cylinders will raise the platform with the trailer on it, and the garbage will come out much like a dump trailer. This requires the land fill machines to push away the garbage that comes out of the trailer so that more can fall on the ground.

Like I said, it requires cooperation between the landfill owner and the trash hauler, but when implemented it works very well. I am not familiar what one of these tippers costs, but they require a four-cylinder engine, two large cylinders and a large pump to raise the platform. But there is no weight restriction on a tipper and it stays on the landfill property, which is private. What it does enable the hauler to do is eliminate the slat-and-clip problems of a live bottom trailer, as well as the weight of the pump and hydraulics on the tractor and trailer, allowing the hauler an additional 5000 pounds of payload. When one section of a dump fills up, the tipper can be moved to a different location. Do the math and you find out that for every ten loads the trash hauler is probably picking up one additional load by not having all this deadweight.

Jack also insisted on space at the landfill that would allow additional trailers to be parked. Governmental rules restricted dumping after 5 p.m. and before 6 a.m., so the parking of loaded trailers, each covered with a tarp to prevent trash from blowing all over, allowed him to run each tractor on a two-shift day, twelve hours each shift. So each tractor in the Chicago area had three trailers, and if you've ever been to a landfill, you can imagine the mad rush at 6 a.m. in the morning to empty the trailers that are full. But this was the answer needed to solve the problem of removing the trash from the transfer station located in the city and bringing it to the landfill.

These solutions seem simple enough, but many times they are hard to implement in a large corporation. No one seems to want to try something new because everybody likes their salaries and nobody wants to make waves or rock the boat. If you asked me why General Motors went bankrupt, this is a perfect example. Why keep making Oldsmobiles that nobody buys? Because people connected with that division of GM figured, "I still got a job. Let's not shake things up." Except, now they don't have a job because somebody finally had to take an ax to the Oldsmobile division, as well as Pontiac, and plug some of the leaks in that corporate boat. This type of behavior happens not only in car making. It also happens in any kind of widget-making industry you can watch go down the tubes.

Jack Burns was just the right guy to make the right changes, and his company, BMI, began to implement all these game plans to make heads or tails out of the transfer hauling business. The problem with most of these changes is they cannot be patented. I once asked him about his design of the two-part trailer back door, and he just shrugged and said, "Well, you can't patent an idea." The concept of leaving the trailers at the landfill rests on the trailer manufacturer because the landing dollies have to be strong enough to hold the weight of the trailer as well is its contents.

And then, of course, there is the personnel needed to implement these ideas. You have to have mechanics that know how to troubleshoot and are willing to go out at all hours of the day or night to repair trucks that have broken down, so that the highway does not become littered with BMI trucks that are not running. And Jack was able to employ just such people. His shop was able to repair both the tractor and trailer, and, if necessary, do a complete rebuild of the trailers, including the wheels and suspensions. His repair shop for the tractors held shelves of standardized parts. One size windshield would fit all of the trucks. His engines were all the same, as well as the transmissions and rear ends.

An example of his operation: one time after retirement, I got a call on a Friday afternoon. Could I take a pickup truck, either my own or one of theirs, to Union City, Tennessee? The cargo was a four-cylinder John Deere engine. My instructions were to be there by 7 a.m. Saturday morning, and I was to meet their mechanic, and he would take me to the local landfill, where the injection pump from the John Deere engine on my pickup was to be installed on a new engine that been put on a tipper at the landfill. If this did not work and the engine would not start, I was to wait while they removed the engine from the tipper, installed the John Deere engine in the tipper and got it running. Then I would come back to Chicago with the other new engine.

Got that? It had a be explained to me a couple times too. But I made it down to Union City overnight, and at 6 a.m. the mechanic woke me up, and we went to a landfill which I would've never found on my own. There were the John Deere mechanics waiting for me, and they took the injection pump out of the engine I had and installed it on the tipper engine. Then they poured fuel into it, primed it and fired it up, and the tipper began to operate again. When I turned around, there was a line of twelve trucks waiting to get on that tipper. Because of Jack's initiative, the corporations who initially had bought the tippers decided that it would be best to let Jack Burns buy them back from the corporation and do the maintenance, as well as purchase new tippers in the future. So he took on a responsibility which in the past had been on the shoulders of the corporation.

    Just a side note: once Jack Burns showed the transfer industry how to do things, the competition was able to copy his ideas very well. For a while, every Tom, Dick and Harry would buy trailers with two-part gates; now most landfills have tippers, and the walking floor is only used where tippers are not feasible.

    One of my trips for Jack required that I go to Salt Lake City, Utah. Salt Lake City has a unique situation, as they allow hauling of doubles, the front trailer being fifty-three feet and the back being forty-eight feet, and to somebody who is into trucks and machines, it is a work of art. It's something to watch how the driver and the transfer personnel work hand-in-hand for a trip to the landfill. When I walked inside their garage, which was located next to the transfer station, I met Calvin, the general manager, who really had a handle on his business. The garage was neat, everything in place, and after a brief conversation with Calvin, he said, "If you don't need me, I have things to do." And he was gone. When I got back to Chicago, I asked Jack, "How did you find this guy?" Jack said, "I went on the Internet, and his name came up. He had had some trucking experience, was a real topline guy, and I hired him." Then and there, I realized this is a gift. I have trouble hiring people when I've known them for four or five months

Jack's expertise helped me a lot with Anchor2. By sheer coincidence and in the trying to hustle up work, I asked him to become one of my customers. At first he said, "No, we throw all our stuff on the bottom of a trailer and fill that trailer with transfer station garbage, so it's not that big a deal. We don't generate that much." But about a month later, I got a call from him. Could I bring him a 2-yard container? "Of course," I said. "No problem." What had happened was: they had found out that some sensitive papers had flown out of a trailer on its return from the landfill. Remember the open back door? Well, you get the picture. It would be better for me to haul his trash, as opposed to somebody finding company papers at 71st and the Dan Ryan, or wherever.

Thus began more of a longer relationship: the 2-yarder became a six and a two, then a second two, and finally twice-a-week service, Monday and Thursday. On the Thursday pickup I would usually arrive at lunchtime, and I would either take my McDonald's hamburgers or I would pack a lunch from home, so I could sit down at the picnic table inside the shop and eat lunch with the BMI crew. Sometimes Jack would be there with Henry, his VP in charge of operations, and we would talk shop and cry on each other's shoulders, and I would complain about the grief I was having with the Mack I had. On one of those Thursdays, Jack handed me the phone and said, "I have dialed the salesman at Kenworth. Tell them exactly what you want."

Which I did. After haggling a little bit about the trade-in on my Mack, the down payment was made, and four months later I had a brand new Kenworth waiting to have the body from the Mack mounted on it. I had seen a similar truck that had been bought by GBI (Greenbriar Industries), and it made my mouth water, a 20-yard body with a short front Kenworth, capable of navigating narrow alleys, yet stout enough to do the job. The only change I made was I bought a standard transmission.

To this day, the owner of GBI still drives that same truck of his almost every day, and every time I see him, with his orange gloves and hardhat, there's a big smile on my face. My hats off to him, eighty years old and still piloting that rig. He's been to the mountain, meaning he owned a fleet of trucks. Then he sold those trucks, has been the boss, has laid under the truck, and in his golden years, is still enjoying himself.

For me, putting that first Kenworth on the street was a godsend. It required very little upkeep. It was one of those trucks that you make sure it's got oil and fuel, turn the key, and go do your job. No longer did I have to pump big bucks into repairs of the chassis. The body had been pretty much dialed in, and all I had to do was haul garbage. Eric had graduated from college and came on full time. He worked 10-hour days, forty hours a week, Mondays, Wednesdays, Fridays and Saturdays, off on Tuesday. I hired Jeff, who came by way of a driver from Trash Management, his brother-in-law. Jeff had a good full-time job, not very hard, so he was looking for something on Saturday. I was able to give him a Monday night of five hours and a Saturday of about six or seven. This kept Eric's overtime at bay, and everybody was happy.

This arrangement worked so well, I decided that maybe it was time to replace my White/GMC, which had replaced the Crane Carrier. When the mortgage on the first Kenworth came down to about a year and a half, I placed an order for a second Kenworth, almost identical to the first one, except for an automatic transmission. It took about four months to build this, and I then had an '83 Leach body mounted on it, and the White GMC went in trade on this new truck. The lessons of the past surely came into play with having new equipment. I know the body was 21 years older than the chassis I bought, but the body is basically steel and cylinders, and had been rebuilt prior to the remount.

My son Owen, who had not gone into this business, once commented to me that trash hauling always afforded somebody the opportunity to make pretty good money on the side doing such things as painting containers, washing trucks, running errands, being a helper. So when my brother Mark asked if I had something for his daughter Shabana to do, I said, "Yeah, she can paint the body on the truck that I just remounted." The cost of a paint job for a truck at that time was about $5,000. The body of a truck, being the widest and highest part of the vehicle, was subject to the most abuse from going down narrow alleys, or having trees scratch it. I told my brother, "I'll give her $1000. It should take her a couple of days." She and Mark did it in two days, and I was happy and she was happy.

My daughter Tricia did the same thing when she and Kurt were deciding to get married. I pitched the same proposal to her on a truck I had acquired from Prescott. The body was red, and I wanted it black. I did not want to spend $4000 to have it painted, so I made her the same offer, and on a Saturday morning she and I went to Home Depot, and bought a couple of Wagner power sprayers, a couple of gallons of black Rustoleum. By 3 o'clock in the afternoon we had painted the complete body. The power sprayers were cheap enough that we threw them away after we were done. Eric Captian had prepared the body prior to us painting, so that part was not in the equation.

During one of my lunch breaks at BMI, Jack and Henry were moaning that they could not find good office help. My daughter had completed one year of college at North Park and decided she did not want to live on campus, so she bought a good car and switched to the University of Illinois, Circle Campus. She was still unclear about what she wanted to do for a living. No, I did not offer her a job driving a trash truck, but on one bright sunny afternoon while waiting in extremely heavy traffic to make the transition from the Kennedy to the Dan Ryan, I came alongside the BMI company pickup truck, and Jack was sitting in the passenger seat and Henry was driving. I yelled out, "You still need decent office help?" "Yes, we do," Jack answered. So I dialed home with my trusty brick phone, which weighed about 2 pounds, and got ahold of my daughter and said, "Go over to BMI and put your application in for office help. Yes, you can list me as a reference, and yes they know you are coming."

She got the job in the office at first on a part-time basis while attending classes in the morning at U of I, Circle, much like her father in the days of De Normandie, when I was going to school and working part time. Only because she is smarter than I am, she would grab lunch and be at work in the afternoon. Several months went by, and at one of our Thursday lunch times, Henry asked me, "Do you mind if your daughter would drop out of college and come to work here full-time?" I said I would talk it over with her. And when we had the talk, she indicated that college was not her cup of tea, mainly because she did not know what she was going to college for, and I indicated that Henry had asked if it was all right if she dropped out of college? "Yeah," she said, jumping at the chance. I'm not even sure she finished out that semester, but she and that company fit together. Maybe the farm system that I talked about previously was still in place even though the trash hauling business had gone through some dynamic changes. (She later got a degree in accounting while working for BMI.)

BMI had some very interesting Christmas parties. No, not the kind where you went to some restaurant and ate food that you shouldn't eat, and people drank like fish because they weren't paying for it. Jack was a non-drinker and stuck fast to his principles. What he did was have a demolition derby in his back forty. Both suppliers and employees, and anyone else who was invited, would bring a car painted funny and race around like wild Indians. Afterward we would have pizza in the barn.

The last derby was held in 2007, and I noticed fifty brand-new Kenworth tractors parked in a row [at the back of the field, or where?], and I asked my daughter, "Why is it you've got fifty trucks parked, doing nothing?" She would usually tell me if something in a different city was coming up, but this time she said, "I have no clue." But as I was going home and for the next couple of days, I began to think about something: the end of 2007 was the year that…well, for lack of a better word…the government was turning truck engines into junk. More about that a little later.

For me, the light went on, and the next Thursday, when I was eating lunch around the shop table, I casually asked Jack, "Did you buy those fifty trucks in anticipation of the government deadline?" He did not give me a direct answer. Just a little smile. As I left I continued to think this thing over. Not only was the deadline going to add $13,000 to each new truck for the "new technology," but, remember what I said earlier, things that are put out there prematurely without proper testing of their application, are going to be used "as is," a very tricky, dangerous situation, and I will talk about that later. In fact, used trucks at that time with 100,000 miles on them were bringing almost the price of new ones.

So I got ahold of the salesman at the Kenworth dealership and placed an order for a new chassis similar to the one I had bought in 2004, with the stipulation that he was to put the order in at the last possible moment, but that I was to get the truck built before the deadline. I assumed that it would take about eight or ten months to build. Well, guess what? It came in four. Remember my telling you about free money? This was still 2007, before the crash. I requested an interest-only loan for the first year, and the remainder to be paid in the next four. Kenworth agreed, and I accepted delivery of this truck. The body which my daughter and I had painted several months prior was transferred to the new truck and Kenworth took the old truck in trade, giving me a fraction of the price I had originally paid for the complete unit from Prescott. I really didn't need this truck, but add a $13,000 savings, and it would have been a foolish not to purchase it, and a few months later the talks with Prescott for a possible buyout had once again resumed. So after Pat and I discussed it, we felt that possibly this would be the best option to take as a preamble for my eventual retirement.

John Watkins

Several years after my retirement I received a call from Jack Burns, and he asked me if I was up for taking a flight to a small town in Tennessee near Murfreesboro. I mentioned earlier that Jack had got his jet pilot's license, and he had purchased a small Cessna jet, and if you have to travel, I can see the appeal of corporate America in using a jet to fly around the country. In about two hours we were at a small airport in Tennessee, and the Fixed Base Operation allowed us to use a car. The purpose of our visit was to go to see John Watkins, the former mechanic at City Disposal. John had cancer, and with cancer it is always a question mark. I have noticed many people who have the Big C wear a brave front, but within a short time you are attending their funeral.

There were six of us: Jack, his brothers Pete and Henry, and two other people who had known John in the past. There was a luncheon in the church, served by John's wife Joann, and some ladies she had gotten together. We sat around and talked about old times, and when we noticed that we had worn John out, we all got up and said our goodbyes and gave John a hug, and flew back home.

I had met John prior, when I was contemplating selling out to City Disposal. At that time John lived in Michigan, and when City Disposal moved to 118th St., John set his travel trailer in back of the garage and would work afternoons and evenings and then sleep in the daytime. On the weekends he would go back home to Michigan.

John was an artist; he could do most anything with trucks. One time Martin and Norbert bought a new front loader, and I did not like how it operated. So I talked them into letting John remove the body, rebuild the cylinders, replace the hoses and put floors and walls inside the body. Remember, a truck body is nothing more than steel and cylinders. The chassis is the item that should be new or almost new to ensure a proper operation.

Later, John had a falling out with Martin and Norbert and left to try several other ventures. Just after I started Anchor2, John called me and asked me if I knew of anyone looking for a driver/mechanic. He listed salary requirements and who he did not want to work for, and on one of my lunches at BMI, I mentioned to one of BMI's mechanics that John had called me, and Jack called me back and said, "Where is he living?" My reply was, "Tennessee," but that John was always willing to pick up his trailer and move wherever the action was.

Jack explained that relocation was not necessary. BMI had just acquired a small operation in a town near where John was living, so it was a perfect fit. I gave Jack the number John had given me, and the two of them got together. As I've said in the past, Jack was always able to find a perfect fit for each location. In this case, Jack put John in charge of the operation. Up until that flight I had only talked to John on the phone and never face-to-face. A week after the flight to Tennessee, Jack called me again and asked if I was willing to make another flight because John had passed away. Of course I said "yes," and from time to time I think about how talented he was and how little recognition he may have got for his immense talent.

Frank Mayer

This was another person who was extremely talented. He worked for a Leach distributor. Early on, he decided that he could strike out on his own and save most of the small operators the extreme cost of the repairs done by "the authorized dealership." In the early days Frank had a truck body, which he would put on your chassis while he rebuilt your own body. He could do the switch overnight, so that you would have a running, functional truck the next morning. This was a godsend for the one- and two-truck operators. Then he would cut all the old steel off of your body shell, repack your cylinders if necessary, replace your hoses pipes and other hardware, and could even paint the thing the color of your choice.

For several years he was able to keep up with the pace of the small operators who were on a growth spurt. At a fraction of the cost, and in half the time, Frank and his talented crew could perform the tasks that in the past were done by the authorized dealer. When the smaller companies began, one at a time, to sell to the larger corporations, Frank began to watch his market share dissipate, and after an extremely heavy fine levied by OSHA for some nit-picky infraction, Frank began to rethink his position of being an employer. He dismissed all of his employees, and promised himself that he would not do any work that would require him to hire someone on a full-time basis. Thereby, whatever he did would result in the money going into Frank's pocket. Even working by himself, Frank is a real artist, and the results of his work are quite widely known, and when you mention his name in trash hauling circles, everybody knows of his work and who he is, and it would be wrong not to have mentioned him and the quality of his work.

Jack Switzer

This acquaintance came quite by accident. After my retirement, I suggested…well, maybe my brothers did, but we all agreed pretty quickly, that a boat trip with just the six of us would be a good idea. Pat and I had done Mississippi River trips from the Quad Cities up to St. Paul three times prior, and they were very good, fun trips. The six brothers thought that because we had had such a good childhood together and still got along well, it would be nice to some extended time together, just the six of us.

We put in at Savannah, Illinois, and headed to St. Paul, and arrived there in very short time because we were doing about 100 miles a day, as opposed to about 50 when Pat and I did it. Bruce had just come back from a volunteer medical trip to Africa right before our boat trip and was eager to sleep in his own bed, but pushing every day got a little bit under Peter's skin, and on the way back we were picked up at the marina in Red Wing, Minnesota, by someone who owned the nearby restaurant, and Peter said, "I don't care about you guys, but I'm going to stay in this high-end hotel overnight." (We had been sleeping on the boats, on the ground and on docks.) I was in agreement with Peter, so I said to him, "Okay, I'll share the cost of the room with you, providing they give us a ride back to the marina tomorrow morning." Next morning, after taking a shower and putting on our fuzzy terrycloth bathrobes, Peter and I received a phone call from brother John. He said, "You had better get down to the marina now," and I inquired if the one of the boats had sank or if some catastrophe had happened, and his reply was, "No, just get down here."

When Peter and I arrived at the marina, nothing seemed amiss, and we walked toward the boat, where John introduced me to a man named Jack Switzer, whose occupation was head sales manager at

McNeilus Corporation, who manufacturers the latest, and I might add, the best trash hauling body in the business. (My opinion; others may beg to differ.) How did John know about my feelings for the McNeilus Corporation? Because during the filming of my last days before I retired, I had told John extensively how the company had gotten feedback from not only the owners, but also the drivers and mechanics, in order to improve their product. I had pointed out to John how they used stainless pins for the connections of the blades, how they had also incorporated stainless steel piping, and several other small, unnoticeable improvements which made this body, in my estimation, much superior to its predecessors. I had also told John that someday I would like to meet somebody in management from this company which had resisted the temptation to cut corners in order to save money, and tell him how well their philosophy had worked out. This cutting of corners is done a lot in corporate America, and at first it is not noticeable, but in the long run it does irreparable damage. Ever wonder why Toyota is the most popular car in America? In the 1980s Chevrolet was the winner, hands down, but complacency set in, and the temptation to cheapen everything turned their product into an also-ran.

  That morning John reminded me of what I had said about that McNeilus Corporation and introduced me to Jack Switzer, who had a boat in the slip next to where our boats were parked in the marina at Red Wing, Minnesota. John said, "Remember how you wanted to talk to someone at that corporation? Well, this is the man you were looking for, and now you can tell him." We invited Jack to sit down and have breakfast with us while I babbled on about his product. At first he declined, saying he had the pick up his daughter from piano lessons, but then relented since Bruce was making some mean pancakes. Jack sat down on the picnic bench while I talked about being introduced to McNeilus late in my career. (The

Sterling/McNeilus body was the first of their products that I had worked on at Prescott, only two years earlier.)

    Jack and I talked about the demise of the Leach dynasty, how it had began as a family-owned corporation started many years ago by Elmer Leach. How it had gone from Oshkosh to Canada, had been acquired by the LaBrie Corporation, and was now being produced in Mexico, almost like a product without a country. Now Leach had the philosophy that said: let's see how cheap we can make it. And anyone who works on or around these refuse bodies will attest to the fact that many times key components would break, unexplained, without abuse. And the sales figures also will attest to this. The once mighty leader, which had captured the refuse body industry, now was scrambling to keep its market share. There is a saying that most companies will fail when they are passed on to the third generation, and there's a lot of truth to this. I don't care if it's in trash hauling, car making, or running a department store. Each generation is less willing to think outside the box, and each generation seems to become more and more complacent. And the final result is that business ceases to be a leader.

    As we talked between bites of pancakes and sips of coffee, it was a thrill to listen to Jack and share war stories, and about an hour after I met Jack, we shook hands and bid each other goodbye. I was so glad to have made this chance encounter, and I thank John for putting two and two together and alerting me to the man I had been hoping to meet. Several months later my brother Bruce came to town, and we went out to dinner with our wives. He handed me a box, and in the box was a model McNeilus truck that Bruce had ordered from Jack Switzer as a gift for me, and I proudly display this model on the shelf in my humble office. From time to time I will send just a short note to Jack on Facebook telling him to keep up the good work.

CHAPTER 38 – RETIREMENT

So in July 2007, only a few months after I had purchased that new Kenworth, Pat and I signed the deal to turn over the assets of Anchor2—my three Kenworths—to Prescott, and I became an employee of Prescott. I drove the three trucks to the Prescott yard and began my final year of employment. Kind of funny. Prescott was buying one of their old bodies back. But a tear came to my eye one day when I noticed two of the Kenworths at the top of the 111th Street bridge getting on the Bishop Ford Expressway to make their southbound journey to Florida with dealer tags on them. Later I noticed in one of the trade magazines that the '04 was up for sale. I never did find out what happened to the '07 with the almost-new chassis.

Once again being employed was not a bad deal. I had learned how to take orders. There were a few wrinkles in trying to get some of the things on the truck changed, and the Kenworth—which to me looked beautiful--was replaced with a couple of Sterlings, which were practically brand-new, body and chassis. Each was identical and had very low miles on it, somewhere around 27,000-miles. The only drawback was the color: school bus yellow, and we all took a bunch of ribbing for that. But when Trash Management acquired Prescott, they sent them to the paint shop. And even though I don't like green paint, the green and white combination makes those two trucks the best looking of the Chicago Trash Management fleet. Prescott had put aluminum wheels on them, as well as stainless mirrors, and they still catch my eye as they go up and onto the expressway. Not because I drove them, but because they are just plain good looking trucks.

The last year of my employment was very uneventful, except for the fact that my son Chris, who was living in California, was trying to get residency in the country of Slovenia, where Pat's father came from. I asked him to help me through the winter snow, and I would be willing to pay him out of my own pocket. At the time, he was living on the North Side of Chicago, so I would make the first load by myself and go to the transfer station dump, then pick him up at 31st St.

With Chris, I got a little taste of how things were between me and my father. Chris had totally different ideas than I did, and on any given day a disagreement could erupt into a very verbal argument, and the following day he might decide that he wasn't going to work with me because of something I had said the day before. He had learned to live very frugally and did not need a lot of money to exist. So after about four months—through the critical part of the winter—he packed up and moved to Slovenia, and I finished the last three months of my employment with Prescott by myself.

I retired the first week of September, the Friday before Labor Day, and because of the rich heritage of what this business has given me, I regret that there are only a few (five) snapshots of my grandfather and uncles, that gave me a little more insight into my rich heritage. It wasn't till the book *Dutch Chicago* came out and I read the section on the Dutch in the garbage business, that I realized that on my paternal grandfather's side there were a Congo and a Nicholas Deckinga, and after asking a couple of cousins in the Chicago area, I could not get a definite answer on who these two relatives of mine were.

I was told to contact my cousin Marlene Deckinga, who is kind of the keeper of the Deckinga side of the family tree, just like my wife Pat seems to be the keeper of the Laning side, and I'm thankful for that. Marlene told me that Congo was a brother to Nicholas, and Nicholas was my great grandfather, and hats off to Robert Swierenga for writing the book, *Dutch Chicago* and doing such a thorough job of running down these family trees, though I don't think at the time he was writing the book, he realized he was doing so many of us such a big service. Thanks again, Professor Swierenga.

Well, I don't know what the future holds, and I know it appears to be self-serving, but as my retirement loomed, I figured: *what can it hurt to photograph my last day of work in trash hauling and first day of retirement?* My brother John, who lives in northern Michigan, is a very good photographer, and I invited him to come and spend the last weekend of my trash career while operating a movie camera.

The day started out rather mundanely: stopping for breakfast at the McDonald's near my home at 12:30 a.m. and placing my order at the drive-up window: a double quarter-pounder with cheese and fries, half of which I fed to the dog named Trash, who kept an eye on the place at Prescott. For the next twelve hours, John sat alongside me, camera rolling, while I proceeded to scratch my face about 10,000 times, blow my nose another 500 times, and began to realize why my grandfather years and years ago would always grab my knee and try to settle me down. I remember my father could sit on the front porch of the cottage or the house on Aberdeen Street, and just look over at some object for hours. Me? I didn't have the patience to sit there for five minutes. This was probably why we could never get along very well. I wanted him to move faster, and he wanted me to slow down.

But if the world was full of people like me, it would be terrible, and if the world was full of people like my father it, would be equally unnerving, and this is why God made each of us with our own personalities, and if you have a strong faith in the Lord and put your trust in him, let him be your guide.

As John was filming, we would tell people what was going on and why, and if they would not like to be seen in a movie of my last day, then we would definitely not film them. At 7 a.m. we arrived at Lawful Gardens, a huge housing development on 35th St.. This was a six-day a week pick-up, and on this particular morning the janitor held John back and said to me, "They want to see you in the basement." This was highly unusual because I had never been asked to go down there in the past. When I got down there, much to my surprise, there was a conference room with several dozen donuts and several boxes of coffee and a sign that said, "Happy Retirement, O!" It definitely took my breath away to be remembered by people who I had not thought would even notice me. Dominic, who was the manager of the building, had orchestrated this going-away party, and Dominic, I will always remember you for your thoughtfulness and generosity. You made it extra nice when you gave me an envelope with a few bucks in it to put gas in my retirement boat, and these are things which I can never erase from my mind.

I already knew about the going away party that Prescott had planned that same afternoon, so when John and I got in from my route, the mechanic shop had been transformed into a banquet hall with beef and chicken, soft drinks, coffee. My thanks to Mick and Will for their hospitality and generosity. These memories too will never be forgotten, unless of course I get Alzheimer's, which I plan to do someday.

After the Prescott party was over, John and I went to Holiday boats, where I had previously arranged to have my boat put into working order so that I could once again use it. I had almost forgotten I had one because it had been six years since I had last used it. All that time, it had been kept inside, so I wasn't worried about the outward appearance. But mechanically, I wanted to make sure that thing ran because John and I planned to take it to Burnham Harbor, where I had made arrangements to rent a slip for the Labor

Day weekend. Being one of the first holidays I did not have to work, I wanted to wake up and savor not having to punch in.

What a glorious sight on that Monday morning to wake up with the sun streaming in over the backside of Soldier Field, knowing I did not have to get up and do a day's work! John's wife Nancy and my wife Pat had slept at home and came later in the day to pick us up and go for dinner in downtown Chicago. You've heard of people doing pub crawl's? Well, that evening the four of us did "stop crawl." We went back to the Fisher building, John Marshall Law, the printing company which happened to be the first stop in the morning on Desplaines and Adams. Now this warehouse had been transformed into a modern high-rise. When we arrived at what was known as Sam L Bingham, it had been transformed into a parking lot for a high-rise building. Even the street name had been updated. No longer was it known as Sherman Place. It is now know as Financial Place. The ladies of the evening must have thought we were crazy, standing in the middle of Plymouth Court, one guy with a video camera in his hand, the other guy pointing at doors in the sidewalk, and buildings that were long gone.

CHAPTER 39 – THE FUNERAL

While I was writing this book, I received a phone call that my cousin JoAnn (Laning) Huizenga had passed away at age 75. Only a week earlier, I had received notice that she was suffering from cancer. Her sister Sharon, who had died less than eleven months prior, had lived with her cancer for about four years. So, when I heard about Jo's cancer, I felt I would still have time to touch base with her, and was praying that God would spare her many more years. But this was not to be. I made the journey to her funeral, a trip of 1000 miles one way.

The funeral was a reflection on how much I enjoyed my relationship not only with my uncles, but also with their children. Just prior to leaving the church luncheon that was held after the funeral, I asked Jo's husband Bernie, who had spent his adult life hauling trash, how many of his children (three sons and a daughter) now made a living in the trash hauling business. "Two sons," was his reply, and he added that their daughter was married to a guy who fixed the trash hauling trucks.

I then scanned the room and remembered Jo's brother Kenny and his wife had sold a business several years prior to Trash Management, and now were back into trash hauling again with the help of Kenny's two sons. I was introduced to one of them and gave him a thumbs up. I also remembered that JoAnn had a younger brother—my cousin David, who had sold a business some years prior, and moved to Florida and was driving for someone down there. I then began to think of my other cousins, on both side of my family, and was reminded that several others had taken up the profession of trash hauling, following in the footsteps of their fathers, my uncles.

Uncle Pete Laning

This uncle, like his brother Clarence, had gone into the mission field, but afterwards he found out that the mission field was not his cup of tea. He moved his family to Michigan and built a small trash hauling business with the help of his son Butch and his son-in-law Dan. Uncle Pete's health began to fail and the operation was sold. I'm not too sure about the details, but I had heard Trash Management had bought it. Shortly thereafter my uncle died, and both his son and his son-in-law went into a different line of work.

Uncle Murph Laning

His one-truck operation was sold when his health also started to fail. It was sold to an individual who ran it for a while, then sold it to a larger group. I am not sure if it was sold the first time to one of the public companies or was done so latter.

But neither of Murph's two boys, or his son-in- law, made trash hauling a part of their life's work.

Uncle Al Laning

After he shut the key off and said, "I am not doing this anymore," Uncle Al worked in an occupation far removed from trash hauling. He and my aunt traveled after he retired, and none of his sons, or his sons-in-law did trash hauling again. I am almost sure that when he died, Uncle Al was well into his 80s. Years prior he saw that this business could take its toll on people. I was privileged to have many a good conversation with him, and made a point to pay him and my Aunt Ruth several visits when they came to town.

Uncle Slim Laning

Slim was always plagued by health problems, but lived way beyond 60.
He passed the business name of Peter Laning Sons to his son Junior and his son-in-law Jim, who for years ran it very successfully. When the Ally began their buying spree, Junior and Jim decided to sell to Ally. Jim, Slim's son-in-law, was given a position as a sales manager in the Chicago region, which he kept doing until his retirement in 2015. He enjoyed a very rewarding time there for many years.

Jim has three sons. Jim Jr stayed at Ally and is still employed as a semi driver. Son Mike is the owner of a roll-off company at the present time. Son Matt started a packer route in 1998, at the same time I started Anchor2, and he ran it very well for sixteen years by himself, then he too sold the operation to Ally and is still with them. Jim's one daughter was married to a guy who worked for Ally for a short time.

Slim's son Junior also worked for Ally as a transfer driver, but died very early—in his 40s—while sweeping a transfer trailer before returning to the transfer site. He left a widow and three young daughters. That was not a pleasant time in the Laning history.

But Junior's middle daughter married a guy named "Stretch" who now works in the trash business, switching bodies, changing engines and troubleshooting.

Uncle Buck and Auntie Gert (Laning) Campbell

Uncle Buck had worked for Uncle Slim many years prior, till him and Slim had a falling out. Uncle Buck never did work on a garbage truck again. For him, driving a semi was considerably easier. They had four children: two boys, two girls. Neither of the sons-in-law went into the trash hauling business. One son, Henry, began hauling special/hazardous waste, and moved to Denver with his wife and eventually started a trash hauling business. Henry sold his semi and bought a garbage truck, and from scratch built a small company with the expertise he had learned from his exposure to the trash hauling operations in the Chicago area. Henry had one son, Chris, and his wife had a son named Jason, and while out there in Denver Henry and his wife parted company, and he sold his trash hauling business—I'm not sure to whom—and move back to the Chicago area with both of his sons.

Henry still works as a semi driver for Stericycle, hauling special wastes, and has remarried to a farm girl named Ruth. Jason worked for a company hauling residential grass, but this is very seasonal in the North, and Jason was laid off, and as of today, I do not know if he has returned to that business. Chris, on the other hand, has worked in trash hauling for several years, and he is the guy capable of hauling 1500 homes a day. Last I heard, though, he was given a truck with a mechanical arm, and I do not know his current home count, but it sure makes his job a lot easier.

Uncle Pete Lindemulder

As I recounted in the earlier chapters, I was closest to this uncle. His influence on me was probably greater than my own father. His personality matched mine; he liked destroying things. (I mean that in a very positive way. You can really crush things with a packer blade!) He came from a family that had hauled trash, just like he was doing, and two of his brothers were also involved in trash pickup. One even worked for him for a very long time. Uncle Pete was responsible for much of the money that I made as a pre- and teenager. If I needed $75 to pay my way for summer camp, I would go see him, and he would ask me how much I needed, and I would tell him to hang onto the money till I had enough to go to camp. So I had a very good relationship with him.

He had purchased his operation from my other uncle, Peter Laning when my uncle decided to enter the mission field. Pete Lindy was a hustler, and spent long days making his operation (Duke Scavenger) work. He died young (53), and when he did, I was at a loss, because he had given me sound advice, as well as other help, when I needed it. His son, Peter Jr, purchased the operation from his father a few years before his death, and built it up even further. Once again, when Ally was on its acquisition tear, Peter could see that this was a very good opportunity, so he sold to Ally and went to work for them. Peter Jr rose up through the ranks at Ally and was sitting at the head table up until his death, also at an early age. Looking back, I can see the hand of the Lord on many of the decisions both myself and my relatives made concerning the buying and selling of trash companies. Peter Junior's son, Peter 3, was my boss at Prescott and left Prescott when it was required by TM, and later went into a business that was in direct competition with Stericycle, in the transportation and disposal of medical wastes.

Uncle Deck

Shortly before Uncle Deck's retirement, he sold to Ally also, and after his retirement he worked, delivering truck parts, which gave him access to many of the trash truck garages that he knew from the old days. His second daughter, Betty, is married to All Vander Laan, who used to own a trash hauling company. Al sold to Slim's son and son-in-law, Junior and Jim, in the mid-90s.

Uncle Deck's son Clarence worked side-by-side with me at City Disposal, and when City was sold, he went along with that acquisition. He stayed there for some time and later moved to another company, where he still is gainfully employed. Our paths cross quite often. One of the last conversations I had with Uncle Deck was in 1998 when I informed him that I was going to start up again, and I noticed a tear in his eye when he said, "Boy, I wish I could join you. I sure do miss that business." By then, he had lost his mobility and was confined to a wheelchair.

On the flight back from my cousin JoAnn's funeral, I sat next to a middle aged guy who I later learned was an air marshal, and I mentioned the nature of my flight. I also said just how short life is, and one must enjoy every day like it's your last. I mentioned that the Lord puts you on this earth at a given time, and he calls you home at his time. That time seems so short, and life goes by so quickly. As I was getting off the plane, I told him to enjoy his day. His reply was, "I will sure try. Those are very profound words that you said to me." Looking back now as I am writing, I think about all the uncles that have gone to glory before me, and all I can say is, "Where did the time go?"

CHAPTER 40 - BLESSING

When I look back, I see that some people have a—for lack of a better word—love, or passion, for picking up trash. Or maybe it's just that they said it's better to be employed for a long period of time, not having to worry about your job being exported to a foreign country, or being laid off when a particular job is complete and waiting at home for the next one to begin without the benefit of a paycheck. I used to say, "Remember, this job cannot be exported to China or India."

So as I wind this story down, I think of all the people who have gone before me, who have influenced me by what they have said or what they have done to make this business one of the greatest experiences of my life, along with my faith in God, and my family. Some of my experiences have been bad, but most were good, even if I didn't realize it at the time. It's been a very exciting career, and if I had to do it all over again, I might make a few changes along the way, but I would still choose to haul trash.

In the Bible, Proverbs 22, verse 29, says: "Do you see someone skilled in their work? They will serve before kings, they will not serve before officials of low rank." To me this passage says it all; when you mention that you spent a lifetime hauling trash, that you bought and sold four companies and they were all trash hauling companies, the image you portray is that you got rich. Did I get rich? Yes, of course.

But the term "rich" to most people conjures up an image of someone who has an excessive amount of money. This is not my case. The essay I wrote at Lindbloom Technical High School, way back when I was struggling through summer school, still resonates, and the way I defined success then is the way I would still define it now: do something you enjoy, make it a game, feel good about your accomplishments, and this is success.

I have had a comfortable adult life. The job of hauling someone else's trash has paid my bills, put my children through Christian school, put a roof over our heads, and bought us a few cars. But the riches I'm talking about are the ones that you cannot measure in dollars and cents. I live the American dream. I was able to acquire small companies and build on them and in doing so I met some of the most amazing people, and to me they were all kings.

Here's one story that illustrates the satisfaction I've gotten from doing the best I possibly can, and letting my work speak for me. A few years back, on the south side of Chicago a man had just purchased a building next to the building I was hauling. At the time the City of Chicago did not require us to label our containers, and I was not so much interested in the growth of my business as I was in giving my current customers the most bang for their buck. I did not advertise in the telephone book because the price of ads was rather expensive and I figured word-of-mouth was a much better form of advertisement.

The containers in the building I was hauling were bought from a company called Park-Can, which is located in Silver Lake, Indiana. The only label on my container was their company name plus a serial number. Unbeknownst to me, this man went through the trouble of calling Park-Can with the serial number of that container and asking who had purchased it. They told him and gave him my phone number. He then contacted me and became my customer.

Am I patting myself on the back? In a way, yes. But this is a testimony to my original theory that if you do a good job people will make you rich beyond your wildest dreams, not always in the form of dollars and cents, but in the satisfaction of being able to appear before kings. You see most of the people I have met definitely are kings, and the fact is, hauling trash was the key that opened the door.

TO GOD BE THE GLORY

Acknowledgements

I want to thank the people who have opened the doors for me. At the time they may not have realized how much they were helping me. Many people I never got to thank. And also, thanks to the people that closed doors on me, because this gave me cause to reflect and go in a different direction. Thanks to all the people who have hauled garbage in the past, who are hauling it now, and who will haul it in the future.

Thanks to Robert Swierenga, author of **Dutch Chicago**, who helped me see that garbage hauling is an interesting topic for many people. And to Larry VanderLeest, author of **Garbio**, thanks for the inspiration to write stories about the day-to-day grind of picking up trash.

Owen Jr and Linda (aka Veronica). Thank you for letting me park the camper in your driveway so that I would have the space and time to begin writing this book. And to John and Nancy for help in editing and layout of the final draft.

To my uncles, all now deceased, who shaped my career and were instrumental in my early childhood, you were my role models.

To my parents and grandparents, also deceased, thank you for my upbringing. And especially to my parents, thanks for giving me five great brothers.

The greatest thanks go to my children and grandchildren, and especially to my wife Pat who is the best part of my whole life story.

www.ingramcontent.com/pod-product-compliance
Lightning Source LLC
Chambersburg PA
CBHW071601080526
44588CB00010B/983